teach®
yourself

zulu
arnett wilkes and
nicholias nkosi

For over 60 years, more than
40 million people have learnt over
750 subjects the **teach yourself**
way, with impressive results.

For UK order enquiries: please contact Bookpoint Ltd, 130 Milton Park, Abingdon, Oxon OX14 4SB. Telephone: +44 (0) 1235 827720, Fax: +44 (0) 1235 400454. Lines are open 9.00–18.00, Monday to Saturday, with a 24-hour message answering service. Details about our titles and how to order are available at www.teachyourself.co.uk

For USA order enquiries: please contact McGraw-Hill Customer Services, P.O. Box 545, Blacklick, OH 43004-0545, USA. Telephone: 1-800-722-4726. Fax: 1-614-755-5645.

For Canada order enquiries: please contact McGraw-Hill Ryerson Ltd, 300 Water St, Whitby, Ontario L1N 9B6, Canada. Telephone: 905 430 5000. Fax: 905 430 5020.

Long renowned as the authoritative source for self-guided learning – with more than 30 million copies sold worldwide – the Teach Yourself series includes over 300 titles in the fields of languages, crafts, hobbies, business, computing and education.

British Library Cataloguing in Publication Data: a catalogue entry for this title is available from The British Library.

Library of Congress Catalog Card Number: on file

First published in UK 1995 by Hodder Headline Ltd, 338 Euston Road, London, NW1 3BH.

First published in US 1996 by Contemporary Books, Aa Division of the McGraw-Hill Companies, 1 Prudential Plaza, 130 East Randolph Street, Chicago, IL 60601 USA.

This edition published 2003.

Typeset by Transet Limited, Coventry, England.
Printed in Great Britain for Hodder & Stoughton Educational, a division of Hodder Headline Ltd, 338 Euston Road, London NW1 3BH by Cox & Wyman Ltd, Reading, Berkshire.

Impression number   10 9 8 7 6 5 4 3 2 1
Year   2008 2007 2006 2005 2004 2003

19

CONTENTS

—— INTRODUCTION ——

African languages spoken in South Africa

South Africa's population comprises many distinctive peoples or population groups, each with its own language. There are also a great many dialects especially in the various indigenous or African languages. Four main African language groups are found in South Africa. Within these language groups nine languages are officially recognised. They are Zulu, Xhosa, Swazi and Southern Ndebele (belonging to what is known as the Nguni language group), Northern Sotho, Tswana and Southern Sotho – also known as seSotho – forming the Sotho language group, and finally Venda and Tsonga.

Although some salient phonetic and grammatical differences exist between the various members of the Nguni and Sotho language groups respectively, they are not so comprehensive as to constitute any great barrier to mutual intelligibility. Thus one finds that speakers of, for instance, the Nguni group have little difficulty in understanding one another – a Swazi speaker, for example, has no difficulty in understanding a Zulu speaker and vice versa. This is, however, not so for speakers belonging to different language groups. In general, a Zulu-speaking person cannot understand a speaker belonging to any of the other language groups and vice versa.

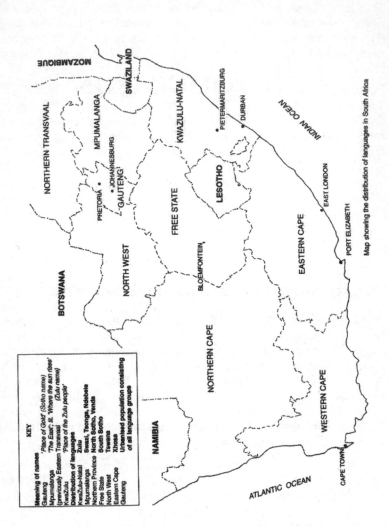

Map showing the distribution of languages in South Africa

KEY

Meaning of names	
Gauteng	'Place of Gold' (Sotho name)
Mpumalanga	'The East'; lit. 'Where the sun rises'
(previously Eastern Transvaal	(Zulu name)
KwaZulu	'Place of the Zulu people'

Distribution of languages	
KwaZulu-Natal	Zulu
Mpumalanga	Swazi, Tsonga, Ndebele
Northern Province	North Sotho, Venda
Free State	South Sotho
North West	Tswana
Eastern Cape	Xhosa
Gauteng	Urbanised population consisting of all language groups

The Nguni languages

The Nguni languages are spoken by more than 20 million people, who reside – with few exceptions – in the south-eastern part of the country, in an area stretching for about 1000 km in a broad coastal belt from Swaziland in the north, right through KwaZulu-Natal, far down into the Eastern Cape in the south.

In the northern part of this territory (consisting of KwaZulu-Natal) Zulu predominates, while Xhosa is the predominating language in the Eastern Cape. Zulu is also the dominating language in the south-eastern part of eMpumalanga as well as on the Witwatersrand (i.e. Johannesburg and adjacent areas). Zulu and Xhosa are numerically the strongest of the Nguni languages. Swazi, which is the main language of neighbouring Swaziland, is mainly spoken in eMpumalanga in an area that is more or less adjacent to the Kruger National Park. IsiNdebele is the Nguni language with the smallest number of speakers, and is mainly spoken in the eMpumalanga and Gauteng provinces.

The Sotho languages

The Sotho-speaking people occupy the interior lands to the west and north-west of the main Nguni area. Northern Sotho is mainly spoken in the Northern province, and Tswana in the North-West province as well as in neighbouring Botswana. Southern Sotho is by and large restricted to the Free State. It is, of course, also the national language of nearby Lesotho.

Venda and Tsonga

Venda is the language with the fewest speakers of the four principal Bantu language groups in the Republic of South Africa and is spoken mainly in the northern districts of the Northern province.

Tsonga is spoken in the Northern province as well as in eMpumalanga. It is also the official language of neighbouring Mozambique.

PRONUNCIATION GUIDE

To acquire the correct pronunciation of Zulu, it is recommended that, whenever possible, the help of a native speaker is enlisted. However, it is good to remember that the main objective is not to acquire a perfect accent of Zulu but to be understood; here are a number of techniques for studying pronunciation:

- Listen carefully to the cassette provided and whenever possible try to repeat aloud the sounds and words pronounced by the mother tongue speaker on the tape.
- Record yourself and compare your pronunciation with that of the mother tongue speaker on the tape.
- Make a list of words that give you pronunciation trouble and practise them.

The first important rule to remember regarding pronunciation in Zulu is that the penultimate syllable of most Zulu words is lengthened. The lengthening of this syllable is clearly audible in words that occur as the final word in the sentence. Compare the following examples on your cassette. Pay special attention to the pronunciation of the penultimate syllable of the final word in the sentence:

Ngisafunda isi**Zu**lu	*I am still learning (to speak) Zulu*
Sihamba **ma**nje	*We are going now*
Amabhasi asuka **ku**phi?	*Where do the buses depart from?*

A wide variety of vowel elisions occur in Zulu, too many to treat in detail here. However, one kind of elision that should perhaps be mentioned is the elision of the second **i** in the noun prefix isi- in nouns with di- or tri-syllabic stems. For example:

isikole > iskole   *school*

isiSkotilandi > isKotilandi   *Scotland*

Vowels

a   is pronounced somewhat as in bark; e.g. **ubaba** *(father)*
e   has two pronunciations. When followed by the vowel **i** or **u** it is
    pronounced somewhat as in bed; e.g. **-thengile** *(bought)*. When
    followed by the vowel **a** its pronunciation sounds much like that
    of the **a** in cat; e.g. **-letha** *(bring)*
i   is pronounced approximately as in see; e.g. -thi *(say)*
o   has two pronunciations. It is pronounced somewhat as in saw
    when it is followed by an **a**; e.g. **-bona** *(see)*. When followed by an
    i or **u** it is pronounced much as in the northern English no.
u   resembles the northern English sound in food; e.g. **ufudu**
    (tortoise)

Semi-vowels

y   is pronounced as in yes; e.g. **yebo** *(yes)*
w   is pronounced as in want; e.g. **wena** *(you)*

Consonants

Only those consonants that may cause pronunciation problems are
given below.

f   is pronounced as in fall; e.g. **ifu** *(cloud)*
v   is pronounced as in van; e.g. **vala** *(close)*
sh   is pronounced as in shall; e.g. **shaya** *(hit)*
tsh is pronounced somewhat as the initial **ch** in church
th   is aspirated and pronounced much like the **t** in tea; e.g. **thatha**
     (take)
t   is pronounced somewhat like the **t** in steam; e.g. **intombi** *(girl)*
ph   is aspirated and pronounced much like the **p** in pen; e.g. **pheka**
     (cook)
p   is pronounced somewhat like the **p** in spoon but without any
     aspiration; e.g. **impisi** *(hyena)*
kh   is pronounced much like the **c** in can; e.g. **ikhanda** *(head)*

k has two pronunciations. The 'soft-k' is something between English **k** and **g**; e.g. **ukuvuka** (*to wake up*). The so-called 'sharp-k' has no equivalent in English. It sounds somewhat like the **c** in **c**at but without any aspiration and normally occurs after **n**, as in e.g. **inkunzi** (*bull*)

g is pronounced more or less as in **g**ain; e.g. **ugogo** (*grandmother*)

n is pronounced as in English. However, when it precedes a **k** or a **g** it is pronounced more or less like the **ng** in si**ng**; e.g. **inkomo** (*beast*)

ng is pronounced as in fi**ng**er; e.g. **ingane** (*child*)

ny is pronounced as in Vi**gn**ette; e.g. **inyoni** (*bird*)

d is pronounced much like the **d** in **d**uck; e.g. **amadoda** (*men*)

b has two pronunciations. In combination with **m** it sounds like the **b** in English; e.g. **hamba** (*go, walk*), **imbuzi** (*goat*). On its own it is pronounced with implosion, i.e. with a slightly ingressive airstream; e.g. **ubaba** (*father*), **ubani?** (*who?*)

bh sounds like something between **b** (as for instance in **b**all) and **p** (as in **p**ot). Although it is written **bh** there is no aspiration in this sound; e.g. **ibhola** (*ball*), **ibhokisi** (*box*)

h is pronounced as in **h**and; e.g. **hamba** (*go*)

hh is the *voiced* equivalent of **h** and occurs in words such as **ihhashi** (*horse*), **hhayi** (*no!*)

hl is pronounced very much as **ll** in the Welsh **Ll**anelli. This sound is pronounced by pressing the tongue just behind the upper teeth as if to articulate **l** then, while holding it there, blow the air over both sides of the tongue; e.g. **-hlala** (*sit*)

dl is the *voiced* form of **hl**. It sounds much like **d** + **hl** pronounced simultaneously; e.g. **-dlala** (*play*)

j is pronounced as in **j**ust; e.g. **ukujabula** (*to be glad*)

Click sounds

c To pronounce this sound:
(i) place the tip of the tongue against the upper front teeth and gum.
(ii) Depress the centre of the tongue.
(iii) Release the tip of the tongue drawing it slightly backward.
This click resembles the English click of annoyance written as **tut-tut**; e.g. **-cela** (*request*)

q To pronounce this sound:
(i) Press the upper part of the tongue-tip against the part between the teeth ridge and the hard palate.
(ii) Raise the back of the tongue so that it touches the soft palate.
(iii) Depress the centre of the tongue.
(iv) Release the tip of the tongue sharply downwards.
This click resembles the sound of drawing a cork from a bottle: e.g. **qala** (*begin, start*)

x To pronounce this click:
(i) Place the upper part of the tongue-tip against the part between the teeth ridge and the hard palate.
(ii) Raise the back of the tongue towards the soft palate.
(iii) Withdraw one side of the tongue from the upper teeth.
This sound is generally used in urging a horse; e.g. **xoxa** (*chat, converse*)

| When aspirated these clicks are written: | **ch** | **qh** | **xh** |
| Nasalised they are written: | **nc** | **nq** | **nx** |

(Note that the nasal and the click are pronounced simultaneously as a single sound)

| With voicing: | **gc** | **gq** | **gx** |

1
UNJANI?

How are you? (Greetings)

In this unit you will learn how to

- exchange greetings and address people
- say goodbye to people
- ask about someone's health
- use some personal pronouns

 ———— **Ingxoxo (*Dialogue*)** ————

Greetings form an important part of Zulu people's social life. It is highly unusual for persons to engage in conversation, no matter how brief it may be, without first greeting each other and enquiring about each other's health.

In the following dialogue, Stephen (a tourist) and Albert (a waiter in the hotel where Stephen stays) exchange greetings. Stephen is about to leave.

Albert   Sawubona Mnumzane.
Stephen   Yebo.
Albert   Unjani?

Stephen	Ngikhona, wena unjani?
Albert	Nami ngikhona. Ulale kamnandi na?
Stephen	Yebo.
Albert	Uyahamba manje?
Stephen	Yebo.
Albert	Hamba kahle.
Stephen	Sala kahle.

Sawubona	*Good day*	**Hamba kahle**	*Go well*
mnumzane	*sir*	**Sala kahle**	*Stay well*
Ngikhona	*I'm fine*	**yebo**	*yes*
Ulale kamnandi na?	*Did you sleep well?*	**Unjani?**	*How are you?*
Uyahamba manje?	*Are you leaving/going now?*	**Wena unjani?**	*How are you?* ('you' emphasised)
		nami	*I also/I too*

Ulimi (*Language usage*)

1 Forms of greeting

The most important greeting word in Zulu when addressing a single person is **sawubona** which may also be expressed as **sakubona**. When we greet more than one person we say **sanibona** or **sanibonani** (pronounced **sanbonaan'**). These forms of greeting can be used at any time of day and night as they can mean *good morning, good afternoon, good evening*, or simply *hello*.

In reply to a greeting it is customary to say **yebo** (*yes*) or **yebo, sawubona** (singular) or **yebo, sanibonani** (plural).

2 Forms of address

It is important to use the correct form of address when greeting people in Zulu. Here are a few common terms of address which you as a student of Zulu should know:

mnumzana/e *sir*	ma *madam* – used when addressing an older woman, is less formal than **nkosikazi** above
nkosikazi *madam* (a married woman)	mfowethu *my brother*
nkosazana *miss*	dadewethu *my sister*
baba *sir* – used when addressing an older man, is less formal than **mnumzana** above	madoda *men*
	mfana *boy, young man*
	mntanami *my child*

When we greet friends we may, of course, use their personal names. In addition to their traditional name (**igama lesiNtu**), most Blacks in South Africa also have a so-called Christian (i.e. Western or White person's) name (**igama lesiLungu**). Like most other loan-words such names are normally adapted to the Zulu sound system. So, *Joseph* is often pronounced as **Josefa**, *David* as **Davidi**, *Lisbeth* as **Lisbethe**, etc. The original pronounciation may, however, be retained.

In informal situations where a person's name is not known, Blacks often address each other with **mfowethu** (in the case of a male person), and **dadewethu** or simply **dade** (in the case of a female person). **Ma** is another favourite greeting form for married female persons. In most metropolitan areas the slang forms **bhuti** (short for Afrikaans **boetie** *brother*) and **sisi** (*sister*) are also frequently used.

3 Saying goodbye

When saying goodbye to someone who is leaving, you say **Hamba kahle** (Lit. *Go well*).

When saying goodbye to someone who is staying behind, you say **Sala kahle** (Lit. *Stay well*).

To say goodbye to more than one person you simply add **-ni** to the verb **hamba** or **sala**:

| Hamba**ni** kahle | (when they are leaving) |
| Sala**ni** kahle | (when you are leaving). |

4 Asking about someone's health

There are various ways in which to enquire about one another's well-being in Zulu. Some of the most frequently used expressions are:

Singular

Unjani?	*How are you?*
Ngikhona	*I'm fine* (Lit. *I'm there.*)
Wena unjani?	*(And) How are you?* ('you' emphasised)
Nami ngikhona	*I'm fine too.*

In addition to **Unjani?** one may also ask:

Usaphila na?	*Are you still fine?* (Lit. *Are you still alive?*)
Yebo, ngisaphila.	*I am still fine.* (Lit. *Yes, I'm still alive*)
Wena uphila njani?	*How are you doing?* ('you' emphasised) (Lit. *How do you live?*)

or:

Uphila njani?	*How are you?* (Lit. *How do you live?*)

| Ngiyaphila | *I'm OK.* (Lit. *I am living.*) |

or:

| Kunjani? | *How is it (with you)?* |
| Kulungile | *It's OK (with me).* |

Plural

| Ninjani? | *How are you?* |
| Sikhona (or Siyaphila) | *We are fine.* |

or:

| Nisaphila na? | *Yebo, sisaphila.* |

Instead of using **njani?** or **-phila** in your response to a question about your well-being you can also say:

| Ngingezwa kini. | *May I hear how things are at your home.* |

or:

| Singezwa kini. | *May we hear how things are at your home.* |

| Sawubona bhut' John, ninjani? | *Good day brother John, how are you?* (pl.) |
| Sikhona. Singezwa kini. | *We are fine. May we hear how things are at your home.* |

5 Personal pronouns

The equivalents of the English pronouns *I, you, we, it, he/she* and *they* are not complete words in Zulu. They are formatives, or, to use their grammatical name, concords, i.e. they are constituent parts of words. Here are some concordial pronouns that you have already encountered as well as one or two new ones which you will be using soon.

ngi-	*I*	**u-**	*he/she*
u-	*you*	**ba-**	*they*
ni-	*you* (pl.)	**ku-**	*it*
si-	*we*		

In Zulu there is no grammatical distinction between masculine and feminine. Note also that the pronouns *he/she* and *you* (singular) are both **u-** in Zulu except that in case of the latter the **u-** is pronounced with a low tone while in case of the former it is pronounced with a high tone.

——— Umsebenzi *(Exercises)* ———

1 Let's practise the material you have studied thus far by exercising the following dialogues. In the first one, Thandi and her friend Fikile (two girls), greet each other. Let's imagine you are Thandi. How would you respond to what Fikile says?

   Fikile: Thandi:
   (a) Sawubona Thandi   ——
   (b) Unjani?   ——
   (c) Nami ngikhona, sala kahle ——

2 In the second dialogue, Sibusiso greets a couple of his (male) friends (**amadoda** *men*). You are Sibusiso. Try to enact his role in this dialogue by bearing in mind how his friends respond.

   Sibusiso: Amadoda:
   (a) ——   Yebo.
   (b) ——?   Sikhona, wena unjani?
   (c) ——

3 How would you say hello to the following people?

   (a) your boss at the office
   (b) your friend Mandla
   (c) a married woman (in a formal way)
   (d) an unfamiliar male person
   (e) an unmarried young woman (in an informal way)
   (f) an elderly gentleman

4 How would you say goodbye (you are leaving) to the following people?

   (a) your friend Raymond
   (b) people you have just met

5 You are speaking to Paul and Mary. Ask them how they are and tell them that you are fine.

6 How do you say in Zulu:

    (*a*) How are they?
    (*b*) He/She is fine.
    (*c*) They are fine.
    (*d*) We are fine.
    (*e*) How are you? (pl.)
    (*f*) It's OK.

7 Correct, rewrite and then translate the following:

    (*a*) Sanibonani mfowethu.
    (*b*) Sala kahle bafana (*boys*).
    (*c*) Ngiphila.

8 Complete the missing dialogue.

2
— WENA UNGUBANI? —
Who are you? (personal identification)

In this unit you will learn how to

- ask someone's name and surname
- ask someone's identity and where he or she comes from
- use Zulu praise names
- form singular and plural nouns

────────── Ingxoxo ──────────

Asking someone's name and where he or she comes from is something that crops up regularly in many a conversation, as for instance in the following dialogue between Michael Cohen from England and Sam Ndlovu from Ladysmith, South Africa. They have met briefly before and now use the opportunity to become more closely acquainted. Having first greeted each other as is customary, they continue by asking each other's names and surnames and where they each hail from.

Michael Ngubani igama lakho baba?
Sam Igama lami nguSam, mnumzana.
Michael Sam bani?
Sam NginguSam Ndlovu mnumzana. Wena ungubani?
Michael NginguMichael.

Sam	Michael bani?
Michael	Michael Cohen.
Sam	Uphumaphi?
Michael	Ngiphuma phesheya.
Sam	[somewhat surprised] O! Uphuma phesheya! Kuphi phesheya?
Michael	Ngiphuma eNgilandi. Wena uphumaphi Sam?
Saml	Mina ngiphuma eMnambithi.

Ngubani igama lakho? *What is your name?*	**Uphumaphi?** *Where do you come from?*
Igama lami nguSam *My name is Sam*	**-phuma** *come from*
Sam bani? *Sam who?*	**Phesheya** *Overseas*
NginguSam Ndlovu *I'm Sam Ndlovu*	**Kuphi?** *Where?*
Wena ungubani? *Who are you?*	**eNgilandi** *England*
Wena *You (emphasised)*	**Mina** *I (emphasised)*
	eMnambithi *Ladysmith* (a town in KwaZulu-Natal)

Ulimi

1 Asking someone's name

To ask someone's name (**igama**) you say:

Ngubani igama lakho?   Lit. *It is who the name of you?*

or:

Lithini igama lakho?   Lit. *It says what your name?*

To this you may reply by adding **Ngingu-** (*I am ...*) to your personal name.

NginguPeter
NginguJohn
NginguMandla
NginguThandi

Or you may wish to reply more fully by saying: **Igama lami ngu** ... (*My name is ...*).

Igama lami nguStephen.   *My name is Stephen.*

Or you can put **ngingu-** before your name and **igama lami** after it.

NginguStephen igama lami   Lit. *I'm Stephen my name.*

2   Asking someone's surname

To ask someone's surname (**isibongo**) you use:

Ngubani isibongo sakho?   *What's your surname?*

or:

Sithini isibongo sakho?   *What's your surname?*

To this you may reply:

Isibongo sami nguJones   *My surname is Jones*

or:

SinguJones   *It is Jones*

or:

NginguJones (isibongo sami)   *I'm Jones (my surname)*

To ask a third person's name or surname is similar, except that instead of the possessive pronoun **-kho** (*you* sing.) and **-mi** (*my*) you use the third person possessive pronoun **-khe** (*his / her*).

Ngubani igama la**khe**?
Igama la**khe** nguSamuel.   *His name is Samuel.*
UnguSamuel igama lakhe.   *He is Samuel his name (that is).*

Ngubani isibongo sa**khe**?
Isibongo sa**khe** nguKhathi.   *His surname is Khathi.*
UnguKhathi isibongo sakhe.   *He is Khathi his surname (that is).*

3   Asking someone who (s)he is

To ask someone's identity you can simply say **Ungubani?** (*Who are you?* Lit. *You are who?*) as in the following dialogue where Meshack Masondo and Themba Nkosi are introducing themselves to one another.

4 Sam who?

When a person tells you his or her name and you would also like to know his or her surname, you simply put the interrogative **bani?** after the person's name as is done in the dialogue at the beginning of this unit.

5 The emphatic pronouns wena and mina

Wena is used to emphasise the second person singular, **mina** to emphasise the first person singular:

Wena uphumaphi? *Where do you come from?*
('you' emphasised)

Mina ngiphuma eNgilandi. *Í come from England.*
('I' emphasised)

6 Asking someone's praise name

Praise names (**izithakazelo**) are a prominent feature of Zulu culture, and, in fact, of all clans belonging to the Nguni language group.

Every adult male person in Zulu society has a praise name. All eligible male persons belonging to the same family clan (i.e. persons sharing a common surname) have the same **isithakazelo**. For instance, the **isithakazelo** of all adult male persons with the surname **Khumalo** is **Mntungwa**; those whose surname is **Ntuli** have **Mphemba** as their **isithakazelo**, and so on. It is interesting to know that President Mandela, being a member of the Xhosa-speaking group, is also known by the name **Madiba** which is the praise name of the Mandela clan. **Isithakazelos** are only used by men folk, women never call men by their praise names. Zulus are without exception delighted when they are called by their **isithakazelo** and are usually pleasantly surprised if foreigners know their praise names. It is consequently strongly recommended to find out what a clan's **isithakazelo** is. (You can do this by first asking any Zulu male person what is **isibongo** (*surname/clan name*) is and then what his **isithakazelo** is). Make a point of using a person's **isithakazelo** as often as possible in your conversation with him.

The following are a few examples of popular Zulu surnames and their accompanying **isithakazelos**:

Cele – Ndosi
Dlomo – Mkhabela
Buthelezi – Shenge
Nkosi – Dlamini
Ndlovu – Gatsheni

To find out what someone's praise name is, you ask **sithini isithakazelo sakho?**

You	Ngubani isibongo sakho, Sam?
Sam	NginguKubheka, mnumzana.
You	Sithini isithakazelo sakho?
Sam	SinguKhathide (or NginguKhathide or NguKhathide), mnumzana.

7 Definite and indefinite articles

It is important to note at this stage that Zulu differs from languages such as English in that it doesn't distinguish between definite and indefinite nouns by means of articles such as *the* and *a*. In other words, a noun like **inja**, for instance, can either mean *the dog* or *a dog* depending on the context in which it occurs.

8 Initial vowel of nouns

As you will have noticed above, all nouns in Zulu normally begin with a vowel. However, when we address a person or persons, the noun referring to such a person or persons discards its initial vowel.

sawubona	(u)mfana
sanibonani	(a)madoda
sawubona	(u)baba

9 The noun class system of Zulu

A striking feature of Zulu and all other Bantu languages is the fact that their nouns are classified into various categories or noun classes. There are 18 such noun classes in Zulu, of which some are singular and others plural classes. There are also two neutral classes which are neither singular nor plural. Each noun class has what is known as a class prefix which is a formative that is attached to the beginning of the noun, in fact, to the noun stem. The class prefix indicates to which noun class a noun belongs and at the same time also whether a noun is a singular, plural or a neutral noun. In most instances these prefixes operate in pairs, one being the singular prefix and the other the plural prefix.

The following system of noun class prefixes is found in Zulu:

Singular prefixes		Plural prefixes	
Class 1	**um(u)-**	Class 2	**aba-**
Class 1a	**u-**	Class 2a	**o-**
Class 3	**um(u)-**	Class 4	**imi-**
Class 5	**i(li)-**	Class 6	**ama-**
Class 7	**isi-**	Class 8	**izi-**
Class 9	**in-/im-**	Class 10	**izin-/izim-**
Class 11	**u(lu)-**		
Class 14	**ubu-**		
Class 15	**uku-**		

Note that nouns in class 11 take their plural in class 10, and that only nouns signifying human beings belong to classes 1 and 2.

Let's look at a few examples of how these class prefixes distinguish between singular, plural and neutral nouns in Zulu.

umu-ntu	*person*	**aba**-ntu	*people*
um-lungu	*White person*	**abe**-lungu	*White people*
u-baba	*father*	**o**-baba	*fathers*
um-fula	*river*	**imi**-fula	*rivers*
i(li)-bhayisikili	*bicycle*	**ama**-bhayisikili	*bicycles*
isi-kole	*school*	**izi**-kole	*schools*
in-dlu	*house*	**izin**-dlu	*houses*
u(lu)-debe	*lip*	**izin**-debe	*lips*
ubu-ntu	*human nature*		
uku-hamba	*travelling*		

Note that when the stem of nouns belonging to classes 1 and 3 consists of only one syllable, the class prefix of these nouns is **umu-**; and when the stem consists of more than one syllable (which is normally the case) the class prefix is **um-**.

um-lungu   but   **umu**-ntu

Note also the variant form of the prefix of class 2 in words such as **abe**-lungu. This variant form is, however, confined to only a small number of nouns in this class.

A limited number of nouns in class 9 have irregular plural forms in class 6.

indoda *man*	but	**ama**doda *men*
inkosi *chief*	but	**ama**khosi *chiefs*
intombazane *girl*	but	**ama**ntombazana *girls*

Finally, it is important to know that most loanwords (from, for instance, English and Afrikaans) occur in the **ili**-class. If one does not know the Zulu name of something one may (as a last resort) 'Zulufy' an English noun by simply putting **i-** in front of it.

iRadio
iFour-wheel drive
istation

Umsebenzi

1 How would you respond in Zulu if someone asks/says to you:

   (a) Sawubona mnumzane/nkosazana.
   (b) Unjani?
   (c) Usaphila na?
   (d) Ngubani igama lakho?
   (e) Ngubani isibongo sakho?
   (f) Hamba kahle.
   (g) Ungubani wena?

2 Imagine you are Joseph Gumede and you meet someone you don't know. How would you:

   (a) introduce yourself to him?
   (b) ask him his name and surname?
   (c) ask him where he comes from?
   (d) tell him where you come from?
   (e) bid him goodbye?

3 Give the plural form.

umfazi *woman*	**umu**zi *village*
ibhasikidi *basket*	iwashi *watch*
isitolo *store*	**in**doda *man*
umntwana *child*	**um**khonto *spear*
imoto (class 9) *car*	**u**baba *father*

4 Rewrite the following nouns in the singular:

abantu *people*	**izin**kwa *breads*
amarandi *Rands* (money)	**izin**komo *cattle*
imimese *knives*	**abe**Suthu *Sotho people*
amakamelo *rooms*	**aman**tombazana *girls*

5 Correct (where necessary) and rewrite each of the following sentences:

Hambani kahle Simon.
Ngubani igama lakho? Igama lami Sally.
Isibongo lami nguPeters.

Sawubona ubaba.
Uphila njani? Ngiphila.
Ubani wena?

6 How will you ask Desmond Khumalo what his surname and what his praise name is? Do you remember what the Khumalo's praise name is?

3
UYAKWAZI UKUKHULUMA ISINGISI NA?

Can you speak English?

In this unit you will learn

- how to ask someone whether he or she is able (or not able) to do something
- how to ask what language a person speaks
- what to say when you do not understand what someone says to you in Zulu
- nouns denoting languages
- how to ask what a person's nationality is

 ——————————— **Ingxoxo** ———————————

Janet Smith is about to take up a full-time job and is considering employing a nanny-cum-housekeeper to relieve her of some of her household chores. She talks to her friend Sophie Ngubane who knows of someone who might be interested in the work. Among other things, Janet is interested to learn from Sophie whether Sophie's acquaintance is fond of children, if she's married and knows how to cook, what her language proficiency is and her nationality (i.e. her tribal affinity), and when she will be able to start should Janet decide to employ her.

Janet	Ungubani lo mngane wakho Sophie?
Sophie	UnguGertrude igama lakhe.
Janet	Uthanda abantwana lo Gertrude?
Sophie	Kakhulu! nkosikazi.
Janet	Ushadile na?
Sophie	Yebo, ushadile.
Janet	Uyakwazi ukupheka?
Sophie	Angazi kodwa ngiqinisile ukuthi uyakwazi.
Janet	Uyakwazi ukukhuluma isiNgisi lo mame?
Sophie	Yebo, uyakwazi.
Janet	IsiBhunu-ke?
Sophie	Uyasazi kodwa hayi kakhulu.
Janet	Ungumhlobo muni?
Sophie	UngumZulu uGertrude.
Janet	Angaqala nini?
Sophie	Angazi kodwa ngizombuza.
Janet	Ngiyabonga Sophie. Mtshele uGertrude ukuthi ngithanda ukumbona.
Sophie	Kulungile, ngizomtshela.

Ungubani lo mngane wakho?
Who is she (i.e. *What is the name of*) *this friend of yours?*

UnguGertrude igama lakhe
Gertrude is her name (Lit. *She is Gertrude her name.*)

Uthanda abantwana lo Gertrude?
Is she fond of children this Gertrude?

Kakhulu! *Very much!*

Ushadile na? *Is she married?*

Uyakwazi ukupheka? *Can she cook?* (Lit. *Does she know how to cook?*)

Angazi *I don't know*

kodwa *but*

Ngiqinisile *I'm sure*

ukuthi *that*

uyakwazi *she knows/can*

Uyakwazi ukukhuluma isiNgisi lo mame? *Can this lady speak English?* (Lit. *Does this lady know how to speak English?*)

Umame (term of respect used in addressing a married woman)

IsiBhunu-ke? (*And*) *Afrikaans?*

Uyasazi kodwa hayi kakhulu *She knows it but not much*

Ungumhlobo muni? *What nationality is she?*

UngumZulu *She's a Zulu*

Angaqala nini? *When can she start?*

Angazi kodwa ngizombuza *I don't know but I'll ask her*

Mtshele ukuthi ngithanda ukumbona *Tell her that I would like to see her*

Kulungile ngizomtshela *OK, I'll tell her*

1 Can you ...? (i.e. are you able to ...?)

1.1 Do/Can you speak English?

To ask someone whether he or she or a third person (in class 1 or 1a) can (i.e. is able to/knows how to) perform a certain action, you say **Uyakwazi uku...?** (Lit. *Do you know how to...?*) followed by the name of the action the person is to perform.

Uyakwazi ukukhuluma isiNgisi mnumzane?	*Do (Can) you speak English, sir?* (-khuluma isiNgisi *speak English*)
Uyakwazi ukupheka Paulina?	*Do you know how to cook (i.e. Can you cook), Paulina?* (-pheka *cook*)
Uyakwazi ukufunda Maria?	*Do you know how to (i.e. Can you) read, Maria?*

Note that the initial vowel of a noun denoting the addressee is dropped, as in the case of **mnumzane**, **Paulina** and **Maria** above. (See also Unit 2, Section 8.)

When this question concerns a third person (in class 1 or 1a), the same construction is used except that the third person singular concord **u-** (*he / she*) – (i.e. the initial **u-** in **uyakwazi**) – is pronounced with a high tone – the second person singular concord **u-** (*you*) is pronounced with a low tone – while the initial vowel of the person's name (if mentioned) is retained.

U**Frank uyakwazi uku**lungisa izibane?	*Does Frank know how to fix the lights?*
U**Doris uyakwazi uku**-ayina?	*Does Doris know how to iron?*

Note that Zulu has **no grammatical gender** as far as its pronominal system is concerned, **i.e. it does not distinguish between masculine** (=he) **and feminine** (=she) pronouns. Both these pronouns are expressed by the same concordial pronoun, i.e. **u-**.

1.2 Yes, I can (speak English)

To say you are able to do something, you simply replace the initial second person singular concord **u-** (*you*) of **uyakwazi** by the first person singular concord **ngi-** (*I*), i.e. **ngiyakwazi**.

Uyakwazi ukukhuluma isiNgisi Josefa?	*Do you speak English, Joseph?*
Yebo, **ngi**yakwazi	*Yes, I do.* (=*can*) (*speak English*)
Uyakwazi ukushayela imoto Marvin?	*Can you drive a car, Marvin?*
Yebo, **ngi**yakwazi mnumzane.	*Yes I can, sir.*

1.3 No, I can't (speak English)

In the negative of the first person singular we start with an **a-** and omit the **-ya-**.

Uyakwazi ukukhuluma isiNgisi?	*Do you know (how to speak) English?*
Cha, **angi**kwazi.	*No, I don't.*

In the negative of the third person singular (in class 1 or 1a), you replace the initial **u-** with **aka-** and also omit the **-ya-**.

Umlungu (class 1) **u**yakwazi ukukhuluma isiZulu na?	*Can the White person speak Zulu?*
Cha, **aka**kwazi.	*No, he can't.*
ULydia (class 1a) **u**yakwazi ukushayela imoto na?	*Does Lydia know how to drive a car?*
Cha, **aka**kwazi.	*No, she doesn't.*

2 Do you speak ...?

2.1 Do you know Zulu?

To ask whether someone **knows** (how to speak) a language, you use the stem **-azi** (*know*) and say **Uyasazi...** followed by the name of the language.

Uyasazi isiZulu na?	*Do you know Zulu?*

This you can answer by saying:

Yebo, **ngi**yasazi.	*Yes, I know it.*

In the negative you begin with **a-** and omit the **-ya-** (as in 1.3 above).

Cha, **angisaz**i.   *No, I don't understand it.*

2.2   Yes, a little. I'm still learning (to speak) it

Beginners who try to communicate in Zulu are often asked by mother tongue speakers whether they know Zulu (**Uyasazi isiZulu na?**). You can respond to such questions by saying:

Yebo, ngiyasazi kodwa hayi   *Yes I know it, but not very*
kakhulu.   *well.*

or:

Ngisazi kancane. Ngisasifunda.   *I know it a little. I'm still*
                                                    learning it.

Instead of **Uyasazi isiZulu na?** you can also be asked **Ukhuluma isiZulu na?** (*Do you speak Zulu?*), to which you can reply:

Ngisikhuluma kancane.   *I speak it a little. I'm still*
  Ngisasifunda.   *learning it.*

Another and also very idiomatic way to say that you are still a beginner as far as speaking Zulu is concerned is to use the verbal stem **-cathula** (*toddle, learn to walk*).

Angisikhulumi kahle kakhulu.   *I do not speak it so well, I'm still*
  Ngisacathula.   *learning to walk (i.e. I'm still a*
                                                    beginner).

2.3   Where have you learned to speak Zulu?

Beginners are also frequently asked where they've learned to speak Zulu (**Usifundephi isiZulu?**).

To this you may reply:

Ngisifunde encwadini.   *I've learned it from a book.*
Ngisifunde esikoleni.   *I've learned it at school.*
Ngisifunde epulazini.   *I've learned it on a farm.*

3   What language do you speak?

South Africa is a multilingual country with no less than 11 official languages. Visitors to this country are often confused by the multitude of tongues they hear and are seldom if ever able to distinguish between most of them. To enquire what language a person speaks, you can ask:

> Ukhulumani?   *What (language) do you speak?*

The answer will usually be **Ngikhuluma...** followed by the name of the language.

> Ukhulumani? Ngikhuluma   *What (language) do you speak?*
> isiXhosa.   *I speak Xhosa.*

Another way to gain the above information is to ask:

> Nikhulumani ekhaya?   *What (language) do you (people)*
>   *speak at home?*

4   Sorry, I do not understand what you are saying

When someone speaks to you in Zulu and you do not understand what the person is saying, you may reply:

> Ngiyaxolisa kodwa angiqondi   *Sorry, but I do not understand*
> kahle usho ukuthini.   *what you are saying.*

If you want someone to repeat what he or she has said because you did not understand it very well, you can ask:

> Awuphinde. Angiqondi kahle.   *Please repeat. I do not understand*
>   *(you) very well.*

or:

> Awukhulume kancane, angiqondi   *Please speak (more) slowly, I do*
> kahle. Ngisafunda ukukhuluma   *not understand so well. I am still*
> isiZulu.   *learning to speak Zulu.*

5   Nouns denoting languages

All nouns in Zulu denoting languages begin with the prefix **isi-**.

isiNgisi *English*	isiZulu *Zulu*
isiBhunu *Afrikaans*	isiXhosa *Xhosa*
isiFulentshi *French*	isiSwati *Swazi*
isiNdebele *Ndebele*	isiTsonga *Tsonga*
isiSuthu (Southern) *Sotho*	isiTswana *Tswana*
isiVenda *Venda*	isiPedi *Pedi (Northern) Sotho*
isiJalimane *German*	

All the above languages ,with the exception of French and German, are official languages in South Africa.

6 What nationality are you?

To ask someone's nationality, you say **Ungumhlobo muni?** or **Ungowasiphi isizwe?**

The answer to such a question usually begins with **Ngingu-** or **Ngiyi-** (*I am ...*). **Ngingu-** is used when the noun denoting the nationality begins with **u-**, while **ngiyi-** is used when such nouns start with **i-**.

NgingumZulu.	*I'm a Zulu.* (umZulu *Zulu person*)
NgiyiNgisi.	*I'm English.* (iNgisi *Englishman*)
NgiyiNdebele.	*I am an Ndebele-speaking person.*

6.1 Names of nationalities

Here are the names of a few European nationalities as well as a few (tribal) nationalities found in South Africa.

umNgisi (or iNgisi) *Englishman* (**ama**Ngisi pl.)	umXhosa *Xhosa-speaking person* (**ama**Xhosa pl.)
isiKoshi *Scotsman*	iNdebele *Ndebele-speaking person* (**ama**Ndebele pl.)
iJalimane *German*	
umHholandi *Dutchman* (**aba**Hholandi pl.)	umTswana *Tswana-speaking person* (**abe**Tswana pl.)
iFulentshi *Frenchman*	umPedi *Pedi-speaking person*
iBhunu *Afrikaner*	umSuthu *Suthu-speaking person* (**abe**Suthu pl.)
umZulu *Zulu-speaking person* (**ama**Zulu pl.)	umTsonga *Tsonga-speaking person*
umSwati *Swazi-speaking person* (**ama**Swati pl.)	umVenda *Venda-speaking person*

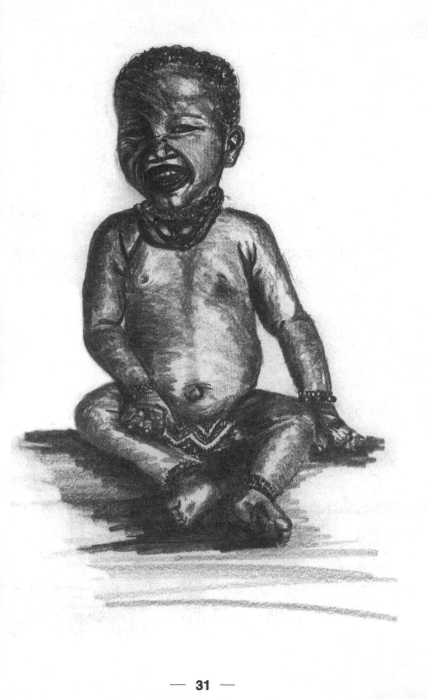

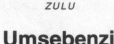 —————— **Umsebenzi** ——————

1 Complete the following dialogue between Linda and Thandiwe by providing the missing words.

Linda	____ mhlobo muni Thandiwe?
Thandiwe	NgiyiNdebele Linda.
Linda	____ kuphi?
Thandiwe	Ngiphuma KwaNdebele.
Linda	Nikhuluma isiZulu ekhaya (*at home*)?
Thandiwe	Cha, sikhuluma isiNdebele ekhaya. Nina nikhulumani ekhaya?
Linda	____ isiNgisi [and] nesiBhunu. Uyasazi isiBhunu Thandiwe?
Thandiwe	Ngiya ____ kodwa hayi kakhulu.

2 How would you ask someone whether he or she can speak the following languages:

(*a*) French
(*b*) Afrikaans
(*c*) Xhosa
(*d*) Zulu?

3 How would you say to someone that you know the following languages:

(*a*) English
(*b*) Zulu
(*c*) Sotho?

But that you don't know the following languages:

(*a*) German
(*b*) Venda
(*c*) Afrikaans?

4 When someone addresses you in Zulu and you do not understand what he or she is saying, how will you tell him or her that you do not understand?

5 You have arived at Durban airport and have taken a taxi to your hotel. On your way you engage in conversation with the driver. You ask him (*a*) what his name is and he tells you (*b*) it is

Mzilikazi. He ask you (c) where you come from and you answer (d) you are from Johannesburg (**eGoli**). You ask (e) what nationality he is and he replies (f) he is a Zulu. You conclude by asking him (g) where he comes from and he answers (h) **eMlazi** (a main township near Durban).

Write a suitable dialogue based on the information given above.

4
— NGINGAKUSIZA NA? —
Can I help you?

In this unit you will learn how to

- offer help
- say 'Thank you', 'Yes, please' and 'No, thank you'
- ask what price something is
- say 'each' meaning 'one'
- use another way to say goodbye
- say 'and'

Ingxoxo

Fruit and vegetable stalls are a familiar sight along many of South Africa's tourist routes and are often frequented by travellers. In the following dialogue, a traveller (Mrs Webb) wants to buy some fruit and vegetables from an adult female vendor.

Vendor	Ngingakusiza ngani nkosikazi?
Mrs Webb	Ngifuna uhlaza nezithelo.
Vendor	Ufunani?
Mrs Webb	Ngifuna utamatisi nokwatapheya. Yimalini utamatisi?
Vendor	Yi-R3 iphakethe.
Mrs Webb	Kulungile. Ngizothatha iphakethe. Yimalini ukwatapheya ngamunye?

Vendor	Yi-R1 ngamunye.
Mrs Webb	Ngizothatha munye.
Vendor	Ufuna nani futhi?
Mrs Webb	Lutho. Ngiyabonga.
Vendor	Awufuni uphayinaphu?
Mrs Webb	Cha, ngiyabonga.
Vendor	Kukhona okunye na?
Mrs Webb	Cha, yilokho kuphela.
Vendor	Ngiyabonga.

Ngingakusiza ngani? *With what may I help you?/What can I do for you?*	**Yimalini ukwatapheya ngamunye?** *How much for one avocado pear?*
ngani? *with what?*	**Yi-R1 ngamunye** *It's R1 for one*
Ngifuna *I want/need*	**Ngizothatha munye** *I will take one (avocado)*
uhlaza *vegetables*	
nezithelo *and fruit*	**Ufuna nani futhi?** *What else do you want?*
Ufunani? *What do you want?*	**Lutho. Ngiyabonga** *Nothing. (I say) Thank you*
utamatisi *tomatoes*	
nokwatapheya *and avocados*	**Awufuni uphayinaphu?** *Don't you want some pineapples?*
Yimalini? *How much does it cost? (Lit. How much money is it?)*	
Yi-R3 *It is R3*	**Cha, ngiyabonga** *No, thank you*
iphakethe *a packet*	**Kukhona okunye na?** *Is there anything else?*
Kulungile *OK*	**Yilokho kuphela** *That is all*
Ngizothatha iphakethe *I'll take a packet*	

Ulimi

1 Can I help you?

To ask whether you *can* or *may* help someone you say:

Ngingakusiza na?   *Can I help you?*

Or you can ask *With what can I help you?* in which case you have to add **ngani?** (*with what?*).

Ngingakusiza ngani na?

Note that the **na** may be omitted. (See also Unit 6.)

2 Yes, please/No, thank you

Zulu has no separate word for please. It makes use of, for instance, the stem **-jabula** (*be happy*) for this purpose.

Ngingakusiza na Simon?   *Can I help you Simon?*
Ngingajabula mnumzana.   *Yes, please, sir. (Lit. I can be happy, sir)*

For *No, thank you* you say **Cha, ngiyabonga**.

Ufuna itiye?	*Do you want some tea?*
Cha, ngiyabonga.	*No, thank you.*

3 Saying thank you

To thank someone for services rendered you say:

Ngiyabonga	*(I) Thank you*

or:

Siyakubonga	*(We) Thank you*

When you want to emphasise your gratitude you add **kakhulu** and omit **-ya-**, as in:

Ngibonga kakhulu.	*Thank you very much.*

The person who is thanked may then politely reply:

Nami ngiyabonga.	*I too say thank you.*

It is important to note that in Zulu one does not normally say thank you for something as is often done in English, e.g. *'Thank you for the food, thank you for the cool drink'*. To thank someone in Zulu you say **Ngiyabonga**. When you want to mention the thing you are thankful for, you simply say it after **-bonga** and also leave out the **-ya-**.

Ngibonga **usizo lwakho**.	*Thank you for **your assistance/ help***
Sibonga **usizo lwenu**.	*Thank you for **your** (pl.) **assistance/for helping us**.*
Ngibonga **itiye**.	*Thank you for **the tea**.*
Sibonga **imali**.	*We thank you for **the money**.*

4 That is all, thank you

When shopping you are often asked by the people who attend to you whether there is anything else you need. You will be asked:

Kukhona okunye na?	*Is there anything else?*

If there is nothing else you want you can reply:

Cha, yilokho kuphela.   *No (thank you), that is all.*

or:

Cha, sekwanele.   *No (thank you), it is (now)*
                                         (enough =) all.

5   Asking prices

To ask what something costs, you can say **Yimalini** (*It is how much money?*) followed by the name of the particular object, as in:

Yimalini amapentshisi?   *How much (money) are the*
                                         peaches? (i.e. What's the price
                                         of the peaches?)

Yimalini ubhanana?   *How much are the bananas?*

Another possibility is to use the subject concord (see Unit 6.4) of the noun denoting the object or thing whose price you want to know.

Ubiza malini **u**bhanana?   *How much are the bananas?*
Abiza malini **ama**zambane?   *How much are the potatoes?*
Libiza malini **i(li)**lokwe?   *How much is the dress?*
Zibiza malini **izi**cathulo?   *How much are the shoes?*

6   Saying how much something is

6.1   It's R5/It costs R5

When you are asked **Yimalini?** and you want to give the amount in English in your answer you always start with **yi-** followed by the amount in English.

Yimalini u-anyanisi?   *How much are the onions?*
Yi-R5
Yimalini ukholifulawa?   *How much is the cauliflower?*
Yi-R3

6.2   R1 each; I'll take one

When you go shopping you might want to find out the price of *one of many* of the same thing. On such occasions you would ask: *How much for (each) one?* In Zulu this is **Yimalini?** followed by:

(a) **Ngamunye** if the name of the article in question is a noun in class 1a, i.e. a noun with the prefix **u-**.

Yimalini uphayinaphu (class 1a) ngamunye?	*How much are the pineapples each?*
Yi-R1.50 ngamunye.	*It's R1.50 for one (i.e. They're R1.50 each).*

(b) **Ngalinye** if the name of the article is a noun in the **i(li)**-class, i.e. class 5.

Yimalini amaposikhadi ngalinye (iposikhadi)?	*How much are the postcards (for) each (one)?*
Yi-75 cents ngalinye (iposikhadi).	*They are 75 cents each (postcard).*

With nouns in the **isi**-class (class 7) you say **ngasinye**, and with nouns in the **in**-class (class 9) you say **ngayinye**. Note also that the stem **-nye** only operates in the singular classes.

7 Names of vegetables and fruits

Vegetables		Fruit	
amazambane	*potatoes*	**amapentshisi**	*peaches*
utamatisi	*tomatoes*	**amawolintshi**	*oranges*
ubhontshisi	*beans*	**amahabhula**	*apples*
u-anyanisi	*onions*	**ubhanana**	*bananas*
ukholifulawa	*cauliflower*	**umango**	*mangoes*
amakherothi	*carrots*	**amapulamu**	*plums*
uletisi	*lettuce*	**ukwatapheya**	*avocado pear*
ikhukhamba	*cucumber*	**uphayinaphu**	*pineapple*
amantongomane	*peanuts*	**uphopho**	*paw-paw*

Note that some vegetable and fruit names are given in the singular. This is so because these words have a collective meaning.

8 Another way to say goodbye

In Unit 1 you learned how to say *Goodbye*. Here's another way to do so.

When you are leaving you say:

Usale kahle.	*You must stay well* (sing.).
Nisale kahle.	*You must stay well* (pl.).

When (s)he or they are leaving you say:

Uhambe kahle.	*You must go well* (sing.).
Nihambe kahle.	*You must go well* (pl.).

When saying goodbye to someone we often express the wish that we will see each other again soon. To do so in Zulu you say:

Sobonana futhi.	*We'll see each other again.*
Hamba kahle baba Velaphi, sobonana futhi.	*Go well baba Velaphi, we'll see each other again (soon).*

9 And

Expressing the concept *and* in Zulu, as in 'fruit *and* vegetables, bread *and* butter', you make use of a preposition-like formative **na** which combines with the succeeding noun in the following way:

(*a*) When the following noun begins with **u-** the **na** changes to **no** and the **u-** is dropped.

Isithelo **no**hlaza	*Fruit and vegetables* (**u**hlaza *vegetables*)
Ushukela **no**bisi	*Sugar and milk* (**u**bisi *milk*)

- (*b*) When the following noun begins with **i-** the **na** changes to **ne** and the **i-** is dropped.

Uhlaza **ne**sithelo	*Vegetables and fruit* (**i**sithelo *fruit*)
IsiZulu **ne**siSuthu	*Zulu and Suthu* (**i**siSuthu is a Sotho language)

(*c*) When the following noun begins with **a-** the **na** remains unchanged.

Abafana **na**mantombazane	*Boys and girls* (**a**mantombazane *girls*)
Amadoda **na**bafazi	*Men and women* (**a**bafazi *women*)

Umsebenzi

1 You're doing your weekly shopping and need some fruit and vegetables which you decide to buy at your nearby greengrocer's. (*a*) You are greeted by the shop assistant whom you know by name. (*b*) She asks what she can do for you. (*c*) You tell her that you need (some) vegetables and (some) fruit. (*d*) She asks you what you want. (*e*) You say what you want (select any two kinds of vegetables and one kind of fruit from the picture above). (*f*) You ask the price of the oranges and she replies (*g*) R10 a pocket (**usakazana**). (*h*) She asks whether there is anything else you want and you reply by saying, (*i*) 'That is all, thank you'.

With the above information create a suitable dialogue between you and the greengrocer.

2 Combine each of the following pair of nouns by means of **na** (*and*). Don't forget the sound changes that may occur.

Isinkwa ___bhotela *Bread and butter* (**i**bhotela *butter*)
UJames ___Fikile *James and Fikile*
AmaZulu ___maXhosa *Zulus and Xhosas* (**ama**Xhosa *Xhosa-speaking people*)
Itiye ___khofi *Tea and coffee* (**i**khofi *coffee*)
Usawoti ___pelepele *Salt and pepper* (**u**pelepele *pepper*)

3 Someone asks you: **Ngingakusiza na mnumzana?**
   How would you answer him politely in the positive; and how in the negative?

4 How would you thank someone for:

   (*a*) assisting you
   (*b*) bringing you some *toast* (**isinkwa esithosiwe**)
   (*c*) the *good treatment* you have received (**impatho efudumele**)?

5 ● Give the plural.

   (*a*) **um**lungu *White person*   (*e*) **isi**tolo *shop / store*
   (*b*) **i**(li)thikithi *ticket*   (*f*) **in**komo *beast*
   (*c*) **i**(li)rande *(one) Rand*   (*g*) **in**taba *mountain*
   (*d*) **um**fundisi *minister of religion*

   ● Give the singular.

   (*a*) **aba**ntu *people*   (*f*) **ama**qanda *eggs*
   (*b*) **izin**ja *dogs*   (*g*) **imi**fula *rivers*
   (*c*) **izi**kole *schools*   (*h*) **ama**bhodlela *bottles*
   (*d*) **aban**twana *children*   (*i*) **izin**dawo *places*
   (*e*) **ama**doda *men*   (*j*) **ama**ntombazana *girls*

5

UKUBUKEZA

Revision

1   You and an old acquaintance, Ray Mfeka, meet each other at the station.

   (a)   He greets you first.
   (b)   You respond excitedly (*Mehlomadala, Ray!*).
   (c)   He asks you how you are.
   (d)   You say that you are fine.
   (e)   You would also like to know how things are with him.
   (f)   He replies that he's OK.

With this information, create a suitable dialogue between you and Ray Mfeka.

2   You are holidaying at a seaside resort and have met someone with whom you would like to become better acquainted. How would you:

   (a)   tell him who you are?
   (b)   ask him who he is (name and surname)?
   (c)   tell him where you are from?
   (d)   ask him where he comes from?
   (e)   ask him where he stays (**-hlala**) (at the resort)?

3   You are shopping for groceries. Complete the following dialogue between you and the shop assistant by using the guidelines given in brackets as well as the words and phrases in the box:

ZULU

> -kusiza ngani? kukhona okunye na? (*Is there anything else?*)
> ibhotela (*butter*)   sekwanele (*It is all*) ushizi (*cheese*) -jabula, yimalini?
> yi- (*it is*)

Assistant	Nginga ___.
You	Nginga ___ (*Yes, please*). Ngifuna ___ (*and*) ___.
Assistant	Kulungile.
You	___ ushizi?
Assistant	___ R15 ngekhilogramu (*per kilogram*).
You	Kulungile ngizothatha uhafu wekhilogramu (*half a kilogram*).
Assistant	___? (Is there anything else?)
You	Cha, ___.
Assistant	Ngiyabonga.

4 Give the plural.

(a) **um**ntwana *child*
(b) **in**dlovu *elephant*
(c) **u**malume *uncle*
(d) **isi**timela *train*

(e) **i**tafula *table*
(f) **isi**memo *invitation*
(g) **umu**zi *village*
(h) **i**phinifo *pinafore*

5 Give the singular.

(a) **abe**lungu *White people*
(b) **izi**lwane *animals*
(c) **ama**Zulu *Zulus*
(d) **ama**Ngisi *Englishmen*

(e) **ama**Bhunu *Afrikaners*
(f) **izin**gane *small children*
(g) **imi**khonto *spears*
(h) **o**phopho *paw-paws*

6 ● Give the Zulu word for:

(a) the Zulu language
(b) the English language
(c) bananas
(d) onions
(e) name

(f) the Afrikaans language
(g) the Xhosa language
(h) pineapples
(i) tomatoes
(j) surname

● Briefly say what the following Zulu words and phrases mean:

(a) Angisazi isiZulu
(b) Uyakwazi ukukhuluma isiNgisi na?
(c) Ngubani igama lakho?
(d) Yilokho kuphela?
(e) Ngingakusiza na?
(f) Usaphila na?
(g) Ungubani wena?
(h) NgingumHholandi
(i) NgiyiNgisi
(j) NgiyiJalimane

7 How would you greet each of the following people?

(a) your friend Denise
(b) a married woman
(c) an adult (married) man
(d) an unknown male person (informally)
(e) more than one adult male person
(f) a respected gentleman
(g) a young boy

8 Correct and rewrite each of the following sentences:

(a) Sala kahle bafowethu (*my brothers*)
(b) Hambani kahle baba
(c) Igama lami yiNorman
(d) Isibongo sami yiNyembezi
(e) Ngizazi isiZulu
(f) Angisazi iBhunu
(g) UDavid uyiZulu
(h) Ngibonga
(i) Yimalini? Nga-R5
(j) Ngikhuluma isiNgisi nasiZulu

9 How do you say in Zulu:

(a) Thank you?   (d) No, thank you?
(b) Yes, please?   (e) What's the price?
(c) How are you?   (f) What's your name?

10 A Zulu mother tongue speaker speaks to you in Zulu. As a beginner you do not follow everything that he or she says to you. How will you ask the speaker:

(a) to repeat please, as you do not understand what he or she says?
(b) to speak slowly please as you do not understand so well?

11 Write (a) – (e) below in Zulu:

You have met a Zulu-speaking person called Albert and you are interested to know whether he is also proficient in some of the other African languages spoken in South Africa. You ask him whether:

(a) he (also) knows Tswana
(b) he can (also) speak Xhosa

He replies that:

(c) he knows Tswana but not very well

You ask him:

(d) where he has learned it

He replies that:

(e) he has learned (to speak) it in the townships (**emalokishini**).

6
AWUGCWALISE
Fill up, please (filling up at a petrol service station)

In this unit you will learn

- what to say when buying petrol at a garage
- how to ask politely for something
- how to ask yes/no questions
- what to say when tipping
- how to use the agreement system in Zulu
- the position of subjects in sentences

Ingxoxo

Most garages in South Africa employ petrol pump attendants. Their main task is to attend to the motorist's petrol needs but they also perform other duties such as checking your car's water, oil, battery and tyre pressure, and cleaning the windscreen.

Stephen Hall is on his way to work but notices that his car is low on petrol. He decides to fill up at one of the garages on his way and to use the opportunity also to have his car's water and oil checked – something he hasn't done for quite some time. At the garage he's greeted by Kepisi, one of the petrol pump attendants.

Kepisi	Good morning Sir.
Stephen	Yebo, sawubona ndoda.
Kepisi	Hawu! Ukhuluma isiZulu!
Stephen	Yebo, kancane.
Kepisi	Ngingakusiza ngani?
Stephen	Ngifuna uphetroli.
Kepisi	Wamalini?
Stephen	Awugcwalise bese uhlola amanzi nowoyela.
Kepisi	Kulungile.
	[After the water and oil have been checked:]
Kepisi	Ngiqedile mnumzane.
Stephen	Ugcwalisile na?
Kepisi	Yebo.
Stephen	[noticing that the windscreen is dirty]
	Awusule ifasitele, ngibona lingcolile.
Kepisi	Kulungile.
	[after having cleaned the windscreen:]
	Ufuna umoya?
Stephen	Cha, yilokho kuphela. Ngiyabonga. Ngikhokha kuphi?
Kepisi	Ukhokha kimi mnumzane.
Stephen	Malini?
Kepisi	Yi-R85 mnumzane.
Stephen	[giving the attendant a small tip:] Nasi isipho sakho.
Kepisi	Ngibonga kakhulu mnumzane.
Stephen	Nisale kahle.
Kepisi	Uhambe kahle mnumzane.

*Note: Blacks very often address White people in English or Afrikaans, since most Whites in South Africa cannot speak or understand a Black language. Whites who (unexpectedly) respond in a Black language seldom fail to elicit a favourable reaction from the person they communicate with.

Hawu! (exclamation of joyful surprise) e.g. *Well I never!*	**Ngiqedile** *I've finished*
Ukhuluma isiZulu! *You speak Zulu!*	**Ugcwalisile?** *Have you filled up?*
Yebo, kancane *Yes, a little*	**Awusule ifasitele** *Please wipe the (window =) windscreen*
Ngingakusiza ngani? *With what can I help you?*	**ngibona** *I notice*
Ngifuna uphetroli *I want (some) petrol*	**lingcolile** *it is dirty*
Wamalini? (*Of =) For how much money?*	**Ufuna umoya?** *Do you need air (for the wheels)?*
Awugcwalise *Please* (Lit. *make full*) *fill up (the tank)*	**Cha, yilokho kuphela** *No, that's all*
bese *and then*	**Ngikhokha kuphi?** *Where do I pay?*
uhlola *you inspect/check*	**Ukhokha kimi** *You pay (here) by me*
amanzi *the water*	**Malini?** *How much?*
nowoyela *and oil*	**Nasi isipho sakho** *Here's a (gift =) tip for you* (Lit. *Here's your gift*)
Kulungile *OK*	

Imibuzo (Questions)

Phendula imibuzo elandelayo (*Answer the following questions*):

(a) UStephen uyasazi isiZulu na?
(b) UStephen ufuna uwoyela na?
(c) UStephen ukhokha malini?
(d) Ngubani igama lomuntu osize (*helped*) uStephen?

———————— **Ulimi** ————————

1 Friendly requests

There are two ways of saying *please* when you are asking for something: the first is used when you request someone politely to *do something*, while the second is used when you politely ask someone *for something*.

Please bring us the menu

Attach **awu-** (or **mawu**) to the front of the verb and let the verb end on an **-e**, as for instance in:

> **awu**gcwalis**e** (< -gcwalisa *make full*)
> **awu**sul**e** (< -sula *wipe off*)

in the above dialogue. Compare also:

Awusilethel**e** (< -lethela *bring for*) imeniyu.	**Please** bring us (= -si-) the menu
Awuval**e** (< -vala *close*) umnyango, mnumzane.	**Will you please** close the door, sir?
Awungisiz**e** (< -siza *help*) lapha, baba.	**Please** lend me a hand here, baba.

When the request is directed to the 3rd person singular (Class 1, 1a) you use **maka-**:

> **Makalinde uThandiwe** (*Thandiwe must wait, please*).

Can we have some jam, please?

To ask for something politely you may use the verb stem **-cela** (*request*).

Ngi**cela** usizo.	(*I* **request** (*your*) *help* **please**), i.e. *Will you help me* **please**.
Si**cela** imeniyu.	*Can we have the menu,* **please**?
Si**cela** ujamu.	*Can we have some jam,* **please**?

Remember that you use the above ways of saying *please* when you want to make friendly requests and that they must be distinguished from the *please* we use when saying *Yes, please* (see Unit 4).

2 Asking yes/no questions

Plain statements in Zulu can be turned into yes- or no-questions, i.e. questions requiring a *yes/no* answer, without any change in the word order. Such questions normally have a falling intonation in Zulu and may, in addition, take the interrogative **na** which normally appears at the end of the sentence. Beginners are advised to use this **na** as much as possible when asking questions of this kind as it has the tendency of pulling the intonation downwards.

UyiNgisi **na**?	*Are you an Englishman?*
Ufuna ukungena **na**?	*Do you want to come in?*
Uphuma phesheya **na**?	*Do you come from abroad?*

3 Tipping

Tipping is by no means obligatory in South Africa. However, if service has been good you may want to leave a tip. Most restaurants, for instance, allow customers who prefer to pay by credit card to add a tip to the price of their meal. Many motorists prefer to give the petrol attendant a small tip, especially when 'extra' service has been rendered, like wiping the windscreen. To tip for example a petrol attendant or a waiter in a hotel or a restaurant you may say:

Ngibonga (*or* Sibonga) kakhulu.	*Thank you very much. Here's a*
Nasi isipho sakho.	*present (i.e. tip) for you.*

Instead of **nasi isipho sakho** you can also say:

Nansi imfalakahlana yakho.	*Here's some small change for you.*

or:

Nangu umbhanselo wakho.	*Here's a small something (=tip)*
	for you.

4 The agreement system: the subject concord

Closely related to the noun class system is the agreement system in Zulu, according to which certain words such as verbs and adjectives are linked to the nouns with which they occur. This agreement occurs in the form of a so-called concord which is derived from the noun class prefix with which it partially agrees in form. In the case of verbs you have two kinds of concords. One is the subjectival concord and the other the objectival concord. There are two important things one should know about these concords. First, they link the subject and object nouns to the predicate. Second, they may act as pronouns of the subject and object nouns they refer to. Both these concords form part of the verb. The subject concord, however, is an obligatory part of the verb and must appear in all verbs that have a subject. It occupies the initial position in the verb. Let's look at a few examples of how the subject concord acts as a link between the subject noun and the verb:

Um-fowethu **u**sebenza edolobheni	(*My brother he-works in town*) *My brother works in town.*
U-baba **u**yagula.	(*My father he-is sick*) *My father is sick.*
Aba-ntu **ba**yakhala.	(*The people they-complain*) *The people are complaining.*
I(li)bhasi **li**-hambile na?	(*The bus it-has left?*) *Has the bus left?*
Isi-timela **si**fike ngo-10	(*The train it-arrived at 10 o'clock*) *The train arrived at 10 o'clock.*
In-gane **i**yakhala na?	(*The baby he/she-is crying?*) *Is the baby crying?*

A practical hint for beginners: a quick way to get accustomed to the use of the subject concord in Zulu is to remember that where in English one says for instance *the child is ill*; *the people have left*; *the bus has come*, in Zulu you say '*the child he/she is ill; the people they have left; the bus it has come*', and so on.

5 Tables of subject concords

Subject concords of the different noun classes

noun class		subject concord	example
Class 1	um(u)-	u-	**um**ntwana **u**limele *the child is injured*
Class 2	aba-	ba-	**aba**ntu **ba**yakhala *the people are complaining*
Class 1(a)	u-	u-	**u**baba **u**khathele *father is tired*
Class 2(a)	o-	ba-	**o**dokotela **ba**yasebenza *the doctors are working*
Class 3	um(u)-	u-	**um**mese **u**khaliphile *the knife is sharp*
Class 4	imi-	i-	**imi**mese **i**buthuntu *the knives are blunt*
Class 5	i(li)-	li-	**i**bhasi **li**fikile *the bus has arrived*
Class 6	ama-	a-	**ama**nzi **a**yabanda *the water is cold*
Class 7	isi-	si-	**isi**nkwa **si**phelile *the bread is finished*
Class 8	izi-	zi-	**izi**tolo **zi**valiwe *the shops are closed*
Class 9	in-/im-	i-	**in**yama **i**mnandi *the meat is tasty*
Class 10	izin-/izim-	zi-	**izin**dlovu **zi**nengozi *elephants are dangerous*
Class 11	u(lu)-	lu-	**u**bisi **lu**mnandi *milk is nice*
Class 14	ubu-	bu-	**ubu**so bakhe **bu**ngcolile *his face is dirty*
Class 15	uku-	ku-	**uku**dla **ku**vuthiwe *the food is done*

Note that the subject concords of classes 5 and 11 are derived from an (underlying) part of the respective class prefixes of these classes that seldom, if ever, occurs in the written or spoken language.

When two nouns in class 1 or class 1a together form the subject of the sentence, then the subject concord is **ba-**:

   UJohn noMary bahambile.   John and Mary have left.

Subject concords of the first and second persons

1st p. sing.	ngi-	(**ngi**lambile *I am hungry*)
1st p. pl.	si-	(**si**lahlekile *we are lost*)
2nd p. sing.	u-	(**u**njani? *how are **you**?*)
2nd p. pl.	ni-	(**ni**njani? *how are **you**?*)

For the third person, see the different noun classes above.

6 The position of subjects in sentences

Although the basic position of subjects in Zulu is at the start of the sentence, they may just as well occur at the end (especially when the subject is known to both speaker and listener), i.e. you can say:

UMartha uyagula (or)   *Martha is ill.*
  Uyagula **uMartha**.
Abantu bazohamba kusasa (or) *The people will leave tomorrow.*
  Bazohamba kusasa **abantu**.
IsiZulu sihle kakhulu (or)   *Zulu is (a) very beautiful*
  Sihle kakhulu **isiZulu**.   *(language).*

✔ ———————— Umsebenzi ————————

1 You arrive at a petrol station to put some petrol in your car and also to have your car's tyres, water and oil checked. The attendant asks you (*a*) what he can do for you and you tell him (*b*) that you want some petrol. He asks (*c*) for how much and you ask him (politely) (*d*) to put in (= **-thela**) petrol for R80 (= **We-R80**). After he has done so you request him (again politely) to (*e*) check the water and oil. He asks (*f*) whether he should check the tyres (**ngihlole amasondo?**) and you tell him: (*g*) 'Yes, please'. He does so and asks if (*h*) there is anything else you need (= want) and you reply: (*i*) 'No, that's all, thank you'. (*j*) Finally, do not forget to tip the attendant.

Use the above information to create a suitable dialogue between you and the petrol pump attendant.

2 Complete the following sentences by providing the missing subjectival concord:

  (*a*) USolmon no-Anna ____buyile. *Solmon and Anna have returned.*
  (*b*) **In**yama ____phelile. *The meat is finished.*
  (*c*) **Is**inkwa ____phelile. *The bread is finished.*
  (*d*) **U**(lu)bisi ____phelile. *The milk is finished.*
  (*e*) **I**(li)khofi ____phelile. *The coffee is finished.*
  (*f*) **Im**ali yami ____phelile. *My money is finished.*

(g) **Ama**nzi ____phelile. *The water is finished.*
(h) **Uku**dla ____phelile. *The food is finished.*
(i) **Isi**Zulu ____hle. *Zulu is a beautiful language.*
(j) **Ama**ntombazana ____khathele. *The girls are tired.*
(k) **Abe**lungu na**ba**ntu ____yasizana. *The White people and the Black people help each other.*
(l) **I**(li)zulu ____shisa kakhulu namhlanje. *The weather is very hot today.*

3 You are on your way to work and unexpectedly bump into your old friend Winifred whom you haven't seen for a long time. You greet her first with **Mehlomadala Winifred!** *Good gracious!* (Lit. *Old eyes!*) Complete the following conversation between you and Winifred.

You   Mehlomadala Winifred! ____njani?
Winifred ____khona, wena ____?
You   Nami ____.
Winifred ____njani **aba**zali bakho? (*your parents*)
You   (*They*) ____phila.
Winifred Ngijabulile (*I'm glad*). Ungikhonzele kubo (*You must give them my regards.*)
You   Ngizokwenza njalo (*I'll do so.*)

4 Use two different ways to ask the greengrocer the price of (a) the bananas and (b) the pineapples, and then tell him that you'll take one (pineapple).

5 You are having dinner with family or friends at a rather large table. Ask them politely for each of the following items on the table:

(a) salt (**usawoti**)
(b) water (**amanzi**)
(c) pepper (**upelepele**)
(d) milk (**ubisi**)
(e) cheese (**ushizi**)

7
UNCAMSILE UKHUMBULA
— USUKU LOKUZALWA —
KWAKHE

Ncamsile celebrates her birthday

In this unit you will learn

- how to congratulate people
- how to wish someone well
- how to wish someone a happy Christmas and a prosperous New Year
- some exclamations and how to use them
- how to express the concept 'for'
- a further way to ask about someone's health
- about object concords and how to use them

 ──────────────── **Ingxoxo** ──────────────

Edith and Ken are invited to Edith's friend Ncamsile's birthday party. They arrive at Ncamsile's house and are met at the door.

Ncamsile	[delighted that her friend has come] Hawu! Sawubona sis' Edith. Sawubona bhut' Ken. Ninjani?
Edith	Siyaphila. Sicela kini?
Ncamsile	Nathi siyaphila. Awu! Ngijabula kakhulu uma nifikile.
Edith	Nathi siyajabula. Ngikufisela impilontle nempilonde ngokukhumbula usuku lokuzalwa kwakho.

Ncamsile	Ngiyabonga sis' Edith.
Ken	Nami ngikufisela unwele olude!
Ncamsile	Ngiyabonga bhut' Ken.
Edith	Sikulethele isipho esincane. Sethemba ukuthi uzosithanda.
Ncamsile	[pleasantly surprised] Hawu! Ngibonga kakhulu!

Sis' Edith *Sis (sister) Edith* (see also Unit 1)
Bhut' Ken *Brother Ken*
Sicela kini? *How's it with you?*
Nathi siyaphila *And we too are living* i.e. *OK*
nathi *we too*
Awu! Ngijabula ukuthi ufikile *My! I am happy that you have come*
Ngikufisela impilontle nempilonde Lit. *I wish (for) you a pleasant life and a long life*
impilontle *a pleasant life*
nempilonde (na-impilonde) *and a long life*
ngokukhumbula usuku lokuzalwa kwakho *on your birthday* (Lit. *with remembering your birthday*)
-khumbula *remember*
usuku *day*
ukuzalwa kwakho *the birth of you*
nami *I too*
unwele olude *May you live long* (Lit. *Long hair* – an idiomatic expression often used in congratulatory contexts)
Sikulethele isipho esincane *We brought (for) you a small present*
isipho *present*
esincane *small (present)*
Sethemba ... *We trust ...*
-ethemba *trust*
ukuthi *that*
uzokusithanda *you will like it*
Hawu! (exclamation of pleasant surprise)

Imibuzo

1 Kuyiqiniso noma akusilo? (*True or false?*) Correct and rewrite the false ones.

(a) UNcamsile ukhumbula usuku lokuzalwa kwakhe
(b) U-Edith noKen abajabuli kakhulu
(c) U-Edith noKen bafisela uNcamsile okuhle
(d) UNcamsile ufisela u-Edith okuhle

2 Phendula imibuzo elandelayo:

(a) U-Edith ufiselani uNcamsile? (**-ni** *what?*)
(b) UKen ufiselani uNcamsile?
(c) U-Edith noKen bamletheleni uNcamsile?
(d) UNcamsile ukhumbulani?

SIKUFISELA IMPILONTLE NEMPILONDE NGOKUKHUMBULA USUKU LOKUZALWA KWAKHO. MAVIS

1   Congratulating people/wishing them well

There are various expressions you may use to congratulate people or to wish them well. Here are few suggestions.

1.1   I/We wish you ...

This is expressed as follows:

Ngikufisela .../Sikufisela ...   *I / We wish (for) you*
                                    (sing.) (= **-ku-**) ....

Sinifisela ...   *We wish (for) you* (pl.) (= **-ni-**) ...

To this you may add **okuhle kodwa** *only the best*, e.g.:

Sikufisela okuhle kodwa.   *We wish (for) you only the best.*

or **usuku oluhle** *a nice day*, e.g.:

Nginifisela usuku oluhle.   *I wish (for) you (pl.) a nice day.*

or **impilontle** *a beautiful / prosperous life*, e.g.:

Ngikufisela impilontle.   *I wish (for) you a prosperous life (i.e. health and happiness).*

or **impilonde** *a long life*, e.g.:

Sinifisela impilonde.   *We wish (for) you (pl.) a long life.*

uKhisimuzi omuhle (nonyaka omusha omuhle)! *a happy Christmas (and a prosperous New Year)!*

Sinifisela uKhisimuzi omuhle nonyaka omusha omuhle.   *We wish you a Happy Christmas and a prosperous New Year.*

UKHISIMUZI OMUHLE
NONYAKA OMUSHA OMUHLE

A HAPPY CHRISTMAS
AND A PROSPEROUS NEW YEAR

In English you sometimes say *Cheers!* when sharing a drink with friends. In Zulu you say **Impilontle!**

1.2 Congratulations!

When congratulating someone you can either say **Halala!** *Congratulations!*, e.g.

Halala Ron! Wenze kahle.   *Congratulations Ron! You have done well.*

or use the verbal stem **-halalisela** as in:

Siyakuhalalisela Angela!   *We congratulate you, Angela!*
                           (**-ku** = *you*)

1.3 Congratulations on ...

When you want to say *Congratulations on* you use **nga-** for *on*.
However, this **nga-** becomes **ngo-** when followed by a noun starting
with **u-**, and it becomes **nge-** when followed by a noun beginning with
i-.

Halala ngokukhumbula   *Congratulations on (the*
  (< nga-ukukhumbula) usuku   *remembrance of) your birthday,*
  lokuzalwa kwakho, Paul.   *Paul.*

or:

Sikuhalalisela   *We (I) congratulate you on*
  (Ngikuhalalisela) ngosuku   *your birthday.*
  lokuzalwa kwakho.

2 Pronunciation of sisi and bhuti

The words **sisi** (*sister*) and **bhuti** (*brother*) which are popular forms of
address among contemporaries, especially in metropolitan areas, are
frequently pronounced without their final vowel.

Sawubona sis' Pamela   *Good day, sister Pamela.*
Halala sis' Nomsa   *Congratulations, sister Nomsa.*

Ngiyabonga bhut' John   *Thank you, brother John.*
Uphi ubhut' Jake?   *Where is brother Jake?*

In the last example **ubhut' Jake** is not addressed, which explains
why the initial **u-** is not omitted.

3 Exclamations!

Exclamations are a regular ingredient of Zulu. Here are a few popular
examples.

(emphatic) negation

Hhayi/Hhayibo!/Hhayikhona!	No! Most definitely not!

Hhayikhona! Akunjalo. *No! It's not so. You are lying!*
Ukhuluma amanga! (Lit. *You are talking lies*)
Hhayibo! Angifuni. ***Definitely not!*** *I don't want to.*

drawing someone's attention

We!	Hey!

We Mike! Ngiyakufuna. ***Hey*** *Mike! I'm looking for you.*
We bafana! Thulani! ***Hey*** *boys! Be quiet!*

wonder/surprise

Hawu!	Hurrah!, My word!, Good heavens!

Hawu! Bafikile! ***Hurrah!*** *They have come!*

Awu!	My!

Awu! Uphasile Sipho! *My! You have passed, Sipho!*

Mehlomadala!   (Lit. *Old eyes*) What a pleasure! Good gracious! (at meeting an old acquaintance)

Mehlomadala! Sakubona Lindi! *What a pleasure to see you again*
Unjani? *after such a long time, Lindi!*
How are you?

This last exclamation is very popular. You use it when greeting people whom you have not seen for a fairly long time.

pardon

| **Nxephe** | *Pardon!, Never mind! Sorry!* |

Nxephe mfowethu, angifuni
ukukuphazamisa.

*Sorry brother! I don't mean to
bother you.*

4 Expressing the concept 'for'

In Zulu, the concept *for*, as in 'I work for him', is expressed by changing the final vowel **-a** of the verb stem to **-ela**.

- -fis**a** *wish, desire*   -fis**ela** *wish for*
- -leth**a** *bring*   -leth**ela** *bring for*
- -sebenz**a** *work*   -sebenz**ela** work for

Ngisebenz**ela** iGolden City
Furnishers.

*I work for Golden City
Furnishers.*

- -biz**a** *call*   -biz**ela** *call for*

Ngizo**ku**biz**ela** ithekisi.

*I'll call a taxi **for you**.*

In the past tense **-ela** becomes **-ele**:

Sitheng**ele** umama isipho.

*We bought (**for**) mother a
present.*

Ngisebenz**ele** uHulumeni.

*I worked **for** the Government.*

-ela also becomes **-ele** when used in friendly requests:

Awu**si**leth**ele** imeniyu.   *Please bring (**for**) us the menu.*
Awu**ngi**phath**ele** ibhotela.   *Please pass (**for**) me the butter.*

Finally it must be noted that not all verbs that end in **-ela** incorporate the concept *for*, e.g.:

-tshela   *tell*
-vela   *come from*

5 The object concords

In English when you do not want to repeat the name of a person or an object in your discourse, you use a pronoun instead, as in 'Do you know **Mr Ntuli?** Yes, I know **him**', where the object noun *Mr Ntuli* has been replaced with the object pronoun *him*.

In Zulu you do not use pronouns to replace object nouns in your discourse, but you use object concords instead. Like its counterpart the subject concord (see Unit 6), the object concord is not an independent word but forms part of the verb. Its position in the verb is immediately before the verb stem as can be seen here:

- Ufuna **uGilbert?**   *Do you want **Gilbert?***
  Yebo, ngi-ya-**m**-funa.   *Yes, (I-**him**-want =) I want **him**.*
- Uthanda **amazambane?**   *Do you like **potatoes?***
  Yebo, ngi-ya-**wa**-thanda.   *Yes, (I-**them**-like =) I like **them**.*
- Ukhuluma **isiZulu** na?   *Do you speak **Zulu?***
  Yebo, ngi-ya-**si**-khuluma.   *Yes, (I-**it**-speak =) I speak **it**.*

Notice the difference in word order between Zulu and English. In English the object pronoun comes after the verb, as in 'I know *him*, We like *it*', whereas in Zulu it comes before the verb (stem): I *him* know, We *it* like.

Like the subject concords, the object concords are derived from the noun class prefix, which is why many objectival concords have the same or almost the same form as their subjectival counterparts.

noun class		subject concord	object concord
1st p. sing.		ngi–	–ngi–
1st p. pl.		si–	–si–
2nd p. sing.		u–	–ku–
2nd p. pl.		ni–	–ni–
Class 1	um(u)–	u–	–m–
Class 2	aba–	ba–	–ba–
Class 1a	u–	u–	–m–
Class 2a	o–	ba–	–ba–
Class 3	um(u)–	u–	–wu–
Class 4	imi–	i–	–yi–
Class 5	i(li)–	li–	–li–
Class 6	ama–	a–	–wa–
Class 7	isi–	si–	–si–
Class 8	izi–	zi–	–zi–
Class 9	in–/im–	i–	–yi–
Class 10	izin–/izim–	zi–	–zi–
Class 11	u(lu)–	lu–	–lu–
Class14	u(bu)–	bu–	–bu–
Class 15	uku–	ku–	–ku–

Subject concords that consist of a vowel only get **w-** or **y-** before them when they are used as object concords. Note, however, the form of the object concord in the case of classes 1 and 1(a).

Before vowel verb stems (see Unit 13) the vowel-part of most object concords is discarded, except in the case of the concords **-ku-** and **-lu-** which change to **-kw-** and **-lw-** respectively when appearing before vowel verb stems that begin with **a** or **e**:

Ngiya**kw**azi (< ngi-ya-**ku**-azi)   *I know you*
Uya**ng**azi na? (< u-ya-**ngi**-azi)   *Do you know me?*

Let's briefly exercise the use of some of the object concords listed above by providing the missing concord in the following examples. Note what the noun class prefix looks like before deciding on the appropriate object concord.

- Utshele **um**numzane Khumalo na?   *Have you told **Mr Khumalo**?*
  Yebo, ngi___tshelile.   *Yes, I have told **him**.*
- Ukhuluma **isi**Ngisi?   *Do you speak **English**?*
  Yebo, ngiya___khuluma.   *Yes, I speak **it**.*
- Ubone **i(li)**bhubesi na?   *Did you see **the lion**?*
  Yebo, ngi___bonile.   *Yes, I saw **it**.*
- Siya___fisela usuku oluhle Maria.   *We wish (for) **you** a nice day, Maria.*
- Siya___fisela usuku oluhle.   *We wish (for) **you** (pl.) a pleasant day.*
- Asi___azi (**u**baba Gumede).   *We do not know **him (baba Gumede** that is).*
- Ulethe **imali** (class 9) yami Zodwa?   *Did you bring my **money**, Zodwa?*
  Yebo, ngi___lethile.   *Yes, I brought **it**.*
- Usa___khumbula Simon?   *Do you still remember **me** Simon?*
- Yebo, ngiya___khumbula.   *Yes, I remember **you** (sing.).*

Umsebenzi

1 It's your friend Mary's wedding anniversary. Write a card to congratulate her and her husband on (=**nga-**) this happy occasion (**ukukhumbula usuku lokushada kwenu**) and to wish them (**ni** = *you*) a long and prosperous life. Begin your card with:

Mary othandekayo   *Dearest Mary*

And end it:

Yimi   *It is I*
Umngane wakho   *Your friend*
_____   (your name)

UROBERT DLOMO UFISA UKUNIMEMELA
EDILINI   LOSUKU LOKUZALWA
MHLA KA-24 SEPTEMBA NGO 8
KUSIHLWA ELONG LANE STREET, ARCADIA

ROBERT DLOMO WOULD LIKE YOU TO COME TO HIS
BIRTHDAY PARTY
ON 24 SEPTEMBER AT 8 P.M.
LONG LANE STREET, ARCADIA

2 Supply the appropriate exclamation

(a) ____ Susan! Yisikhathi eside sagcinana! (surprised)   *Hello Susan. It's such a long time since we've seen each other.*

(b) ____ Weta! Woza lapha! *Hey waiter! Come here (please)!*

(c) ____! Angiyi mina *No way! I'm not going*

(d) ____! Sicela ukwedlula *Please excuse us / Sorry! We would like to pass*

3 Complete each of the following sentences by filling in the appropriate object concord of the first and second person:

(a) Uya____ funa, Chris? *Are you looking for **me**, Chris?*

(b) Yebo, ngiya____funa. *Yes, I am looking for **you**.*

(c) Baya____biza na? *Are they calling **us**?*

(d) Yebo, baya____biza. *Yes they are calling **you** (pl.).*

(e) Uya____azi na? *Do you know **me**?*

(f) Yebo, ngiya____azi. *Yes, I know **you**.*

(g) Uya____khumbula na? *Do you remember **us**?*

(h) Yebo, ngiya____khumbula. *Yes, I remember **you** (pl.).*

(i) Uya____khumbula, Nonhlanhla? *Do you remember **me**, Nonhlanhla?*

(j) Yebo, ngiya____khumbula. *Yes, I remember **you** (sing.).*

(k) Nginga____siza na mnumzana? *Can I help **you**, sir?*

(l) Ngizo____fonela kusasa. *I will phone **you** tomorrow.*

4 Complete each of the following sentences by providing the missing object concord of classes 1 or 1a as the case may be:

(a) Angi____azi (lo muntu). *I do not know **him** (this person).*

(b) Ngizo____tshela kusasa. *I will tell **her** tomorrow.*

(c) Awu____bize. *Please call **him**.*

(d) Awu____tshele ukuthi siyamfuna. *Please tell **her** that we are looking for her.*

5 It is Christmas time. How will you wish a Zulu-speaking friend of yours a happy Christmas and a prosperous New Year?

6 It is your friend Mzilikazi Nxumalo's birthday. Send him a card in which you wish him a happy birthday.

7 ● Ask your friend Jacob to do the following for you:

(a) bring (**-letha**) you some tea (**itiye**)

(b) open (**-vula**) the gate (**isango**)

(c) call Joseph

● Tell Jacob that you will do (a) – (c) above for him.

8

IKHONA NA ISTONEY JINJABHIYA?

Do you have Stoney ginger beer?

In this unit you will learn how to

- ask whether something/someone is available
- say it is or it is not available
- ask where someone/something is
- say 'Here he/she/it is'/'There he/she/it is'
- ask whether someone has any small change
- say something is open, closed or locked
- form and use the present tense

Ingxoxo

It's a typical South African summer's day – hot and dry. Nomsa is on a long-distance journey by car. She's thirsty and decides to buy a cool drink. As many South African garages sell soft drinks she decides to buy one at the next garage and also to get some petrol and make use of the toilet facilities. She speaks to the attendant.

Nomsa	Nithengisa i-cooldrinki?
Attendant	Yebo.
Nomsa	Ijinjabhiya ikhona?
Attendant	Yebo ikhona.
Nomsa	Inhloboni?

Attendant	Yi-Stoney.
Nomsa	Iyabanda na?
Attendant	Yebo, ibanda kakhulu.
Nomsa	Kulungile. Ngizoyithatha.
Attendant	Ufuna (amathini) amangaki?
Nomsa	Ngifuna linye.
	[receiving the cool drink from the attendant]
	Ngiyabonga. Yimalini?
Attendant	Yi-R2.
Nomsa	Uphethe ushintshi?
Attendant	Wamalini?
Nomsa	We-R50.
Attendant	Yebo.
Nomsa	[handing the attendant a R50 note] Nansi (imali).
Attendant	Ngiyabonga dade.
Nomsa	Ithoyilethe likhona na?
Attendant	Yebo.
Nomsa	Likuphi?
Attendant	[pointing to the toilet] Nanto.
Nomsa	Livuliwe?
Attendant	Cha, nanku ukhiye.
Nomsa	Ngiyabonga.

Nithengisa i-cooldrinki? *Do you sell cool drink/soft drinks?*
Ijinjibhiya ikhona na? *Do you have ginger beer?*
Yebo, ikhona *Yes, we have*
Inhloboni? *What kind is it* (i.e. *Which brand is it?*)
Yi-Stoney *It is Stoney* (a well-known ginger beer brand name)
Iyabanda na? *Is it cold?*
Ngizoyithatha *I'll take it*
Ufuna (amathini) amangaki? *How many (cans) do you want?*

Ngifuna linye kuphela *I want only one (can)*
Yi-R2 *It is R2*
Uphethe ushintshi na? *Do you have any change on you?*
Wamalini? *(Of =) For how much money?*
We-R50 *For 50 Rands*
Ithoyilethe likhona na? *Is there a toilet (here)?*
Likuphi? *Where is it?*
Nanto *There it is*
Livuliwe na? *Is it open?*

Imibuzo

Kuyiqiniso noma akusilo? Correct and rewrite the false ones.

(*a*)   UNomsa ufuna ukuthenga i-cooldrinki
(*b*)   UNomsa ufuna ushintshi we-R20
(*c*)   UNomsa ucela amanzi
(*d*)   Ithoyilethe livaliwe
(*e*)   UNomsa ukhokhe (paid) R2.50

——————————— **Ulimi** ———————————

1   Asking questions with khona

1.1   Asking whether something is present

When you need or are interested in something and you want to find out whether it is available or nearby, you use the stem **khona** (together with its subject concord referring to the thing in question). In English you often begin such questions with *Is there ...?* or with *Do you have ...?*

U(**lu**)cingo **lukhona** na?	***Is there/Do you have*** *a telephone (here / nearby)?*
I(**li**)thoyilethe **likhona** na?	***Is there*** *a toilet (here)?*
I-Tourist Bureau **ikhona** na?	***Is there*** *a Tourist Bureau (here / nearby)?*
Likhona na izu?	***Is there*** *a zoo here?*
I-Coke **ikhona** na?	***Do you have*** *Coca-Cola?*
U(**lu**)bisi **lukhona** na?	***Do you have*** *milk?*

Note that the subject noun may either follow or precede **khona**.

1.2   Saying something is present

When the answer to a **khona**-question is positive, you simply reply by using the subject concord (appearing in the question) plus **khona**.

Ucingo lukhona na?
Yebo, **lukhona.**   *Yes, there is one.*
Amanzi anosoda (soda water)
  akhona na? Yebo, **akhona.**   *Yes, there is.*
ICoca Cola ikhona na?
  Yebo, **ikhona.**   *Yes, we have/there is.*
I-Tourist Bureau ikhona na?
  Yebo, **ikhona.**   *Yes, there is.*

1.3   Saying something is not present

When the answer to any **khona**-question is negative, you put **a-**
before the subjectival concord and discard the **na** of khona. Note that
the subject concord **u-** of class 3 becomes **wu-**; that of class 9 **yi-**; and
that of class 6 **we-** in the negative.

Ikhona i-Coke na? Cha, **ayikho** (< a-ikho).
Lukhona ucingo na? Cha, **alukho.**
Ukhona uthosi [class 3] (*toast*)? Cha, **awukho.**
Akhona **ama**nzi [class 6] abandayo (*cold water*) na? Cha, **awekho.**
Inyama (*meat*) [class 9] ikhona na? Cha, **ayikho.**

1.4   Asking whether someone is present

To ask whether someone is present, you use the stem **khona** together
with the subject concord of the noun referring to the person or persons you are looking for. When the person is a noun in classes 1 or 1a
the subject concord is **u-**, and when the person is a noun in classes 2
or 2a the subject concord is **ba-**.

UJabulani [class 1a] **ukhona** na?   *Is Jabulani here?*
U**M**numzane [class 1] Kruger   *Is Mr Kruger here?*
  ukhona na?
Abantwana [class 2] **ba**khona   *Are the children here?*
  na?

1.5   Saying someone is not present

Saying someone (signified by a noun in classes 1, 1a, 2 or 2a) is not
present, **ukhona** becomes **akekho** and **bakhona** becomes **abekho.**

USheila ukhona na?
  Cha, akekho.   *No **she isn't**.*
Udokotela ukhona na?
  Cha, akekho.   *No, **he isn't**.*
Abantwana bakhona na?
  Cha, **abekho.**   *No, **they aren't**.*
Ubaba nomama bakhona na?
  Cha, **abekho.**   *No, **they aren't**.*

Note that in the last example the subject concord of class 2 is used because **ubaba nomama** (*father and mother*) is a plural subject and as both nouns are in class 1a their plural is taken in class 2.

1.6 There is no one there

When you want to say that there is no one at a particular place, you say **Akunamuntu lapha/lapho** *There is no one here/there.* Or you can use the idiomatic expression:

  Kukhala ibhungane   *A beetle is buzzing there*

Beetles buzz when there is no sound of human voices around. So this is said when you come to a place, e.g. someone's home, and you find nobody there.

The expression may also be used when you telephone someone and find there is no answer. Note that in the past tense you say **Kukhale ibhungane**.

2 Loanwords and noun class membership

The lack of sufficient terminology, especially words signifying modern concepts, is in many ways still a serious problem in Zulu. To make up for this shortcoming, nouns are often borrowed from English and then used either unchanged or in a Zulufied form but always provided with the necessary class prefix. Thus, you have **iTourist Bureau, ikompiyutha** (*computer*), **inyuziphepha** (*newspaper*), and so on. Some speakers prefer to put these loanwords in class 5 (in which case they take the subject concord **li-**), while others prefer to put them in class 9 (in which case they take the subject concord **i-**).

3   Asking where someone/something is

To ask where someone or something is you use the interrogative (question) word **-phi?** (or **kuphi?** *Where?* in the case of places) and add to it the subject concord of the thing or person whose location you want to know.

Uphi **u**Davide?	*Where is David?*
Likuphi **i(li)**posihhovisi?	*Where's the post office?*
Luphi **u(lu)**bisi?	*Where's the milk?*
Baphi **aba**ntwana?	*Where are the children?*

4   (T)here he/she it is

If you are asked where a certain person or thing is you may respond by making use of special words that indicate the person or thing in question, provided such a person or thing is in sight. However, before you do so you first have to take into account to which noun class the noun in question belongs. If for instance it belongs to the **in-**class (class 9), we say **nansi**; to the **i(li)**-class (class 5), we say **nanti**.

Iphi **imali** yami?	*Where is my money?*
Nansi.	*Here it is.*

or

Nansi imali yakho.	*Here is your money.*

If the noun occurs in the **um-** or **u-** class (classes 1 and 1a respectively) and signifies humans, you say **nangu**.

Uphi **u**Paulina?	*Where is Paulina?*
Nangu.	*Here she is.*

or

Nangu u Paulina.	*Here is Paulina.*

The following are a few *Here is...* words for nouns belonging to some of the more popular noun classes.

Class 1	Nangu	Nangu umfana/umnumzana/umlungu
Class 1a	Nangu	Nangu uSamuel/umama/ubaba Khumalo
Class 5	Nanti	Nanti ibhotela/ibhasi/iposihhovisi
Class 6	Nanka	Nanka amanzi/amathikithi/amantombazana
Class 7	Nasi	Nasi isipho/isinkwa/isitolo
Class 9	Nansi	Nansi imali/imoto/indawo
Class 11	Nantu	Nantu ubisi

The words **nanti** and **nantu** have alternative forms, namely **nali** and **nalu** respectively.

umlungu *White person*	**ibhotela** *butter*
ubaba Khumalo *Mr Khumalo*	**iposihhovisi** *post office*
amathikithi *tickets*	**isinkwa** *bread*
amantombazana *girls*	**isitolo** *store*
indawo *place*	**ubisi** *milk*

To say *There is/are...* you simply replace the final vowel of the *Here is/are...* words with an **o**.

Uphi uJonathan?	*Where is Jonathan?*
Nango.	*There he is.*
Likuphi iposihhovisi?	*Where is the post office?*
Nanto.	*There it is.*
Nanto ibhasi manje!	*There is the bus now!*

5 Asking whether someone has any small change

When talking about money you may either say the amount in English or you may put an **i-** before the English name, for example:

ngiphethe **R10**   (*ten Rand*)

or

ngiphethe **i-R10**

The stem **-phethe** signifies *to have with you* (i.e. in your pocket, bag, etc. or in your hand). To ask whether someone has any small change with him you say:

Uphethe ushintshi na?   *Do you have any change on you?*

The same applies to any other lightweight article that can be carried.

Uphethe amathikithi/imali na?   *Do you have the tickets / money with you?*

In the negative, **a-** is added to the front of the positive verb.

Angiphethe ugwayi.   *I don't have any cigarettes with me.*

Asiphethe imali.   *We don't have any money with us.*

5.1   (Change) For how much?

The question **Uphethe ushintshi na?** (*Do you have any change on you?*) very often elicits the counter-question *For how much?*

Wamalini?   (Malini? *How much money?*)

To answer this question, **we-** is placed before the amount to be changed, e.g. **we-R20, we-R50**.

You	Uphethe ushintshi na, mfana?
Umfana	Wamalini?
You	We-R20.

5.2   Change for R20

If you want to know whether a person has small change for a certain amount of money, you ask:

Unotshintshi we-R20 na?/Uphethe utshintshi we-R20 na?

6   Is ... open/closed

To ask whether something is open or closed, like shops, Government departments, offices, doors, and so on you use the verb stems **-vuliwe** (*be open*) and **-valiwe** (*be closed*).

Izitolo **zivuliwe** namhlanje noma **zivaliwe**?   *Are the shops open or closed today?*
Ikhefi **livaliwe** na?   *Is the café closed?*
Onke amahhovisi **avaliwe** namhlanje.   *All offices are closed today.*

In the negative you simply put **a-** in front of the verb.

Cha, ikhefi **alivaliwe**.   *No, the café is not closed.*

It is important to distinguish between closed and locked. If something is locked you use the verb stem **-khiyiwe**.

Umnyango **ukhiyiwe**.	*The door is locked.*
Ihhovisi lakhe **likhiyiwe**.	*His office is locked.*

7 Expressing the present tense

The present tense in Zulu can be either marked or unmarked. When it is marked, **-ya-** is inserted in the verb just after the subjectival concord.

Liya**banda**.	*It is cold* (-banda *be cold*).
Baya**sebenza**.	*They are working.*
Uya**khala**.	*He is crying.*
Siya**hamba**.	*We are leaving.*

There are two important rules to note concerning the use of this present tense **-ya-**. First, **-ya-** never occurs in the negative; secondly, it must always be used in the present tense when no other words follow on the verb.

When the present tense verb is followed by another word or words the **-ya-** is normally omitted.

Ufuna imali?	*Do you want money?*
Ngibonga kakhulu.	*Thank you very much.*
Libanda kakhulu.	*It* (e.g. *the weather*) *is very cold.*

Note, however, that this rule does not apply when the verb is followed by a noun denoting the person to whom you are talking (the addressee).

Siya**bonga** baba.	*Thank you, sir.*
Ngiya**jabula** Moses.	*I'm glad, Moses.*

────── Umsebenzi ──────

1 Provide the missing parts in the following dialogue. Dudu Mkhize wants to borrow some money from her sister Agnes to buy a magazine.

Dudu	Uphethe imali Agnes?
Agnes	Yebo.
Dudu	Ngicela nje ungiboleke imali. (*Will you please lend me some money?*)
Agnes	Ufuna _____? (*How much do you want?*)
Dudu	Ngicela i-R10.
Agnes	Angi_____ i-R10, Ngi_____ i-R5 kuphela. (*I don't have R10 on me, I only have R5.*) Kuzolunga na? (*Will it be OK?*)
Dudu	Cha, ngifuna i-R10. Ubaba _____ na? (*Is father here?*)
Agnes	Cha, a_____.
Dudu	Nomama-ke? (*And mother?*)
Agnes	U_____.
Dudu	Ngizocela kuye. (*I'll ask her.*)

2 Remembering the rule about the present tense **-ya-** how would you express the following in Zulu:

   (a) I am working (**-sebenza**)
   (b) I am working today (**namhlanje**)
   (c) I am sick (**-gula**)
   (d) I am going (**-ya**)
   (e) I am going to town (**edolobheni**)

3 How would you ask someone:

   (a) whether there is a telephone/a doctor/an expensive restaurant (**irestouranti elibizayo**) nearby
   (b) for a beer (**ubhiya**) please (use **-cela** for this)
   (c) whether someone has change for R20?

4 How would you reply in the negative to the following questions:

   (a) Ucingo **lukhona** na?
   (b) **Likhona** iposihhovisi na?
   (c) **Akhona** amanzi na?
   (d) Isitimela (*train*) **sikhona** na?
   (e) Imali **ikhona** na?

5 How would you ask where the following people and things are:

   (a) Umnumzane Clayton
   (b) Isikhwama semali sami (*My purse*)
   (c) Inja kaLeonard (*Leonard's dog*)
   (d) I-oda lethu (*Our order*)

   (e) Imeneja (*Manager*)
   (f) Umama ((*My*) *Mother*)
   (g) UDavid
   (h) Abantwana

6 How would you say *There he is* and *There it is* in respect of all the persons and things mentioned in 5 above?

7 How will you tell someone that:

   (a) the stores are closed today
       but that
   (b) the supermarkets (**amasupamakethe**) are open?

9

— USEBENZANI JAMES? —

What do you do for a living, James?

In this unit you will learn how to

- ask someone's occupation
- say what your occupation is
- express the future tense
- ask 'what?'-questions
- ask/tell what time it is
- say that you are obliged to do something
- apologise
- form and use the negative of the present tense

Ingxoxo

James Mazibuko and Godfrey Nene are having a drink in a local pub. They have just been introduced by a mutual friend and are having a social chat.

James   Ngingakuthengela isiphuzo na Godfrey?
Godfrey Ngingajabula James.
James   Ungathanda ukuphuzani?
Godfrey Uwiski onamanzi uzolunga.
James   [after having ordered, James continues with the conversation] Usebenza kuphi Godfrey?

Godfrey	Ngisebenza eHoliday Inn.
James	Kuphi?
Godfrey	EThekwini.
James	Usebenzani lapho?
Godfrey	Ngiyi-accountant. Wena usebenzani?
James	Mina ngingumthengisi.
Godfrey	Umthengisi wani?
James	Ngingumthengisi wezimoto.
Godfrey	[noticing that James has finished his drink, offers to buy him another one.] Ufun'esinye isiphuzo na?
James	[remembering he has another appointment] Cha, angifuni mfowethu, nganelisiwe.
Godfrey	Uqinisile?
James	Yebo. Yisikhathi bani manje?
Godfrey	Ngu-2.30.
James	Ungixolele mfowethu, ngisendleleni.
Godfrey	Ujahephi?
James	Ngifanele ngiyobona ikhasimende lami.
Godfrey	Uyabuya?
James	Cha, angethembi kanjalo.
Godfrey	Uhambe kahle. Bekumnandi ukuhlangana nawe.
James	Ngibonga isiphuzo. Sobonana futhi. Usale kahle.

Ngingakuthengela isiphuzo na? *Can I buy (for) you a drink?*
Ngingajabula *Yes, please (Lit. I can be happy)*
Ungathanda ukuphuzani? *What would you prefer to drink?*
Uwiski onamanzi uzolunga *Whisky with water will be fine*
Usebenza kuphi? *Where do you work?*
Usebenzani? *What do you do for a living?/What work do you do?/What is your occupation?*
Ngiyi-accountant *I'm an accountant*
Ngingumthengisi *I'm a salesman*
wani? *of what?*
wezimoto *of cars*
esinye isiphuzo *another drink*

Angifuni *I don't want*
Nganelisiwe *I'm satisfied (i.e. I had enough)*
Uqinisile? *Are you sure?*
Yisikhathi bani manje? *What's the time now?*
Ungixolele *Please excuse me/Pardon me*
Ngisendleleni *I'm on my way*
Ujahephi? *Where are you going in such a hurry?*
Ngifanele ngiyobona ikhasimende lami *I must go and see a customer of mine*
ikhasimende *customer*
Uyabuya? *Are you coming back?*
Angethembi kanjalo *I don't believe so*
=ethemba *believe, trust, hope*

> **Bekumnandi ukuhlangana nawe**
> *It was good meeting you (to have met you)*
> **Ngibonga isiphuzo** *Thanks (for) the drink*
>
> **Sobonana futhi** *We'll see each other again (some other time)*

Imibuzo

Kuyiqiniso noma akusilo? Correct and rewrite the false ones.

(a) UGodfrey ucele uwiski onosoda
(b) UJames usebenza eThekwini
(c) UJames uthengisa izimoto
(d) UGodfrey ungumthengisi wezimoto
(e) UJames uyobona ikhasimende lakhe (*his*)

Ulimi

1 Asking someone's occupation

To find out what someone's occupation is, you ask:

Usebenzani? *What work do you do?*

If you know where a person works and you would like to know what kind of work he or she does, you ask:

Usebenza njengani? Lit. *You work as a what?*
Usebenza njengani lapho, Mabel? *What are you there, Mabel?*
(Lit. *You work as a what there?*)

2 Saying what your occupation is

If the noun signifying an occupation starts with **u-** (which it often does) you prefix it with **ng-**; and when it starts with **-i** you prefix it with **y-** (not forgetting to add the necessary subject concord before it).

Ngi**ngu**somabhizinizi. *I'm a businessman.*
URobert u**ngu**mthengisi wezimoto. *Robert is a car salesman.*

Umfana wami **ungu**makhaniki.	*My son is a mechanic.*
Ngi**yi**-accountant.	*I'm an accountant.*
Ngi**yi**sisitela.	*I'm a nursing sister.*
[pronounced ngiyisistela]	

Note:
- There is no word for *is, am* or *are* in Zulu
- Where no recognised Zulu name exists for a profession, speakers often make use of the English word and then simply add the prefix **yi-** or (in limited instances) **ngu-** to it.

Ngiyi-Marketing Consultant
Ngiyi-Subject Adviser
Uyi-Research Officer

When you want to say that you are employed as a ... (e.g. as a clerk), you combine the word **njenga-** with the name of the profession. Note that when the name of the profession starts with **u-**, **njenga-** changes to **njengo-**; and when the name starts with **i-**, **njenga-** changes to **njenge-**.

Ngisebenza **njengomabhalane**.	*I work as a clerk*
	(umabhalane *clerk*).
Usebenza **njenge-technician**.	*He works as a technician.*

3 It is (so-and-so) who ...

To say, '*it is so-and-so who...*' you put a **ngu-** before the name of the person and let the following verb start with **o-**. For example:

NguCharmaine **o**phuma eCape Town.	*It is Charmaine who comes from Cape Town.*
Ngu-Alfred **o**fundisa isiZulu.	*It is Alfred who teaches Zulu.*
NguNomasonto **o**sebenza lapho.	*It is Nomasonto who works there.*

If the word following **o-** is a noun the same rule given in (2) above applies:

NguThandi **o**n**g**utisha.	*It is Thandi who is a teacher.*
NguPhilemon o**yi**sitshudeni eWits.	*It is Philemon who is a student at Wits (University).*

When you want to say, '*It is I who...*', you begin with **Yimi** followed by **engi...** .

Yimi engisebenza KaNgwane.   *It is I who work in KaNgwane.*
Yimi engiphuma   *It is I who come from*
   eMgungundlovu.   *Pietermaritzburg.* (uMgungundlovu).

4   Asking what?-questions

What?-questions are formed by adding **-ni?** (*what?*) to the end of the
verb.

Bafuna**ni?**	***What*** *do they want* (=-funa?)
Ufuna ukuphuza**ni?**	***What*** *do you want to drink* (=-phuza)?
Wenza**ni?**	***What*** *are you doing* (=-enza)?
Ufuna ukwenza**ni?**	***What*** *do you want to do?*
Usebenza**ni?**	***What*** *are you working* (=-sebenza)? (i.e. *What kind* *of work do you do?*)

Note that the present tense **ya** never occurs in *what-* verbs.

5   Future tense

The future tense in Zulu is denoted by any one of several formatives
that form part of the verb, namely: **-zo-**, **-zoku-**, **-yoku-** or **-yo-**.

Ngi**zo**mtshela.	*I will tell him / her.*
Ngi**yo**qala kusasa.	*I will start tomorrow.*
Ngi**zoku**buya ngeSonto.	*I will come back on Sunday.*

6   Asking what time it is

There are several ways of asking what the time is. You can say any of
the following:

   Yisikhathi bani manje?
   Sithini isikhathi manje?
   Ngubani isikhathi manje?
   Yisikhathini manje?

Like most words with the prefix **isi-**, **isikhathi** is usually pronounced
as **iskhathi**.

You may answer this question by putting **ngu-** in front of the time given in English.

Ngu-2
Ngu-8.25

7 Saying that you must do something

To say that you *must do* (are obliged to do) something, you use the verb **ngifanele** (*I must*) followed by a verb that begins with the same subject concord, i.e. **ngi-**, and that ends with **-e**.

Ngifanele ngihambe manje. *I must go now.*
Ngifanele ngisebenze kakhulu. *I must work very hard.*

When you want to say *he/we/you must* ..., you use other appropriate subject concords not forgetting that the verb following **-fanele** must contain the same subject concord as **-fanele** (except for classes 1 and 1a, see below).

Ufanele **u**vuke ngovivi *You must wake up very early*
kusasa George. *tomorrow George.*
Abantwana **ba**fanele **ba**lungise *The children must tidy up*
ekamelweni labo. *their room.*
Nifanele **ni**bize amaphoyisa. *You* (pl.) *must call the police.*

Note that when you say *I must go and* ... the verb usually includes the future tense formative **-yo-** in which case it ends with **-a** and not with **-e**.

Abantwana **ba**fanele **ba**yolala *The children must go to*
manje. *sleep,* (i.e. *bed*) *now.*

In the case of the third person sing. (classes 1 and 1a), the subject concord of the verb following on **-fanele** is **a-** instead of the usual **u-**.

USamson **u**fanele **a**hambe *Samson must leave today.*
namhlanje.
UPearl **u**fanele **a**lungise *Pearl must tidy up the house*
endlini kusasa. *tomorrow.*

8 Apologising

When you want to apologise for something, you can either use the noun **uxolo** (*pardon/excuse (me)*) or the verb **ngiyaxolisa** which has more or less the same meaning.

Ngiya**xolisa** mnumzane, kodwa angisazi kakhulu isiZulu.	*Sorry sir, but I don't know Zulu very well.*
Siya**xolisa** kodwa asinamali.	*Sorry but we do not have any money.*
Uxolo kepha anginasikhathi manje.	*Sorry but I don't have the time now.*
Uxolo mnumzane, ngicela umgwaqo oya esiteshini	*Pardon me sir, but can you direct me to the railway station?* (Lit. *Excuse me sir, I request the road that goes to the station*)

Asking someone's pardon

If you want someone to pardon you, you can either use **uxolo** (*sorry, pardon*) or say **awungixolele** (*excuse me*)/**awusixolele** (*excuse us*).

| **Awungixolele** nkosikazi kodwa kufanele ngihambe manje. | *Please excuse me madam but I must go now.* |
| **Awusixolele** mnumzane sicele ukwedlula. | *Please excuse us, sir, we want to pass by (please).* |

9 Forming negatives in the present tense

There are basically two ways in which negatives are formed in Zulu: one is with **a-** and the other with **-nga-**. The **a**-negative form is used when we want to make negative statements such as *He/she doesn't smoke, I don't agree,* and so on.

A-negatives are formed from verbs in the present tense by letting the verb begin with **a-** (the **a-** is added to the subject concord) and changing the final vowel of the verb to **-i**.

Angibhem**i**.	*I don't smoke.*
Angethemb**i** kanjalo.	*I don't believe so.* (-ethemba *believe*)
Asifun**i** amanzi.	*We don't want water.*
Abathand**i** le ndawo.	*They don't like this place.*

Note that the subject concords **i-** and **u-** change to **ayi-** and **awu-** respectively in the negative, while the subject concord **a-** of class 6 (**ama-**class) changes to **awa-**.

- 2nd p. sing. Awuhambi manje mnumzane? / *Aren't you going now, sir?* (u-=*you* (sing.)).
- Class 6 Amanzi awabandi kakhulu. / *The water isn't very cold* (-banda *be cold*).
- Class 9 Ingane ayifuni ukudla. / *The child doesn't want to eat* (ukudla *to eat*).

Note, however, that the subject concord **u-** of class 1 and class 1a does not change to **awu-** but becomes **aka-** in the negative.

Ubaba **aka**phuzi. / *Father doesn't drink (alcohol)* (-phuza *drink*).

U-Emma **aka**yi. / *Emma isn't going* (-ya *go*).
Umnumzane Wilson **aka**funi itiye. / *Mr Wilson doesn't want tea* (-funa *want*).

Note that (passive) verbs ending on **-wa** or **-iwe** do not change their final vowel to **-i** in the negative.

Anganelis**iwe**. / *I'm not satisfied.*
Angiz**wa** kahle. / *I don't understand.*
Akubheny**wa** lapha. / *No smoking (allowed) here.*

Saying you (don't) want to do something

When you want to do something you say **Ngifuna uku-** followed by the verb expressing the thing you want to do.

Ngifuna ukukhala. / *I want to complain.*
Sifuna uku-oda. / *We want to order.*

In the negative, the verb **-funa** is negated in the normal way.

Angifuni ukukhala. / *I don't want to complain.*
Asifuni uku-oda manje. / *We don't want to order now.*
UClement **aka**funi ukulalela. / *Clement doesn't want to listen.*

───────────── **Umsebenzi** ─────────────

1 Imagine that you are having a cool drink at a sidewalk café. Suddenly Sally, a former colleague of yours, passes by. She comes to you and you invite her to (*a*) please sit down (= **-hlala phansi**)

ZULU

(i.e. to join you). (*b*) You introduce her to your friend Emelda (**Mangikwazise kumngane wami u-Emelda** – see Unit 11) and then (*c*) ask her whether she would like something to drink (**Ungathanda okuphuzwayo?** – see Unit 12). (*d*) She politely accepts. You ask her (*e*) what she would like to have (to drink). She says that (*f*) a cup of tea with milk (**itiye elinobisi**) will be fine (**-lunga**). You ask (*g*) what sort of work she is doing and she answers that (*h*) she is a receptionist (**umamukeli**). You ask her (*i*) where and she answers (*j*) at a legal practice (**kwa-Arthur Jones & Associates**). She asks you (*k*) what work you are doing and you say that you are a teacher (*l*). She says (*m*) that's fine (**Kuhle lokho**). She looks at the time and asks you (*n*) to please excuse her as (*o*) she has (**-fanele**) to go. (*p*) She thanks you for the tea. Then (*q*) she says goodbye.

Write a suitable dialogue based on the details given above.

2 What will you say when you:

(*a*) thank someone
(*b*) thank someone very much
(*c*) thank someone for his help (**usizo**)?

3 Rewrite the following in the correct form of the present tense:

(*a*) **Ngibonga** *Thank you*
(*b*) **Sibona** *We see / understand*
(*c*) **Uyafunani?** *What do you want?*
(*d*) **Uyafuna imali?** *Do you want money?*

4 Answer each of the following questions in the negative. Answer in full sentences.

(*a*) UGodfrey uphuza ubhiya (*beer*) na?
(*b*) UJames usebenza eGoli na?
(*c*) UMartin ufuna iCoca Cola na?
(*d*) Nikhuluma isiZulu na?
(*e*) Bafuna ukubaleka (=*run away*) na?
(*f*) Lishisa kakhulu (*It's very hot*) na?
(*g*) Kuyabiza (*It is expensive*) na?

5 How will you say you want:

(*a*) the account (**i-akhawundi**)?
(*b*) to sleep (**-lala**)?

(c)   to eat (**-dla**)?

(d)   to listen to the radio (**-lalela umsakazo/irediyo**)?

(e)   the doctor?

6 Supply the appropriate subject concord (and where necessary also the present tense **-ya-**) in each of the following sentences:

(a)   Laba **ba**ntu ____sebenza edolobheni. *These people work in town.*

(b)   Lo **mu**ntu ____sebenza epulazini. *This person works on a farm.*

(c)   Lesi **si**kole ____phume phambili. *This school came first.*

(d)   **Izin**gane ____hlabelela. *The children are singing.*

(e)   **Am**aposikadi ____biza. *The postcards are expensive.*

(f)   **Ama**phephandaba ____thengis**wa** ekhefini. *Newspapers are sold at the café.*

(g)   **I**langa ____khipha inhlanzi emanzini. *The sun takes fish out of the water* (proverb, i.e. *It is very hot*).

7 How do you say you are:

(a)   a teacher (**uthisha**)

(b)   a clerk (**umabhalane**)

(c)   an engineer (**unjiniyela**)

(d)   an attorney (**ummeli**)

(e)   a nurse (**unesi**)?

8 How will you say that:

(a)   it is Solomon who wants ice-cream (**u-ayisikhrimu**)

(b)   it is Mary who asked (**-cele**) for tea (**itiye**)

(c)   it is you who ordered (**-ode**) beer (**ubhiya**)

(d)   it is Kevin who is a doctor?

10
UKUBUKEZA
Revision

1 It is your parents' wedding anniversary (**ukukhumbula usuku lokushada kwenu**). Write a card to congratulate them on the happy occasion.

2 You want to buy a newspaper but you haven't any small change on you. How will you ask the newspaper vendor whether he has any petty cash? If he asks you for how much, how will you tell him this?

3 Send a Christmas card to one of your friends, wishing him/her a happy Christmas and a prosperous New Year.

4 You have pulled in at a garage to put petrol in your car and have your car checked for water. You tell the attendant (*a*) that you want some petrol (**uphetroli**). He asks you (*b*) for how much and you say (*c*) for R80. Your children want to go to the toilet, so you ask the attendant whether (*d*) there is a toilet and he replies that (*e*) there is one. You then ask (*f*) where it is. He shows you where (*g*) (*there it is*). You ask whether (*h*) it is open. (*i*) He replies in the negative and you ask him whether (*j*) he has the key (on him). (*k*) He says yes.

Write an appropriate dialogue based on the information given above.

5   You are looking for the following people and things. How will you
    ask someone whether they are available or in the vicinity:

    (a) uNoNhlanhla (name of person)
    (b) ucingo (*telephone*)
    (c) u(bu)tshwala (*beer*, also traditional African beer)
    (d) uweta (*waiter*)
    (e) amanzi abandayo (*cold water*)
    (f) inyuziphepha (*newspaper*)
    (g) ikhemisi (*chemist*)
    (h) abelungu (*White people*)
    (i) isikole esincane (*primary school*)
    (j) iyunivesithi (*university*)

6   Answer the questions in 5 above, first in the positive (Yes,
    he/it/there... is) and then in the negative (No, he/she/there... is not,
    e.g. **likhona, alikho**).

7   Answer the following questions, first in the positive and then in
    the negative. Do not, however, repeat the object. Refer to it by
    means of the appropraite object concord, e.g. Uthanda
    i-cooldrinki? Yebo, ngiya**yi**thanda:

    (a) Ukhuluma isiSuthu?
    (b) Uyamazi uGeorge Thwala?
    (c) Uthanda uwiski [class 3]?
    (d) Udla inyama yehhashi (*horse-meat*)?
    (e) Ubhema (*smoke*) insangu (dagga)?
    (f) Ufuna iSoweton [class 9]? (name of newspaper)
    (g) Uthanda uJohanna?
    (h) Uthanda umsebenzi [class 3] wakho? (*your work*)
    (i) Wesaba (u-esaba *afraid*) izinja na?
    (j) Ufunda iBhayibheli na? (*Bible*)

8   Rewrite in the negative of the present tense:

    (a) Ngisebenza namhlanje (*today*)
    (b) Ngiya edolobheni (*to town*)
    (c) Ngihlala eGoli
    (d) UNomusa uhlala eThekwini
    (e) ULizzie usebenza kwa-du Toit (*the du Toit's house*)
    (f) Ugogo ugula (*sick*) namhlanje
    (g) Abantwana baya esikoleni (*to school*) namhlanje

(h) Amadoda asebenza kakhulu (*hard*)

(i) Ibhantshi lakhe (*his jacket*) liyabiza (*expensive*)

(j) Ngiyezwa (*I understand*)

9 Rewrite in the positive of the present tense (do not forget the rule about **-ya-**):

(a) Angikhulumi isiNgisi

(b) Angifuni

(c) U-Esther akasebenzi edolobheni

(d) UJohannes akalaleli (*listens to*) irediyo (radio)

(e) Imoto yakhe ayibizi

(f) Angizwa (*I do not understand*)

(g) Angizwa kahle (*very well*)

(h) Abantwana abaguli

(i) Ugogo akaphili kahle (*feeling well*) namhlanje

(j) Asithandi ibhola (*football*)

10 You are having lunch with a friend. Ask him to please pass you:

(a) the tomato sauce (**usoso katamatisi**)

(b) the mustard (**umasitadi**)

11 Say what these people do for a living by using the words in brackets (e.g.: **UPeter uyinjiniya** *Peter is an engineer*)

(a) umfowethu (*my brother*) (**isisebenzi sikaHulumeni** *civil servant*)

(b) ubaba (uprofesa *professor*)

(c) umama (umabhalana *secretary*)

(d) Lindiwe (unesi *nurse*)

(e) Titus (isitshudeni *student*)

12 Give the meaning of these nouns:

(a) umuntu

(b) inja

(c) umuzi

(d) imali

(e) inyama

(f) isitolo

(g) isikolo

(h) umsebenzi

(i) usizo

(j) amanzi

(k) isiSwazi

(l) iphephandaba

(m) ujamu

(n) isinkwa

(o) ushintshi

13 Give the meaning of these expressions:

   (*a*) Yilokho kuphela
   (*b*) Ngicela ubisi
   (*c*) Nangu uJabulani
   (*d*) Ngibonga kakhulu
   (*e*) USharon usebenzani?
   (*f*) Yisikhathi bani manje?
   (*g*) Ngiyaxolisa
   (*h*) Wenzani manje?
   (*i*) Impilontle!
   (*j*) Mehlomadala!

11
NGIJABULELA
UKUKWAZI RON

Pleased to meet you, Ron

In this unit you will learn

- what to say when introducing people
- some Where?-questions
- ask distances between places
- how to express some numbers
- names of some places/countries/buildings/squares

 ——————— **Ingxoxo** ———————

Sam Ndlovu who is from eMnambithi in KwaZulu-Natal is introduced by his friend Neil to two of Neil's friends, Bob and Ron. Ron is from America. In the following social chat Ron asks Sam where he comes from and where exactly this place is located.

Neil Sam, mangikwethule kubangane bami.
[introducing Bob] NguBob lo.
[introducing Ron] NguRon lo.
[to Bob and Ron] NguSam lo.

Sam [speaking to Ron] Ngijabulela ukukwazi, Ron.

Ron Nami ngijabulela ukukwazi.

Neil URon uphuma eMelika.

Sam	[somewhat surprised to meet someone from abroad] O! Uphuma eMelika? Angikaze ngaya khona.
Ron	Uphumaphi wena?
Sam	Ngiphuma eMnambithi.
Ron	[not having heard the name before] Kuphi?
Sam	EMnambithi.
Ron	Kukuphi eMnambithi?
Sam	Kuse-Ladysmith eNatali.
Ron	Kukude ukusuka lapha?
Sam	Yebo, kodwa hayi kakhulu.
Neil	Kungamakhilomitha amangaki kusuka lapha?
Sam	Kungamakhilomitha angu-150.
Neil	Ngiyabonga.

Mangikwethule (ma-ngi-ku-ethule) kubangane bami Let me introduce you to my friends
-ethula introduce
abangane bami my friends
NguBob lo This is Bob
NguRon lo This is Ron
Ngijabulela ukukwazi Pleased to meet you (Lit. I'm glad to know you)
Nami I too
Uphuma eMelika? You come from America?
Angikaze ngaya khona I have never been there
Uphumaphi? Where do you come from?

eMnambithi Ladysmith (a town in KwaZulu-Natal)
Kukuphi eMnambithi? Where is eMnambithi situated?
KuseLadysmith It is (in) Ladysmith
eNatali in Natal
Kukude ukusuka lapha? Is it far from here?
kodwa hayi kakhulu but not very much
Kungamakhilomitha amangaki ukusuka lapha? How many kilometres is it from here?
Kungamakhilomitha angu-150 It is 150 kilometres

Imibuzo

1 **Kuyiqiniso na noma akusilo?** Correct and rewrite the false ones.

(a) URon uphuma eGermany
(b) EMnambithi kuseDurban
(c) USam ujabulela ukumazi uRon
(d) UNeil uyamazi uBob

2 Phendula okulandelayo (Answer the following).

   (*a*) Ngubani ophuma eMelika?
   (*b*) USam uphuma kuphi?
   (*c*) EMnambithi kukuphi?
   (*d*) UNeil wethule ubani kuSam?

Ulimi

1 Introducing people

1.1 Introducing one person

To introduce one person to someone else you say **Mangikwethule ku-...** or **Mangikwazise ku-...** (*Let me introduce you to ...*) followed by the noun (minus its initial vowel) denoting the name of the person or persons to whom the introduction is made.

Mangikwethule kumnyeni wami.	*Let me introduce you to my husband* (=umnyeni).
Mangikwazise kumngane wami uJanet.	*Let me introduce you to my friend* (=umngane) *Janet.*
Mangikwethule kubazali bami.	*May I introduce you to my parents* (abazali bami *my parents*)?

1.2 Introducing more than one person

When you want to introduce more than one person to someone, you say **Manginethule ku...** or **Manginazise ku...**

Manginethule(=ma-ngi-ni-ethule) kumama wami.	*Let me introduce you* (pl.) (=**-ni-**) *to my mother.*
Manginazise (=ma-ngi-ni-azise) kumngane wami uHerbert.	*Let me introduce you* (pl.) *to my friend, Herbert.*

Presenting people individually during introduction you place **ngu-** in front of the person's name and a (demonstrative) **lo** after it.

Mangikwethule kuPeter noJennifer.	*Let me introduce you to Peter and Jennifer.*
NguPeter lo.	*This is Peter.*
NguJennifer lo.	*(And) this is Jennifer.*

1.3 Pleased to meet you

When you are introduced to someone it is customary to respond by saying something like *pleased to meet you, nice to have met you, nice to know you,* and so on. An appropriate response in Zulu is to say

Ngijabulela ukukwazi (Lit. *I'm happy to know you* (sing.) or **Kumnandi ukukwazi**. (*It is nice to know you.*).

Mangikwethule kunkosikazi
Howard.

Let me introduce you to Mrs Howard.

Ngijabulela ukukwazi nkosikazi.

Pleased to meet you, madam (=nkosikazi).

When someone says to you **Ngijabulela ukukwazi**, you can reply by saying **Nami ngijabulela ukukwazi** *I too* (=nami) *am glad to have met you.*

2 Where? questions

2.1 Where are you going to?

Where?-questions are formed by means of **-phi?** which, when occurring with verbs, is attached to the end of the verb.

Uya**phi**?

Where are you going? (**-ya** go)

Uhlala**phi**?

Where do you stay? (**-hlala** stay)

Lisuka**phi** ibhasi?

Where does the bus depart from? (**-suka** depart)

To say that you are not going anywhere, you say **Angiyi ndawo**. (*I am going nowhere*).

Uyaphi manje Zenzele?

Where are you going to, Zenzele?

Angiyi ndawo Jabu.

I am going nowhere, Jabu.

2.2 Where do you come from?

To find out where a person comes from (i.e. where his or her home is) you ask:

Uphumaphi?/Uvelaphi?

Where do you come from?

Ukuphi ngokuhlala?

Where do you reside (i.e. Where is your home)?

2.3 I come from ...

In response to the question *where do you come from?* (i.e. *where is your home?*) you can say **Ngiphuma** or **Ngivela** plus the name of the place (or country).

| Ngiphuma eThekwini. | *I come from Durban.* |
| Sivela eNgilandi. | *We come from England.* |

An alternative way to state where you come from is to say **Ngis- ...** (*I am from ...*), **Sis- ...** (*We are from ...*) and the name of the place or country, followed by **ngokuhlala** (*residing*).

Niphumaphi? **Sise**Germany ngokuhlala.	*We are from Germany.*
Bakuphi ngokuhlala?	*Where do they reside?*
BaseHolland **ngokuhlala**.	*They are from Holland.*

2.4 Asking where something/someone is

The interrogative **-phi?** may also be used to ask the whereabouts of somebody or something. This is done by prefixing the subject concord of the person or thing whose whereabouts are being questioned to **-phi?**

Uphi uweta?	*Where is the waiter?*
Liphi ikamelo lokudlela?	*Where is the dining-room?*
Baphi abantwana?	*Where are the children?*
Iphi imali yami?	*Where's my money?*

2.5 Where is the Post Office?

When you want to know where a certain place (e.g. building) is, you use **kuphi?** instead of **-phi?**

Likuphi iposihhovisi [class 5] lapha?	*Whereabouts is the Post Office?*
Sikuphi isiteshi?	*Whereabouts is the station?*
Akuphi amahhovisi kaMasipala?	*Whereabouts are the municipal offices?*

When you want to know where a certain town is you say **kukuphi** followed by the name of the place.

| Kukuphi eStellenbosch? | *Whereabouts is Stellenbosch?* |
| Kukuphi eSt Lucia? | *Whereabouts is St Lucia?* |

It is important to note that the first **ku-** in this construction is, in fact, the subject concord **ku-** referring to the place name.

If you know where the place is, you may answer with **Kus-...** (*It is in ...*) followed by the name of a place or area where the place in question is situated.

> Kukuphi eStellenbosch?
> KuseKapa.   *It is in the Cape Province.*
> Kukuphi eSt Lucia?
> KuseNatali.   *It is in Natal.*

When the place name begins with **Kwa-** you simply put **ku-** (i.e. the subject concord) in front of it.

> Kukuphi eShowe?   *Whereabouts is eShowe?*
> KuKwaZulu.   *It is in KwaZulu.*

If the place in question is near another place, you say **Kuseduze nas- ...** (*It is near ...*) followed by the name of the other place.

> Kukuphi ePinetown?   *Whereabouts is Pinetown?*
> Kuseduze naseThekwini.   *It is near Durban.*
> Kukuphi eSoweto?   *Whereabouts is Soweto?*
> Kuseduze naseGoli.   *It is near Johannesburg.*

If it is a building whose location you want to describe, you use the subject concord of the noun denoting the building instead of the subject concord **ku-** in **kus-** or in **kuseduze**.

ITourist Bureau **lise**Carlton Centre.	*The Tourist Bureau **is in** the Carlton Centre.*
IHoliday Inn **lise**Marine Parade.	*The Holiday Inn is on Marine Parade.*
IState Theatre **liseduze** naseChurch Square.	*The State Theatre **is near** Church Square.*

3   Asking distances

3.1 Is the Post Office far from here?

The word **kude** (*far*) is used for this purpose. It is preceded by the subject concord of the noun signifying the name of the place in question.

Iposihhovisi likude (ukusuka lapha) na?	I*s the Post Office far (from here)?*
(**ukusuka lapha** may be omitted)	
Isiteshi sikude ukusuka lapha na?	*Is the railway station far from here?*

The answer could be:

Yebo, likude.	*Yes it (the Post Office) is far;*
or	
Cha, alikude, liseduze.	*No, it's not far, it is nearby* (=seduze).

3.2 Asking how far a particular place is

South Africa is a large country and places are often relatively far apart. Calculating the distance between two points with the aid of a road map can be quite awkward at times. It's usually much easier to find out from the local people what the distance is. But beware! It frequently happens that what many of the local inhabitants consider to be not very far may eventually turn out to be much further than you have anticipated.

To enquire how far (i.e. how many *kilometres* = **amakhilomitha amangaki?**) a certain place is from where you are at that particular time, you say:

[Place name] kungamakhilomitha amangaki ukusuka lapha?	*[Place name] is how far (i.e. how many kilometres) from here?*
EGoli kungamakhilomitha amangaki ukusuka lapha?	*How far, (i.e. how many kilometres), is Johannesburg from here? (Lit. Johannesburg is with how many kilometres going from here?)*

Compare also:

EGoli kungamakhilomitha amangaki ukusuka ePitoli?	*How far is Johannesburg from Pretoria?*
EThekwini kungamakhilomitha amangaki ukusuka eGoli?	*How far is Durban from from Johannesburg?*

Note that many of the older speakers still prefer to use the old distance measure **amamayela** (*miles*) instead of the new official term **amakhilomitha** (*kilometres*).

4 Expressing numbers

Zulu possesses a rather complicated numeral system. Many mother tongue speakers prefer to use a less cumbersome system whereby English numerals are used. Native speakers nevertheless admire people (especially Whites) who know how to use the traditional Zulu way of counting. We'll pay more attention to this system at a later stage (see Unit 21). Suffice it to say here that the modern way of expressing numbers in Zulu is by means of **ngu-** plus number (pronounced in English) preceded by a concord referring to the people or things being counted.

To express the number of kilometres you say **angu-** + number.

Kungamakhilomitha amangaki?	*How many kilometres is it?*
Kungamakhilomitha angu-55, angu-100, ...	*It's 55, 100, ... kilometres.*

In fact, all nouns in the **ama-**class (like **amakhilomitha**) are counted in this way.

Ukhokhe malini?	*How many / much did you pay?*
Ngikhokhe **ama**Randi **angu**-25.	*I payed R25.*
Ufuna **ama**pentshisi **ama**ngaki?	*How many peaches do you want?*
Ngifuna **angu**-4.	*I want four (peaches).*

5 Names of places in South Africa and countries

Asking a person where he or she hails from usually elicits the name of a place in the answer. Two kinds of place names in South Africa may conveniently be distinguished: traditional (rural) place names and place names of 'White' cities and towns. The latter can be divided into two groups: places with Zulu names and those with 'Zulufied' English and Afrikaans names. Here are the names of a few important places in South Africa as they are known among Zulu-speaking people.

Places with Zulu names	
Johannesburg EGoli (*the place of gold*)	**Port Elizabeth** EBhayi
	Zululand KwaZulu
Germiston EDukathole	**Amanzimtoti** EManzimtoti (*Sweet Waters*)
Durban EThekwini	**Ladysmith** EMnambithi
Pietermaritzburg EMgungundlovu/EMalitzboko	**East London** EMonti
	Umlazi EMlazi (township near Durban)

Most places in Zulu-speaking areas (like for instance in KwaZulu-Natal) have Zulu names.

Most English and Afrikaans place names may be 'Zulufied' by putting **e-** before the place name while the form of some place names is also slightly modified in order to bring them more in line with the Zulu sound system.

Places with basically English/Afrikaans names		Soweto	ESoweto (< South Western Townships)
Pretoria	EPitoli	**England**	ENgilandi
Nelspruit	ENelspotho	**London**	ELandani
Vryheid	EFilidi	**Scotland**	ESikotilandi
Ermelo	EMlomo	**Germany**	EJalimani/EGermany
Dundee	EDandi	**Holland**	EHolland

6 Names of buildings and squares

Buildings and squares are usually referred to in their locative form, i.e. as locations. This is why **e-** is usually added to the front of their names.

eCarlton Centre
eState Theatre
eChurch Square
eMarine Parade

Umsebenzi

1   You and a friend (Kevin Sharp) meet Oscar Dhlomo whom you have met before. How would you:

(a)   introduce Kevin to Oscar?
(b)   ask Oscar where he comes from?
(c)   tell him where you come from?
(d)   tell Oscar that Kevin is from Scotland
(e)   ask Oscar where the toilet (**ithoyilethe** [class 5]) is?
(f)   ask Oscar whether the First National Bank (**iFirst National Bank** [class 9]) is far from here?

(g) ask Oscar how far (i.e. how many kilometres) the Kruger National Park (**iKruger National Park** [class 9]) is from Pretoria?

(h) tell Oscar you paid R100?

(i) ask Oscar where Kevin is?

(j) tell Oscar your hotel (**ihhotela lethu** *our hotel*) is near the City Hall (**eCity Hall**)?

2 Answer the following questions by using the information given in brackets.

(a) Uphumaphi? (Scotland/Soweto/Durban/Vryheid)

(b) Niyaphi? (Zululand)

(c) EMalitzboko kungamamayela amangaki ukusuka eThekwini? (90)

(d) Ungubani wena?
Nikuphi nina (you (pl.)) ngokuhlala? (London)

(e) Liphi iStandard Bank? (West Street)

(f) Isiteshi sikude na? (No, it's nearby)

(g) Ufuna malini? (R150)

(h) Liphi i-O K Bazaars? (Smith Street)

(i) Uphethe ushintshi? (For how much?)

3 You have a new girl friend (Sheila) whom you like to introduce to your family. You two arrive at your parents' house in Johannesburg and are met by your mother and younger brother Vincent. (a) First you greet your mother and brother and then (b) introduce Sheila to your mother. Sheila responds by saying that (c) she's pleased to meet her. Then you tell Sheila that (d) this is your brother (**umfowethu**) Vincent. Sheila says that (e) it's nice to meet him. Your mother is interested to know (f) where Sheila comes from and she replies that (g) she's from Durban.

Use the above informaton to create a suitable dialogue between you, Sheila and your mother.

4 Supply the missing positive and negative subject concords in the following sentences (see Unit 8, 1.3 and 1.5)

(a) UMoses ____khona na?   Cha, ____kho

(b) Umlungu [class 1] ____khona?   Cha, ____kho

(c) Abelungu [class 2] ____khona?   Cha, ____kho

(d) Ikhemisi [class 5] (*chemist*) ____khona? Cha, ____kho

(e) Isibhedlela (*hospital*) _____khona?   Cha _____kho
(f) Udokotela _____khona?   Cha, _____kho

5 Give the English equivalents for these Zulu words.

(a) umama
(b) mangikwethule
(c) kuseduze
(d) eGoli
(e) uyaphi?
(f) imali
(g) uyakwazi ukukhuluma isiZulu?
(h) ubaba
(i) ngiyajabula
(j) iposihhovisi
(k) eThekwini
(l) uhlalaphi?
(m) iNgisi
(n) umfowethu
(o) uphumaphi?
(p) isiteshi
(q) ePitoli
(r) yimalini?
(s) umZulu

6 Give the plural.

into (*thing*)
isibane (*light/lamp*)
umlungu (*White person*)
ibhayisikili (*bicycle*)
iBhunu (*Afrikaner*)
inyoni (*bird*)
uphayinaphu (*pineapple*)
umuzi (*village*)

7 How would you ask Simon politely to do the following things:

(a) to come in (**-ngena**)
(b) to close the door (**-vala umnyango**)
(c) to call the waiter (**-biza uweta**)
(d) to bring you (=us) some water (**-silethele amanzi**)
(e) to help you (**-ngisize**)

8 How will you ask someone:

(a) where is he going (=**-ya**)
(b) where does he come from (**-phuma**)
(c) where does he stay (=**-hlala**)
(d) where is the dining-room (=**ikamelo lokudlela**)
(e) whether he has any change (=**ushintshi**)
(f) whether he/she can speak Zulu?

12

SICELA IMENIYU

Can we have the menu please?

In this unit you will learn how to

- order a meal in a restaurant
- ask permission to do something
- deny someone permission to do something
- say something is forbidden (public signs)
- ask someone what (s)he would like to have/wants
- say you want/need something
- ask What?-questions
- say you like something and you want to do something
- ask what something tastes like
- say 'I like to...' and 'I want to...'
- use the emphatic pronouns

Ingxoxo

Sipho Ngcobo and his wife Lindiwe have decided to dine out. The following conversation takes place in the restaurant between Sipho and the waiter.

Waiter   [greeting Sipho and his wife] Sanibonani.
Sipho   Sawubona.
Waiter   Nginganinceda ngani?

Sipho	Sicela imeniyu.
Waiter	Nifuna uku-oda?
Sipho	Yebo.
Waiter	Kulungile. Ngisayilanda mnumzane. [after having brought the menu] Nansi imeniyu mnumzane.
Sipho	Ngiyabonga.
	[studying the menu with his wife, Sipho asks:]
	Niphakamisani namhlanje?
Waiter	Namhlanje siphakamisa ipepper steak.
Sipho	Injani ipepper steak?
Waiter	Imnandi kabi kakhulu!
Sipho	Nenhlanzi?
Waiter	Inhlanzi nayo imnandi kakhulu mnumzane. Eqinisweni sinesipesheli senhlanzi namhlanje.
Sipho	Siyini?
Waiter	Yi-King Klip mnumzane
Sipho	[having decided what to order]
	Inkosikazi yami izothatha iKingKlip, mina ngizothatha ipepper steak.
Waiter	Ipepper steak ibe njani? Ivuthwe kancane noma ivuthwe kakhulu?
Sipho	Ivuthwe kancane kodwa ingavuzi igazi.
Waiter	Kulungile mnumzane. Ungathanda amatshipisi noma izambane elithosiwe?
Sipho	Mina ngifuna amatshipisi, inkosikasi yami ifuna izambane elithosiwe.
Waiter	Namasaladi?
Sipho	Yebo, sifuna amasaladi.
Waiter	Nifuna okuphuzwayo?
Sipho	Yebo-ke.
Waiter	Nifuna ukuphuzani?
Sipho	Sifuna iwayini.
Waiter	Kulungile, ngizobiza elinye iweta.
Sipho	Singabhema lapha na?
Waiter	Cha, akubhenywa lapha mnumzane.

Nginganinceda ngani? *Can/may I help you* (pl.)? (**-nceda** *help* is an alternative form for **-siza**)	**Ibe njani?** *How must it (the pepper steak) be?*
Sicela imeniyu *We want the menu please*	**ivuthe kancane** *it* (i.e. *the meat*) *must be under-done* (i.e. *lightly cooked*)
Nifuna uku-oda? *Do you want to order?*	**noma** *or*
Ngisayilanda *I'll quickly go and fetch it*	**ivuthwe kakhulu** *it* (*the meat*) ***must be*** (Lit. *well cooked*) *well done*
Nansi imeniyu *Here's the menu*	**kodwa** *but*
Niphakamisani? *What do you* (pl.) *recommend?*	**ingavuzi igazi** *it must not be under-done* (Lit. *it must not leak blood*)
Namhlanje *Today*	**Ungathanda amatshipisi?** *Would you like some chips?*
Injani ipepper steak? *What's the pepper steak like?*	**izambane elithosiwe** *baked potato*
Imnandi kabi kakhulu *It's very nice,* i.e. *very tasty*	**namasaladi?** *and salad?*
kabi kakhulu *very (much)*	**Nifuna okuphuzwayo?** *Do you want something to drink?*
Nenhlanzi? *And the fish?*	**okuphuzwayo** *something to drink*
Inhlanzi nayo ... *The fish too ...*	**Yebo-ke** *Yes, please*
eqinisweni *in fact*	**Nifuna ukuphuzani?** *What do you want to drink?*
sinesipesheli *we have a special*	**iwayini** *wine*
senhlanzi (of=) *on fish*	**Ngizobiza elinye iweta** *I'll call another waiter*
Siyini? *What is it (the special)?*	**Singabhema lapha?** *May we smoke in here?*
Inkosikazi yami *My wife*	**Cha, akubhenywa lapha** *No, it (i.e. smoking) is prohibited in here*
YiKing Klip *It is King Klip* (a local kind of fish)	
Inkosikazi yami izothatha ... *My wife will take,* i.e. *will have ...*	
mina (emphatic 1st p. sing. pronoun)	

Imibuzo

1 Kuyiqiniso noma akusilo? Correct and rewrite the false ones.

(a) Banesipesheli senyama (*meat*) namhlanje
(b) USipho akathandi iwayini
(c) USipho nenkosikazi yakhe bafuna amasaladi
(d) Kuyabhenywa lapha

2 Phendula okulandelayo. (*Answer the following.*)

(a) Uweta uphakamisani?
(b) USipho nekosikazi yakhe bafuna ukuphuzani?

(c) Siyini isipesheli namhlanje?
(d) Ngubani ofuna izambane elithosiwe?
(e) I-pepper steak ibe njani?

Ulimi

1 Asking permission to do something

To ask whether you *may* do something, the formative **-nga** is inserted in the verb immediately after the subject concord.

Si**nga**-oda manje?	***May*** *we order now?*
Ngi**nga**bhema lapha na?	***May*** *I smoke here?*
U**nga**hamba manje.	*You* ***may*** *go now.*

Note that the subject concord of classes 1 and 1a which is normally **u-** changes to **a-** when combining with the so-called potential formative **-nga-**.

UJojo **anga**hamba manje na?	***May*** *George go now?*
Umfana **anga**ngena na?	***May*** *the boy come in?*

2 I prefer mine under-done/well done

Ordering meat in a restaurant you are usually asked how you would like it, i.e. under-done, well done or medium. To say how you prefer your meat you reply:

Ngithanda ivuthwe kakhudlwana.	*I prefer it medium.*
Ngithanda ivuthwe kakhulu.	*I prefer it well done.*
Ngithanda ivuthwe kancane.	*I prefer it under-done.*

3 Saying you may not do something

When you want to say that someone *may not* do something, you replace **nga-** with **nge-** and let the verb end on **-e**.

U**nge**hambe manje Jonas.	*You* ***may not*** *go now, Jonas.*
U**nge**ngene lapho Catherine	*You* ***may not*** *go in there, Catherine.*
U**nge**bheme lapha baba.	*You* ***may not*** *smoke in here, father.*

4 Saying something is not allowed

To say something is not allowed, you attach the negative formative
aku- to the front of a verb stem appearing in passive form which in
this instance often means a verb ending on **-wa**.

Akungenwa lapha	*No thoroughfare / entrance here* (-ngena *enter*)
Akubhukudwa lapha	*No swimming allowed here* (-bhukuda *swim*)
Akubhenywa lapha	*No smoking allowed in here* (-bhema *smoke*)
Akupakwa lapha	*No parking allowed here* (-paka *park*)

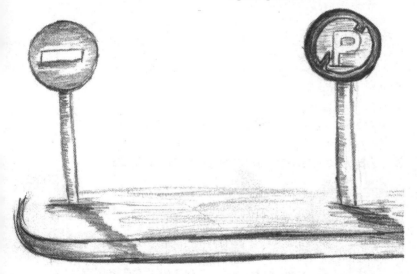

5 Asking someone what (s)he would like to have

To express *would like* as in 'Would you like some tea?', you say
ungathanda (*would you* (sing.) *like*) or **ningathanda** (*would you*
(pl.) *like*), followed by the name of the thing or action desired.

Ungathanda itiye na?	*Would you like some tea?*
Ningathanda iwayini?	*Would you* (pl.) *like some wine?*

Ungathanda okuphuzwayo?	*Would you like something to drink?*

This expression may, of course, also be used in statements.

Ngingathanda izambane elithosiwe.	*I would like to have / I prefer to have a baked potato.*
Singathanda ukuhlala phambili.	*We would like / we prefer to sit in front.*

6 Asking someone what (s)he wants

To ask someone what (s)he wants, you use the stem **-funa** (*want*), add the interrogative **-ni?** (*what?*) to the end of it and the appropriate subject concord to the front.

Ufunani?	*What do you want?*
Nifunani?	*What do you* (pl.) *want?*

7 Saying you want/need something

When you want or need something or someone, you say **ngifuna** (*I want / I need*) or **sifuna** (*we want / we need*) followed by the name of the thing or person you want.

Ngifuna inkomishi yetiye.	*I want a cup of tea.*
Sifuna okuphuzwayo.	*We want something to drink.*
Sifuna amasaladi.	*We want (some) salad.*

Remember that requests with **-funa** are less polite than those with **-cela** (see Unit 6).

8 Saying that you like/prefer something

For this you use the stem **-thanda** (*like*).

Ngithanda itiye.	*I like / prefer tea.*
Bathanda ikhofi.	*They like / prefer coffee.*
Sithanda isiZulu.	*We like Zulu.*

9 Saying you want to (do something)

To say that you *want to do* something, you once again say **ngifuna** followed by a verb starting with **uku-** (*to*).

Ngifun'ukuhamba.	*I want to go.*
Sifun'ukudla.	*We want to eat.*
Sifun'uku-oda manje.	*We want to order now.*
Bafun'ukuvalelisa.	*They want to say goodbye.*

By replacing **-funa** with **-thanda** you say *I like to ...*

Ngithand' ukukhuluma isiZulu.	*I like to speak Zulu.*
Sithand' ukuphuza itiye elinobisi.	*We like to drink tea with milk.*

Note: **uku-** means *to*.

ukudla	*to eat* (**ukudla** also means *food*)
ukuhlala	*to sit*

The construction **-funa uku-** is usually pronounced as **-fun'uku-**, and **-thanda uku** as **-thand'uku-**.

10 Finding out what something tastes like

Visitors to foreign countries are often intrigued by local food and alcoholic drinks, not to mention their often unfamiliar names. To find out what something tastes like (e.g. an item on a menu) you use the stem **-njani?** (*how?*) preceded by the subject concord of the noun referring to the thing you want to know the taste of.

Injani iKing Klip?	*How's the King Klip?*
Linjani ikhasela?	*What is Castle (beer) like?*
Injani iNederburg Riesling?	*How's the Nederburg Riesling* (=wine)

If you want to say *it is nice*, you use the stem **-mnandi**.

Injani ifillet steak? [class 9]	*How's the fillet steak?*
Imnandi.	*It's nice.*
Unjani uphuthini? (*pudding*) [class 3]	*What is the pudding like?*
Umnandi kakhulu.	*It's delicious.*
Lunjani uphuthu [class 11]	*What is the phuthu like?* (traditional thick Zulu porridge)
Lumnandi kakhulu.	*It is very nice.*

— **111** —

Note that Zulu has no word for *is* or *are*.

In the negative you simply prefix **a-** to the positive.

>**Ayi**mnandi (< **a-i**mnandi) i-fillet steak.
>**awu**mnandi (< **a-u**mnandi) uphuthini
>Alumnandi uphuthu.

The change of the subject concords **i** > **yi** and **u** > **wu** comes about naturally when you pronounce **a-i** and **a-u** rapidly.

11 The emphatic pronouns

Zulu has a system of what is known as emphatic pronouns. These pronouns serve to emphasise the nouns or, in the case of the first and second persons, the pronouns.

Mina ngithanda ubisi.	*As for me, **I** like milk.*

To emphasise the first person plural, the pronoun **thina** is used, while the emphatic pronouns **wena** and **yena** are used to emphasise the second person singular and the third person singular (classes 1 and 1a) respectively.

Thina sifuna ikhofi kodwa uPeter [class 1a] **yena** ufuna itiye.	*We want coffee but as for Peter, **he** wants tea.*
Wena ungahlala, **thina** siyahamba.	*You can stay but as for us, we are leaving.*

Every noun class has its own emphatic pronoun which is used to emphasise the nouns of that particular class. Note that these pronouns usually follow the noun they emphasise.

AmaZulu **wona** athanda ukugcina amasiko awo.	*The Zulu people, on the other hand, like to preserve their customs.*
Umama akabhemi kodwa ubaba **yena** uyabhema.	*Mother does not smoke, but father, on the other hand, does smoke.*

Emphatic pronouns

1st p. sing.		mina		1st p. pl.		thina
2nd p. sing		wena		2nd p. pl.		nina
Class 1	**um(u)-**	yena		Class 2	**aba-**	bona
Class 1a	**u-**	yena		Class 2a	**o-**	bona
Class 3	**um(u)-**	wona		Class 4	**imi-**	yona
Class 5	**i(li)-**	wona		Class 6	**ama-**	wona
Class 7	**isi-**	sona		Class 8	**izi-**	zona
Class 9	**In-**	yona		Class 10	**izin-**	zona
Class 11	**u(lu)-**	lona				
Class 14	**ubu-**	bona				
Class 15	**uku-**	khona				

Umsebenzi

1 You are about to have a meal in a steakhouse. It's your turn to order. You speak to the waitress. Complete your part of the dialogue.

Waitress	Sawubona mnumzana.
You	Greet the waitress using a suitable form of address
Waitress	Ngingakusiza ngani?
You	Ask her to bring the menu please. Studying the menu you ask her what she recommends
Waitress	I-T bone steak limnandi kakhulu.
You	Tell her you'll take one
Waitress	Uthanda libe njani?
You	Tell her you prefer (**-thanda**) it to be medium (livuthwe kakhudlwana)
Waitress	Ufun'okuphuzwayo?
You	Yes please
Waitress	Ufunani?
You	Tell her that you would like to have a beer (ubhiya)

2 Give the plural.

(a) umthengisi *salesman*   (e) ihhashi *horse*
(b) isikole *school*   (f) inyoni *bird*
(c) inja *dog*   (g) ikati *cat*
(d) umshini *machine*   (h) utamatisi *tomato*

3 Give the singular.

(a) amadoda *men*
(b) izinto *things*
(c) izitolo *shops*
(d) abantwana *children*

(e) abantu *people*
(f) imizi *villages*
(g) amakhosi *chiefs*
(h) izinkomo *cattle*

4 Give the Zulu for:

(a) telephone
(b) bread
(c) mother
(d) English
(e) milk
(f) butter
(g) my name
(h) Zulu

(i) money
(j) meat
(k) my surname
(l) Afrikaans
(m) water
(n) father
(o) very much

5 How will you tell your Zulu friend that you would like:

(a) to speak Zulu
(b) to read books (**-funda izincwadi**)
(c) to watch TV (**-bukela iTV**)
(d) to play football (**-dlala ibhola**)

6 And how will you tell him/her that you want:

(a) to listen to the radio (**-lalela umsakazo**)
(b) to rest (**-phumula**)
(c) to make a phone call (**ukushaya ucingo**)
(d) a cool drink?

13
SICELA UKU-ODA
IWAYINI

Can we order some wine please?

In this unit you will learn

- how to ask about the form of payment
- how to express satisfaction/dissatisfaction with something
- about the stative form of verbs
- about vowel verb stems

Ingxoxo

In the previous dialogue we met Sipho Ngcobo and his wife Lindiwe while they were dining out. We left just as they were about to order some wine. The following is the conversation between Sipho and the wine steward.

Steward Sawubona mnumzane. Ufuna okuphuzwayo?
Sipho Yebo.
Steward [jokingly] Nomile na?
Sipho Yebo, somile.
Steward Kulungile. Ngizonilethela ilisti yewayini.
  [after having fetched the wine list] Nansi-ke mnumzane.
Sipho Ngiyabonga. [while examining the wine list Sipho asks his wife:] Ungathanda iwayini ebomvu noma emhlophe?

Lindiwe	Akunandaba. Khetha wena.
Sipho	[selects a dry white wine] Mina ngithanda iwayini emhlophe ebabayo. Ilungile yini?
Lindiwe	Yebo, ilungile.
Steward	[brings the wine, pours a little in a glass and enquires whether it tastes all right] Ilungile?
Sipho	Yebo, ilungile. Imnandi.
	[meanwhile the order is served and Sipho is dissatisfied with the way the meat has been prepared and complains to the waiter.] Le nyama ayilungile. Ngicele ukuthi ingavuzi igazi kodwa bheka, iseluhlaza! Awuyibuyisele ekhishini bayipheke kahle.
	[after the matter has been settled and everyone is satisfied]
Steward	Wanelisiwe manje mnumzane?
Sipho	Yebo nganelisiwe.
	[after they've finished their meal Sipho calls the waiter]
Sipho	Weta!
Steward	Yebo, mnumzane.
Sipho	Sicela i-akhawundi. [having received the account] Nginga-khokha nge-credit card noma namukela ukheshe kuphela?
Steward	Samukela kokubili mnumzana.
Sipho	Ngikhokhe kuphi?
Steward	Khokha kimi mnumzane. Nihamba manje?
Sipho	Yebo, sikhathele kancane.
Steward	Nihambe kahle.
Sipho	Ngiyabonga. [handing the waiter the money] Nansi.
Steward	Ngiyabonga mnumzana.

Nifuna okuphuzwayo? *Do you (pl.) want something to drink?*
Nomile na? *Are you thirsty?*
Somile *We are thirsty*
Ngizonlethela ilisti yewayini *I'll bring (for) you (pl.) the wine list*
ilisti *list*
Ungathanda iwayini ebomvu *Would you prefer a red wine*
noma *or*
emhlophe *a white one*
Akunandaba *It doesn't matter*
-khetha *choose*

iwayini ebomvu *red wine*
iwayini emhlophe ebabayo *dry white wine*
-babayo *dry*
Le nyama ayilungile *This meat is not right*
Ngicele ukuthi ingavuzi igazi *I have requested that it must not be underdone*
bheka, iseluhlaza *look, it is still uncooked (= underdone)*
Awuyibuyisele ekhishini *Please return it to the kitchen*

-buyisela *return something to* (*someone/a certain place*)	**-amukela** *accept*
bayipheke kahle *so that they cook* (*-roast*) *it properly*	**kuphela** *only*
wanelisiwe? *are you satisfied?*	**Samukela kokubili** *We accept both*
i-akhawundi *account*	**kokubili** *both*
Ngingakhokha *May I pay* (see also Unit 12)	**Ngikhokhe kuphi?** *Where must I pay?* (see also Unit 11)
-khokha *pay*	**Nihamba manje?** *Are you going now?*
Namukela ukheshe kuphela? *Do you accept cash only?*	**Sikhathele kancane** *We are a little tired*

TABLE MOUNTAIN

1993
SAUVIGNON BLANC

STELLENBOSCH
Produce of South Africa

Imibuzo

Kuyiqiniso na noma akusilo? Correct and rewrite the false ones.

(a) NguSipho ocela imeniyu (see Unit 9)
(b) NguSipho othanda iwayini ebomvu
(c) NguLindiwe othanda iwayini ebomvu kuphela (*only*)
(d) ULindiwe wanelisiwe
(e) ULindiwe ukhala (*complains*) ngokudla (*about the food*)

——————— **Ulimi** ———————

1 May I pay by credit card/cheque?

To enquire about the form of payment, you can use the verb stem
-amukelwa (*be accepted*) or the verb stem **-amukela** (*accept*) or the
verb stem **-amukeleka** (*be acceptable*). When you're about to settle
your account with, for example, your Visa card, you may ask:

    (a) IVisa Card **yamukelwa**   *Is Visa Card accepted here?*
        (i-amukelwa) lapha na?
    (b) **Namukela (ni-amukela)**   *Do you accept Visa Card?*
        iVisa Card na?
    (c) IVisa Card **iyamukeleka** na? *Is Visa Card acceptable?*

When you want to pay by cheque you ask:

    (d) **Namukela** isheke na?   *Do you accept cheques?*

When the answer to (a) is yes, you can say:

    Yebo, **iyamukelwa**   *Yes, it is accepted.*
    (i-ya-amukelwa).   (Note **-ya-** must be used)

When the answer to (b) is yes:

    Yebo, **siyayamukela**   *Yes, we accept it.*
    (si-ya-y(i)-amukela).   (The pronoun (concord) **-y(i)-**
                       refers to the object noun
                       iVisa Card. (See also
                       Unit 7.)

When the answer to (c) is yes:

    Yebo, iyamukeleka.   *Yes, it is acceptable.*

When the answer to (d) is yes:

    Yebo, **siyalamukela**   *Yes, we accept it.*
    (si-ya-l(i)-amukela).   (The pronoun **-li-** refers to
                       isheke *cheque*).

2 Expressing your satisfaction/dissatisfaction with something

When you want to know whether someone is satisfied you ask:

Wanelisiwe na? (=u-anelisiwe)	*Are you (sing.) satisfied?*
Nanelisiwe na? (=ni-anelisiwe)	*Are you (pl.) satisfied?*

For the third person plural you ask:

Banelisiwe na? (=ba-anelisiwe) *Are they satisfied?*

When you want to express your satisfaction with the service you have received, or you want to say that you've had enough to eat or drink, you say:

Nganelisiwe.	*I'm satisfied.*
Sanelisiwe.	*We are satisfied.*

When you are not satisfied you simply say **cha** (*no*) and put **a-** before the positive expression.

Wanelisiwe mnumzana?	*Are you satisfied, sir?*
Cha, anganelisiwe.	*No, I'm not satisfied.*
Nanelisiwe na?	*Are you (pl.) satisfied?*
Cha, asanelisiwe.	*No, we are not satisfied.*

3 The stative form of the verb

Verbs that express a persisting state are known in Zulu as stative verbs. They signify a certain condition or state that someone/something is in, e.g. *I am hungry, we are thirsty, your hands are dirty.* There are several ways in which stative verbs are formed in Zulu.

(*a*) The general rule is to substitute **-ile** for the final vowel of the verb stem.

-lamb**a**	*become hungry*	-lamb**ile**	*be hungry,* e.g. Silambile *We are hungry*
-phuz**a**	*drink*	-phuz**ile**	*be drunk,* e.g. Uphuzile *He is drunk*
-om**a**	*become thirsty*	-om**ile**	*be thirsty* e.g. Ngomile. *I'm thirsty.*
-phel**a**	*get finished*	-phel**ile**	*be finished* e.g. Ukudla kuphelile. *The food is finished.*

(b) Verbs that end on **-ala** or **-atha** change to **-ele** and **-ethe** respectively in the stative.

-l**ala** *go to sleep*	-l**ele** *sleep*, e.g. Izingane zil**ele**. *The children are asleep.*
-khath**ala** *become tired*	-khath**ele** *be tired*, e.g. Sikhathel**ele** kakhulu. *We are very tired.*
-gcw**ala** *become full*	-gcw**ele** *be full*, e.g. Le ndawo igcw**ele** kakhulu. *This place is very full.*
-ph**atha** *hold*	-ph**ethe** *hold / have on you*, e.g. Uph**ethe** imali Ephraim? *Do you have any money on you, Ephraim?*

(c) Verbs that end in **-wa** change to **-iwe** in the stative.

-anelis**wa** *become satisfied*	-anelis**iwe** *be satisfied*, e.g. Nganelisiwe (ngi-anelisiwe). *I'm satisfied.*
-val**wa** *get closed*	-val**iwe** *be closed*, e.g. Izitolo zivaliwe namhlanje. *The shops are closed today.*

It is important to note that the present tense **-ya-** never appears as part of stative verbs.

Note also that the verb stem **-sutha** *satisfied with food* has an irregular stative form in that it ends on **-i**.

Ngiyabonga kodwa **ngisuthi**. *Thank you but I have had enough (to eat).*

Negative of stative verbs

Stative verbs are negated by prefixing the negative formative **a-** to the positive form of the stative verb, bearing in mind the change that the negative creates in the form of some of the subject concords (see also Unit 9).

Silambile > **A**silambile.	*We are not hungry.*
Ngomile (ngi-omile) > **A**ngomile.	*I'm not thirsty.*
UZanele uthokozile > UZanele **aka**thokozile.	*Zanele is not happy.*
Imali iphelile > Imali **ayi**phelile.	*The money is not finished.*
Amadoda aphuzile > Amadoda **awa**phuzile.	*The men are not drunk.*

Abantwana bakhathele
> Abantwana **aba**khathele. *The children are not tired.*
UMandla ulele > UMandla
akalele. *Mandla is not sleeping.*
Ngiphethe imali > **Angi**phethe
mali. *I have no money on me.*

Negative subject concords

1st p. sing.	angi-	1st p. pl.	asi-
2nd p. sing.	awu-	2nd p. pl.	ani-
Class 1 um(u)-	aka-	Class 2 aba-	aba-
Class 1a u-	aka	Class 2a o-	aba
Class 3 um(u)-	awu-	Class 4 imi-	ayi-
Class 5 i(li-)	ali-	Class 6 ama-	awa-
Class 7 isi-	asi-	Class 8 izi-	azi-
Class 9 in-	ayi-	Class 10 izin-	azi-
Class 11 u(lu)-	alu-		
Class 14 u(bu-)	abu-		
Class 15 uku-	aku-		

4 Vowel verb stems

Vowel verb stems are verb stems that begin with a vowel. The reason
why these stems are singled out is because of the change they cause
in the form of the preceding formatives that are added on to them.
The following two rules of thumb apply to the form of the subject and
object concords (see Unit 7) and the present tense **-ya-**:

(*a*) Subject and object concords that consist of a consonant and vowel
(including the present tense **-ya-**) normally discard the vowel.

Si-omile > **S**omile. *We are thirsty.*
Ngi-omile > **Ng**omile. *I'm thirsty.*
Ba-enze kahle > **B**enze kahle. *They have done well.*
Ibhayisikili **li**-ephukile *The bicycle has broken.*
> **l**ephukile.
Izigebengu **zi**-esaba *The burglars are afraid*
> **z**esaba izinja. *of dogs.*
Ngi-ya-si-azi > Ngiyasazi (isiZulu) *I know it* (Zulu that is.)
Si-ya-**ba**-azi > siya**b**azi. *We know them.*
Ba-ya-ngi-azi > Baya**ng**azi. *They know me.*

Note that the subject and object concords of Class 11 (**lu-**) and Class 15 (**ku-**) discard their vowel **u-** before vowel verb stems beginning with an **o-**. Before all other vowels the vowel **u-** changes to **w-**, for example:

Ngi-ya-**ku**-azi > Ngiyakwazi.   *I know you.*
A-si-**lu**-azi > Asilwazi ulimi lwabo. *We do not know their language.*
Ufudu-**lu**-omile > lomile.   *The tortoise is thirsty.*
Ukudla ku-omile > **k**omile.   *The food is dry.*

(*b*) The subject concords **u-** and **i-** change to **w-** and **y-** respectively before vowel verb stems, while the subject concord **a-** falls away.

Umama **u**-alile > **w**alile.   *Mother refused.*
Igane **i**-omile > **y**omile.   *The child is thirsty.*
Amadoda **a**-esaba > esaba kakhulu. *The men are very much afraid.*

Note that the above rules also apply to the negative form of the subject concords.

Ubaba **aka**-esabi > **ak**esabi.   *Father is not afraid.*
Abantwana **aba**-omile > **ab**omile. *The children are not thirsty.*
Lezi **zin**to **azi**-ehlukene >   *These things do not differ.*
  azehlukene.
Isalukazi asiamukeli   *The old woman does not*
  > asamukeli isipho.   *accept the gift.*

☑ ——————— Umsebenzi ———————

1 Change the form of the verb in brackets so that it expresses the concept *for*.

(*a*) (**Awungiphathe**) ibhotela, mama *Please pass (for) me the butter, mother*

(*b*) (**Ngizokubiza**) udokotela *I'll call a doctor for you*

(*c*) (**Ngizokuvala**) umnyango mnumzana *I'll open the door for you, sir*

(*d*) (**Ngizokubheka**) abantwana, nkosikazi *I'll look after the children for you, madam*

(*e*) (**Ngizokwenza**) lokho *I will do that for you*

(*f*) (**Awusilethe**) uthosi, Francis *Please bring us some toast, Francis*

2 Winter is approaching and you want to buy a new heater (**ihitha**). How would you ask the attendant:

  (a) Whether they stock heaters
  (b) How much the heater (which you want to buy) costs
  (c) Whether you can pay by (**=nga**) credit card (*or* = **noma**)
  (d) Whether they accept cheques (**amasheke**)?

3 Complete the following sentences by providing the appropriate subject concord (before the vowel verb stems):

  (a) Laba **ba**ntu ＿＿enze umsebenzi omkhulu *These people did a big job*
  (b) **Isa**lukazi ＿＿amukele imali *The old women accepted the money*
  (c) **i(li)**hembe lami ＿＿omile *My shirt is dry*
  (d) **Izi**cathulo zami a＿＿omile *My shoes are not dry*
  (e) UMark a＿＿azi lutho *Mark knows nothing*
  (f) **A**madoda ＿＿ejwayele le ndawo *The men are accustomed to this place*
  (g) Ubaba a＿＿anelisiwe *Father is not satisfied*
  (h) (Thina) a＿＿azi *We do not know*
  (i) (Mina) a＿＿azi *I do not know*
  (j) Le ndaba [class 9] ＿＿ehlukile *This matter is different*

4 Rewrite each of the following sentences in the stative form

  (a) **Ngiyakhathala** > ＿＿＿＿ *I am (mentally) tired*
  (b) Siyadin**wa** > ＿＿＿＿ *We are (physically) tired*
  (c) Itanki **liyagcwala** > ＿＿＿＿ *The (petrol) tank is full*
  (d) **Kuyalunga** > ＿＿＿＿ *It is OK*
  (e) Abantwana **bayalala** > ＿＿＿＿ *The children are asleep*
  (f) Yonke imali yami **iphela** manje > ＿＿＿＿ *All my money is finished now*
  (g) Bonke abantu **bayathokoza** > ＿＿＿＿ *All the people are happy*
  (h) **Ngiyesutha** > ＿＿＿＿ *I had enough (to eat)*
  (i) Siyabonga, **saneliswa** manje > ＿＿＿＿ *Thank you we are satisfied now*
  (j) **Sikhathazeka** kakhulu > ＿＿＿＿ *We are very worried*

14
NGICELA INDLELA
— EYA EPOSIHHOVISI —

Can you direct me to the
Post Office please?

In this unit you will learn how to
- form and use locative nouns
- express certain relational concepts
- say a place is near another place
- ask/give directions
- say something/someone is in/at ...
- ask Why?-questions
- form and use the positive and negative of the past tense
- say 'and then' and 'until'

Ingxoxo

Themba is on his first visit to Johannesburg and wants to post a letter. He enquires from a young boy (umfana) passing by where the nearest Post Office is.

Themba   Sawubona mfana wami.
Umfana   Yebo, baba.
Themba   Uxolo mfana wami ngicela ungisize.
Umfana   Ngikusize ngani baba?
Themba   Ngibuza iposihhovisi. Ngifuna ukuposa le ncwadi. Ngihambe kanjani uma ngiya khona?

Umfana Hamba njalo ngalo mgwaqo baba. Ungaphambuki. Lapho phambili esitobhini ujikele ngakwesobunxele uqonde ngqo uzokweqa imigwaqo emibili bese ujikela ngakwesokudla. Lapho uzobona iposihhovisi liseduze.

Themba Yibambe lapho mfana wami, ngithi ukubhala lapha phansi. Ngilahlekile kancane.

Umfana Yini ndaba ungaposi incwadi yakho esigxotsheni seposi? Siseduze kakhulu kuneposihhovisi.

Themba Sikuphi?

Umfana Naso-ke ngale komgwaqo eduze nasekhefini.

Themba Hawu! Yini ndaba ubungasho?

Umfana Awungibuzanga baba.

Mfana wami *My (dear) boy*	**bese** *and then*
Uxolo *Excuse me*	**ujikele ngakwesokudla** *and then you (must) turn to the right*
ngicela ungisize *Please help me* (Lit. *I request that you help me*)	
Ngikusize ngani? *With what must I help you?*	**iposihhovisi liseduze** *the Post Office is nearby*
Ngibuza iposihhovisi (*I ask the Post Office=*) *I want to know where the Post Office is*	**Yibambe lapho** *Hold it there*
	ngithi ukubhala lapha phansi *I just want to write (it) down here*
Ngifuna ukuposa *I want to post* (see also Unit 12)	**Ngilahlekile kancane** *I'm a little bit lost*
incwadi *letter*	**Yini ndaba ungaposi incwadi yakho esigxotsheni seposi?** *Why don't you post your letter in a post box?*
Ngihambe kanjani? *How must I go?*	
uma ngiya khona *if I (want to) go there*	**Yini ndaba?** *Why?*
Hamba njalo *Continue*	**isigxobo seposi** *post box* (note the alternative word for *post box*: **ibhokisi leposi**)
ngalo mgwaqo *with this road*	
Ungaphambuki *You must not deviate (from it)*	**Siseduze kakhulu kuneposihhovisi** *It (i.e. post box) is much nearer than the Post Office is*
Lapho phambili *There ahead (of you)*	
esitobhini *at the stop street*	**Sikuphi?** *Where is it (the post box)?*
ujikela ngakwesobunxele *you turn to the left*	**Naso-ke** *There it is* (see also Unit 8)
ujikela *you turn to*	**ngale komgwaqo** *on the other side of the road*
uqonde ngqo *then you (must) carry on straight*	**eduze nasekhefini** *near the café*
uzokweqa (=u-zoku-eqa) imigwaqo emibili *you will cross two streets*	**ikhefi** *café*
	Yini ndaba ubungasho? *Why didn't you say so?*
-eqa *cross over*	**Awungibuzanga** *You didn't ask me*

Imibuzo

Kuyiqiniso noma akusilo? Correct and rewrite the false ones.

(*a*) Isigxobo seposi siseduze nasekhefini
(*b*) UThemba ufuna ukuthenga izitembu (*stamps*)
(*c*) UThemba upose incwadi yakhe eposihhovisi
(*d*) UThemba usize umfana
(*e*) Umfana usize uThemba

Ulimi

1 Forming locative nouns

Locative nouns are nouns that indicate locality and are derived from ordinary nouns in basically two ways, depending on the noun class to which the noun belongs. The translation of Zulu locative nouns in English usually involves prepositions such as *in*, *at*, *to*, *from*, on and so on. Here are two basic rules of locative formation in Zulu.

(*a*) Nouns belonging to classes 1, 1a, 2 and 2a are locativised by replacing the initial vowel of the noun with **ku-**.

kumuntu (< umuntu)	*to, at, by, from, ... the person*
kubantu (< abantu)	*to, at, by, from, ... the people*
kuJoan	*to, at, by, from, ... Joan*

Ngiya **ku**Joan/**ku**baba/**ku**thisha   *I'm going to Joan/my father/*
   kubantu   *the teacher, the people*

(*b*) Nouns belonging to any of the other noun classes are locativised by substituting the initial vowel of the noun with **e-** (a small number of nouns use **o-**) and the final vowel with **-ini**, **-eni** (when the final vowel is **-a**) or **-weni** (when the final vowel is **-o**).

ikhishi > **e**khish**ini**	*in, at, to, from, ... the kitchen*
idolobha > **e**dolobh**eni**	*in, at, to, from, ... town*
isihlalo > **e**sihlal**weni**	*on, at the chair*

Siya **e**dolobh**eni**.   *We are going to town.*

Beka **ekamelweni** (< ikamelo). *Put (it) in the room.*
Bahlezi **ekhishini** (< ikhishi). *They are sitting in the kitchen.*

A limited number of nouns (some of which are place names) only use the **e-** (or **o-** in the case of class 11 nouns) and discard the final **-ini**.

esibhedlela (< isibhedlela)   *in, to, ... hospital*
esitolo (< isitolo)   *in, at, to, ... the shop*
eposihhovisi   *in, at, to, ... the Post Office*
ehhotela   *in, at, ... the hotel*
ekhaya (< ikhaya)   *at, to home*
ebusuku (< ubusuku [class 14]) *at night, in the (late) evening*

An important rule to remember is that whenever a concord, for example a subject concord, appears before a locative noun beginning with **e-** (or **o-**) an **s** is inserted after the (subject) concord.

UMoira **usemsebenzini**   *Moira is at work.*
  (u-s-emsebenzini).
Umama **usendlini** (u-s-endlini). *Mother is in the house.*
Izicathulo zakho **zisekamelweni** *Your shoes are in the room.*
  (zi-s-ekamelweni)

In the case of all other words denoting a locality or place the **s** is omitted.

USharon **ukugogo** (u-ku-gogo). *Sharon is with grandmother.*
Izinja **ziphandle** (zi-phandle). *The dogs are outside.*

2 *Expressing relational concepts*

Relational notions are expressed as follows:

emva kwa-	*after*	**phansi kwa-**	*under*
phambi kwa-	*before*	**phakathi kwa-**	*inside/between*
phezu kwa-	*on top of*	**ngale kwa-**	*across*

The vowel **-a** of the possessive concord **kwa-** changes according to the sound rules pertaining to possessive concords as set out in Unit 19.

emva **kwe**lantshi (< ilantshi) *after lunch*
phambi **kwami**   *before me* (=**mi**) (Unit 19)

phezu **kwentaba**	*on top of the mountain*
phansi **kombhede** (< umbhede)	*under the bed*
phakathi **kwemoto**	*inside the car*
emva **kwamadoda**	*behind the men*
phakathi kwethu	*between us* (=**-ithu**) (see Unit 19)
ngale (kwomgwaqo >) **komgwaqo** (< umgwaqo)	*across the street*

3 The ... is near/next to the ...

To say a place is near another place you use: subject concord + **-seduze nas-** + locative noun.

| I-First National Bank i**seduze nas**eposihhovisi. | *The First National Bank is near (at) the Post Office.* |
| I-Protea Hotel iseduze nasesiteshini. | *The Protea Hotel is near (at) the station.* |

Note that when **eduze** follows a verb, its subject concord is not used and you consequently omit the **s-** of **seduze**.

| Thina sihlala **eduze nas**ebhishini. | *We stay near the beach.* |
| Ngisebenza **eduze nase**-OK Bazaars. | *I work near the OK Bazaars.* |

To say a place is next to another you use **-secaleni nas-**.

| I-OK Bazaars i**secaleni nas**ebhange. | *The OK Bazaars is next to the Bank.* |
| Ikhefi li**secaleni nas**egalaji. | *The café is next to the garage.* |

4 Can you tell me the way to ...?

A very idiomatic and simple way to ask someone to direct you to a particular place is to say **Ngibuza ...** (*I ask ...*) or **Sibuza ...** (*We ask ...*) followed by the name of the place in question.

| Ngibuza i-Standard Bank. | *I would like to know where the Standard Bank is.* (Lit. *I ask the Standard Bank*) |
| Sibuza isiteshi. | *We would like to know where the station is.* (Lit. *We ask the station*) |

Sibuza iHhovisi leziVakashi.   *We want to know where*
(iTourist Bureau)   *the Tourist Bureau is.*

An alternative (more friendly) way to gain this information is to ask
Ngicela indlela eya ... (*I request the road that goes to ...*) followed by
the name of the place that you are looking for. The name of the place
always appears in locative form (see above).

Ngicela indlela eya   *Can you direct me to*
eposihhovisi/eposini   *the Post Office, please?*
(< iposihhovisi/iposi).

Ngicela indlela eya esiteshini   *Can you direct me to the*
(< isiteshi).   *(railway) station, please?*

5   Someone/something is in/at ...

To say someone or something is in or at a certain place or locality you
put **-s-** before the locative noun and use this structure: subject concord + **-s-** + locative noun.

I-Standard Bank (i-**s**-eChurch=)   *The Standard Bank is in*
iseChurch Street.   *Church Street.*
I-Royal Hotel (I-**s**-ekhoneni=)   *The Royal Hotel is at the*
isekhoneni le-Church Street   *corner of Church Street and*
ne-Beach Road.   *Beach Road.*

Ubaba (u-**s**-emsebenzini=) **usemsebenzini** (< umsebenzi).	*Father is at (his) work*
Ibhotela (li-**s**-efrijini=) **lisefrijini** (< ifriji).	*The butter is in the fridge.*
Abantwana (ba-**s**-ekamelweni=) **basekamelweni** (< ikamelo).	*The children are in the room.*
Ummese (u-**s**-ekhishini=) **usekhishini** (< ikhishi).	*The knife is in the kitchen.*

6 Useful expressions when giving/asking directions

You carry on until (= **-ze**) you reach ..... **Uqhubeka uze ufike** .....

Ujikele ngakwesokudla *You turn to your right*

Ujikele ngakwesobunxele *You turn to your left*

Weqe umgwaqo *You cross the street*

Uqonde ngqo *You carry straight on*

Ngalo mgwaqo *With this road*

Wedlule ... *You pass a ...*

Emarobhotini ... *At the robots ...*

Esitobhini ... *At the stop street ...*

Emahlukandlela ... *At the crossroads ...*

Mangibuze mfowethu uya kuphi lo mgwaqo? *Excuse me brother (but) where does this road go to?*

Ngibuza umgwaqo oya ...? *Where is the road that goes to ...?*

Uxolo dade ngibuza umgwaqo oya ... *Excuse me, sister, I'm looking for the road that goes to ...*

Uxolo mnumzane, lo mgwaqo uya .....(place name) na? *Excuse me sir, does this road go to ..... (place name)*

Awungilayele ihhovisi likameneja? *Can you direct me to the manager's office please?*

ngilahlekile *I am lost*

Note: *On the corner of ... and ... streets ...* **Ekhoneni lika-** (+ street name if it is the name of a person) **nelika-** (+ street name if it is the name of a person).

Ekhoneni lika-Smith Street nelika-West Street

or

Ekhoneni **le-** (+ street name if it is not the name of a person) **ne-** (+ street name if it is not the name of a person).

Ekhoneni le-Commercial ne-Field Road.

7 Asking Why?-questions

There are various ways of asking Why?-questions in Zulu. Saying **Yini ndaba?** (or simply **Yini?**) is but one of them. There are two important things to remember about this interrogative. First, when you want to say *don't* with this interrogative (e.g. *Why don't you ...?*) you have to insert **-nga-** just behind the subject concord in the accompanying verb (which ends on **-i** in the present tense negative and **-anga** in the past tense).

Yini ndaba uhamba manje?	*Why are you leaving now?*
Yini ndaba **unga**hamb**i** manje?	*Why don't you leave now?*
Yini ndaba **unga**fik**anga** izolo, Petros?	*Why did you not come yesterday, Petros?*

The second point to remember about **yini ndaba?** is that the subject concords of nouns belonging to classes 1, 1a, 2 and 6 have a slightly different form when used together with this interrogative. The subject concord **u-** of classes 1 and 1a becomes **e-**, the **ba-** of class 2 becomes **be-**, while the subject concord **a-** of class 6 changes to **e-**.

Yini ndaba uJoseph [class 1] esebenza namhlanje?	*Why does Joseph work today?*
Yini abantwana [class 2] **be**ngayi esikoleni namhlanje?	*Why don't the children go (= -ya) to school today?*
Yini ndaba amadoda [class 6] ekhala kangaka?	*Why do the men complain so much?*

8 The past tense

8.1 Positive

The past tense is expressed by **-ile** which is suffixed to the verbal stem.

-bona	*see*	-bon**ile**	*saw*
-pheka	*cook*	-phek**ile**	*cooked*
-phuza	*drink*	-phuz**ile**	*drank*

When another word (or words) follows the verb, an abbreviated version of **-ile**, namely **-e** (which is somewhat accented) is normally used.

Ngimbon**ile**.   *I saw him.*
but:

Ngimbone izolo.	*I saw him yesterday.*
Bahambile.	*They have left.*

but:

Bahambe ngo-12.	*They left at twelve o'clock.*
Babuyile.	*They have come back.*

but

Babuye namhlanje.	*They came back today.*

The short form -e is also used with most so-called Wh?-question words (when?, where?, what?).

Uyephi uJacob?	*Where did Jacob go?* (-ya *go*)
Ufike nini uThokozile?	*When did Thokozile come?* (-fika *come*)
Uboneni Maria?	*What did you see Maria?* (-bona *see*)

8.2 Negative

The negative of the past tense is formed in exactly the same way as the negative of the present tense (see Unit 9) except that the verb ends here in -anga.

Angazanga (a-ngi-az-anga).	*I did not know.* (=-azi)
Abantu ababuyanga.	*The people did not come back.*
UFred akafikanga.	*Fred did not come.*
Inkosi [class 9] yenkantolo ayivumanga.	*The magistrate did not agree.*

Note the past tense negative form of the verb stem -sho (*say (so)*).

akashongo	*he did not say (so)*
angishongo	*I didn't say (so)*

9.1 'Until you ...'

To express 'until you ...' as in '... *until you reach such and such a place*' you use uze followed by a verb ending on -e:

Uqhubeka ngalo mgwaqo uze ufike emarobhothini ...	*You carry on with this road until you come to the traffic lights....*
Sizokulinda uze ubuye.	*We will wait until you return.*

To say '*Until I...*' you replace the second person concord u- with the first person concord ngi-:

Yima lapha ngize ngibuye.	*Wait here until I return.*

9.2 ... and then ...

There are several ways to express the concept *and then* in Zulu. The one that concerns us here is **bese**, which expresses consecutive actions of a non-habitual type.

Awuhlole iwoyela **bese** uhlola amasondo.	*Please check the oil (first) and then check the wheels.*
Uhamba ngalo mgwaqo **bese** ujikela ngakwesobunxele lapho esitobhini.	*You continue with this road and then turn to your left there at the stop street.*

—————— **Umsebenzi** ——————

1 Look at the street guide to Pietermaritzburg overleaf. You are standing on the corner of Berg Street and Commercial Road. As a local inhabitant how would you explain to a visitor how to get from where you're standing to (*a*) the Church of the Vow (**iSonto lesiVumelwano**). and (*b*) the police station.

   Use in your explanation also the following expressions: **ngalo mgwaqo, uqonde ngqo!, ujikele ngakwesokudla** (or **ngakwesobunxele**), **emarobhothini**.

2 You approach a passer-by to ask him to direct you to the station. How would you approach him and how would you ask him where the station is?

   Write a suitable dialogue based on this situation.

3 Rewrite the following sentences in the negative.

   (*a*) U-Emma ukhona
   (*b*) Inyama ikhona
   (*c*) Sifuna uweta
   (*d*) UNkosazana (*Miss*) Zwane ukhuluma iqiniso (*the truth*)
   (*e*) Abelungu bathanda utshwala (*sorgum beer*)
   (*f*) Kushisa kakhulu (*it is very hot*)
   (*g*) Iwayini iyabanda (*be cold*)
   (*h*) Inyuziphepha (*newspaper*) ifikile
   (*i*) UJohannes umtshelile (*told him*)
   (*j*) Amadoda azame (*tried*) kakhulu

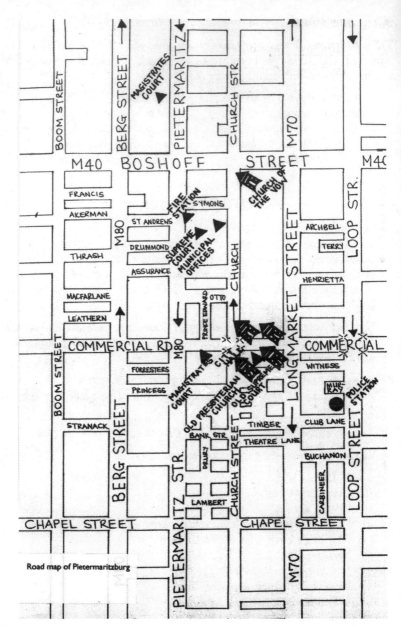

Road map of Pietermaritzburg

4 Complete by providing the missing subject concord.

(a) Izindlovu (*elephants*) ___phuza amanzi

(b) Isikhwama (*purse*) sami ___lahlekile (*lost*)

(c) UHulumeni (*Government*) ___namandla (*is strong*)

(d) Ihembe (*shirt*) lami ___ngcolile (*dirty*)

(e) Isitolo ___valiwe (*closed*)

5 Say that the things below are in the place or at/with the person(s) indicated in brackets.

(a) ushizi *cheese* (ifriji *fridge*)

(b) ibhotela *butter* (itafula *table*)

(c) ummese *knife* (idilowa *drawer*)

(d) uJason (udokotela)

(e) izitsha *dishes* (usinki [class 11] *wash basin*)

(f) abantwana *children* (unina [class 1a] *their mother*)

(g) Marjorie (ikamelo (lakhe) (*her*) *room*)

(h) Imali (isikhwama (sakho) (*your*) *pocket*)

(i) iMalibu Hotel (Marine Parade)

(j) iCapitol Towers Hotel (Corner of Longmarket Street and Church Street)

6 How would you ask someone where the following are:

(a) the Malibu Hotel (iMalibu Hotel)

(b) the railway station (isiteshi)

(c) the police station (ipolisiteshi)

(d) the airport (inkundla yezindiza)

(e) Mrs Dlamini

7 You are on your way to visit the famous Zulu war memorial at iSandlwana in northern KwaZulu-Natal.

You are, however, unsure if you are on the right road leading to your destination. How would you ask one of the local people:

(a) whether this road (i.e. the road you are travelling on) goes to iSandlwana (eSandlwana)

(b) where iSandlwana is?

8 Rewrite in the past tense:

(a) Ubaba uya emsebenzini *Father is going to work*
(b) Sivuka ngo-7 *We wake up at 7 o'clock*
(c) Ibhasi lifika ngo-10 *The bus arrives at 10*
(d) USharon uphuza i-cooldrinki *Sharon is drinking a cool drink*
(e) UWilliam uyahamba *William is leaving*
(f) Ngisebenza eGoli *I work in Johannesburg.*

15

UKUBUKEZA

Revision

1 (*a*) You have invited your new colleague Moses Mthethwa to a barbecue at your house. How would you introduce him to your friends Mark and Judy Strydom? (Do not forget to tell Moses who your friends are.)

(*b*) Mark and Judy are pleased to meet your new colleague and he likewise. How will they express this?

2 (*a*) You are going to have lunch in a Steak House. How will you ask the waiter for the menu? You have decided to order a medium-done rump steak. How will you ask for this? The waiter asks you: **Ufuna ukuphuzani?** What will you tell him?

(*b*) You want to pay by means of your credit card. How will you ask if you may do so?

3 It is your first visit to Durban. How would you ask a Zulu-speaking passer-by where the following places and people are:

(*a*) the Standard Bank
(*b*) the Elangeni Hotel
(*c*) the Aquarium (**i-Aquarium**)
(*d*) the rickshaws (**amalisho**)
(*e*) the road (that goes) to the airport (**enkundleni yezindiza**)

4 • Answer in the positive by using the appropriate object concord.

   (a) Uvale isango na? (*Have you closed the gate?*)

   (b) Ubone ubaba Madiba ku-TV? (*Have you seen baba Madiba* (i.e. *President Mandela*) *on TV?*)

   (c) Uyasazi isiBhunu? (*Do you know Afrikaans?*)

   (d) Uthenge iphephandaba namhlanje? (*Did you buy a newspaper today?*)

   (e) Utshele ubaba Mzilikazi? (*Did you tell baba Mzilikazi?*)

   • Answer the above questions in the negative.

5 (a) You are on your way to Durban and are planning to visit the Hluhluwe Game Reserve (famous for its white and black rhino population). How will you ask a Zulu friend how far Hluhluwe (**eHluhluwe**) is from Durban?

   (b) How will he tell you that the distance is (about) 250 km?

6 Say that you want (**-funa**) to do the following:

   (a) to eat

   (b) to go

   (c) to rest (**-phumula**)

   (d) to sleep (**-lala**)

7 What do these public notices forbid?

   (a) AKUBHENYWA LAPHA

   (b) AKUNGENWA LAPHA

8 You have visitors. How will you ask them whether they would like some tea or coffee?

9 Someone asks you to direct him to the Traffic Department. How will you tell him that he must:

   (a) carry straight on with this road, and then (**bese**)

   (b) turn (to your) right at the corner of Church and New Market Streets?

10 Rewrite in the past tense so that the new sentences reflect the meaning given in brackets.

   (*a*) Ngiya emsebenzini (*I went to work*)
   (*b*) Ngiyabatshela (*I told them*)
   (*c*) Ngenza (ngi-enza) isiphosiso (*I made a mistake*)
   (*d*) Ngikhuluma nobaba Mkhize (*I spoke to baba Mkhize*)

11 Correct and rewrite.

   (*a*) Ngisebenza *I am working*
   (*b*) Ubaba Mabuya uyaqamba amanga *Baba Mabuya is telling lies*
   (*c*) UMaDlamini uyakhalile *MaDlamini complained*

12 Someone asks you where the following people and things are. Say where they are by using the words in brackets:

   (*a*) UThobile (udokotela)
   (*b*) Ubaba wakho (*Your father*) (umsebenzi *work*)

(c) Umama wakho (idolobha *town*)
(d) UNomacala (uMenzi)
(e) Impahla (*goods*) (imoto)
(f) Incwadi (*letter*) (iposi *post*)
(g) Abantwana (phandle *outside*)
(h) Izinja (*dogs*) (indlu *house*)

16
SIKHULUMA NGOCINGO

Telephone conversation

In this unit you will learn how to

- speak on the telephone
- form and use demonstrative pronouns
- ask some Who?-questions
- say 'unfortunately' and 'fortunately'
- ask someone to convey a message
- say something is urgent
- ask the size or number of something

—————————— Ingxoxo ——————————

[telephone rings]

H & H   Sawubona. Kuse-H & H Publishers lapha. Ngingakusiza na?

Mark   Ngicela ukukhuluma nomnumzane Thwala.

H & H   Awubambe kancane, ngizokwedlulisela kumabhalane wakhe.

Mark   Ngiyabonga.

H & H   Kusehhovisi likamnumzane Thwala lapha. Ngingakusiza na?

Mark   Ngabe umnumzane Thwala ukhona?

H & H   Cha, ngeshwa akekho. Uye elantshini.

Mark   Ubuya nini?

H & H	Uthe uzobuya emva kwelantshi. Ngubani okhulumayo?
Mark	NguMark okhulumayo.
H & H	Mark bani?
Mark	NginguMark Stephenson.
H & H	Ngingathatha umyalezo Mark?
Mark	Yebo, nkosikazi. Mtshele uRoy (Thwala) ngicela makangi-fonele. Mtshele nokuthi ngithe yindaba ephuthumayo.
H & H	Uyayazi inombolo yocingo lwakho Mark?
Mark	Ngiqinisile uyayazi. Nokho awuyibhale phansi.
H & H	Ithini inombolo yakho?
Mark	Ithi 420-2493.
H & H	Kukuphi lapho?
Mark	KusePitoli.
H & H	I-'code' yakhona ithini?
Mark	Ithi 002.
H & H	Kulungile, ngizomtshela.

Kuse-H & H Publishers lapha *It is (at) H & H Publishers here*

Ngingakusiza na? *Can I help you?*

Ngicela ukukhuluma ... *I please want to speak to ...* (see also Unit 6)

Awubambe kancane *Please hold for a little while* (see also Unit 6)

ngizokwedlulisela *I'll put you through*

kumabhalane wakhe *to his secretary*

umabhalane *secretary*

Kusehhovisi likamnumzane Thwala *It is (at) Mr Thwala's office*

Ngabe umnumzane Thwala ukhona? *Its Mr Thwala there perhaps?*

ngeshwa *unfortunately*

Akekho *He's not here* (see also Unit 8)

Uye elantshini *He went (to lunch=) for lunch*

Ubuya nini? *When will he return?*

Uthe ... *He said ...*

emva kwelantshi *after lunch*

ilantshi *lunch* (note: *the traditional word for lunch is*

indlamini; *however, the loanword* **ilantshi** *is very frequently used in metropolitan areas*)

Ngubani okhulumayo? *Who's speaking?*

NguMark okhulumayo *It is Mark who is speaking*

Mark bani? *Mark who?*

Ngingathatha umyalezo na? *Can I take a message?* (see also Unit 12)

Mtshele uRoy ... *Tell Roy that ...*

ngicela ukuthi ... *I request that ...*

makangifonele *he must please phone (for) me*

yindaba ephuthumayo *it is an urgent matter*

Mtshele nokuthi ngithe ... *Tell him also that I said ...* (note: **-the** *is the past tense of* **-thi**)

uyayazi inombolo yocingo lwakho? *does he know your telephone number?*

inombolo yocingo *telephone number*

Ngiqinisile *I'm certain*

nokho *nevertheless*

-fonela *phone for*

---

awuyibhale phansi *please write it down*	**Ithi ...** *It says ...*
-bhala *write*	**Kukuphi lapho?** *Where is it?*
phansi *down*	(Lit. *It is where there?*)
Ithini inombolo yakho?' *What's your (telephone) number?*	**I-code yakhona ithini?** *What's the code (number) there?*
Ithini ...? *What does it say ...?*	(Lit. *The code of there says what?*)
(i.e. *your telephone number*)	**khona** *there*
(see also Unit 19)	**Kulungile ngizomtshela** *All right, I'll tell him*

Imibuzo

1 Kuyiqiniso noma akusilo? Correct and rewrite the false ones.

(*a*) UMark uhlala eGoli.

(*b*) Umnumzana Thwala ukhona ehhovisi lakhe

(*c*) UMark ufuna ukukhuluma nomnumzana Thwala

(*d*) Umnumzana Thwala akayazi inombolo yocingo lukaMark

(*e*) Umnumzana Thwala uzobuya kusasa (*tomorrow*)

2 Phendula imibuzo elandelayo.

(*a*) UMark ufonela ubani?

(*b*) Umnumzana Thwala uye kuphi?

(c)   Ithini inombolo yocingo lukaMark?
(d)   UMark uhlala kuphi?
(e)   Umnumzana Thwala uzobuya nini?

Ulimi

1   Speaking on the telephone

- People often neglect or forget to identify themselves when speaking over the phone. When you want to know who is speaking you ask:

Ngubani okhulumayo?   *Who is speaking?*

Let's say your name is Tim Watson, so you answer:

NguTim (Watson) okhulumayo.   *It's Tim (Watson) speaking.*

or:

NginguTim (Watson).   *I'm Tim (Watson).*

- Answering the phone often requires identification, whether it be of yourself or of the firm where you are employed. When stating the name of a firm/organisation you usually begin with **Kuse**, followed by the name of the firm or organisation.

KuseProtea Engineering lapha.   *Protea Engineering (here).*
KuseCargo Carriers lapha.   *Cargo Carriers (here).*

If it is a private home, you say **Kukwa-** followed by the surname of the person in whose name the telephone number is listed.

KukwaJohnson lapha.	*It's Johnson's home here.*
KukwaKhumalo lapha.	*It's Khumalo's home here.*

- To request permission to speak to someone over the phone you say **Ngicela ukukhuluma no-** followed by the name of the person.

Ngicela ukukhuluma noJennifer

Ngicela ukukhuluma nomnumzane de Beer

- If someone has dialled the wrong number you can begin by asking:

Ufuna namba bani?   *What number do you want?*

If the caller has dialled the wrong number you can say:

Uxolo, wedukile.   *Sorry, (you are lost, i.e.) you have phoned the wrong number.*

Ngingathatha umyalezo na? *Can I take a message?*
Ngikhuluma nobani? *To whom am I speaking?*
Ufuna ukukhuluma nobani? *Who do you want to speak to?*
Awuphakamise izwi, angikuzwa kahle *Please talk louder, I cannot hear you properly*
Awufone futhi emva kwamaminithi ayishumi *Please phone again say after 10 minutes*
Ufisa ukushiya umyalezo na? *Do you want to leave a message?*

NguJames Cele okhulumayo *James Cele speaking*
Intambo i(sa)gcwele *The line is (still) engaged*
Awubambe *Please hold*
Ngizokwedlulisela (ku- plus name of person) *I'll put you through (to so and so)*
Akunamuntu *There is no answer (There is no one there)*
Ithini inamba yocingo lwakho lwasekhaya? *What is your (home) telephone number?*

---

2 Asking Who?-questions

Whom do you...?

The interrogative **ubani?** in Zulu is used in a different way from its English counterpart *whom?*. Whom?-questions in English usually begin with the interrogative *whom?*, as in *Whom do you want?*, *Whom did you ask?*

In Zulu, on the other hand, **ubani?** (*whom?*) normally comes at the end of the sentence.

Ufuna ubani?	*Whom do you want?*
	(Lit. *You want whom?*)
Ubuze ubani?	*Whom did you ask?*
	(Lit. *You asked whom?*)
Uthanda ubani?	*Whom do you like?*
	(Lit. *You like whom?*)

Who does/doesn't/did ...?

To ask questions like *Who wants something?* or *Who is doing/did something?*, you begin with **Ngubani o-** followed by the verb expressing the thing done.

Ngubani othanda ikhofi?	*Who prefers coffee?*
Ngubani ofuna itiye?	*Who wants some tea?*
Ngubani ocele uthosi?	*Who asked (for) toast?*
Ngubani obize udokotela?	*Who called the doctor?*

In the negative you put **-nga-** after the **o-** and let the verb end on **-i** in the present tense (see Unit 9) or **-anga-** in the past tense (see Unit 14).

Ngubani **onga**funi i-Tab?	*Who doesn't want Tab*
	(a kind of cool drink)?
Ngubani **onga**khokh**anga**?	*Who did not pay* (=-khokha)?

When the answer to these questions is a name, it usually beings with **ngu-**.

Ngubani ofuna amanzi?	*Who wants some water?*
NguJoan	*(It is) Joan*
Ngubani ovela eThekwini?	*Who comes from Durban?*
Ngunkosazana Zungu.	*(It is) Miss Zungu.*

When the answer is *I*, you say **Yimi** *(It is) I*. When it is *He* or *She*, you say **Nguye** (*(It is) He/She*). When it is *We*, you say **Yithi**; and when it is *They*, you say **Yibo**.

Ngubani okhuluma isiZulu?	*Who speaks Zulu?*
Yimi	*(It is) I do*
Ngubani ovela phesheya?	*Who comes from abroad?*

Yibo	*(It is) They do*
Ngubani okhalayo?	*Who is complaining?*
Nguye	*(It is) She does.*

With whom ...?

When you want to say *with whom* you simply replace **ubani?** with **nobani?**

Ufuna ukukhuluma nobani?	*Whom do you want to speak to?* (Lit. *You want to speak with whom?*)
Uhamba nobani?	*Whom are you going with?* (Lit. *You are going with whom?*)
Uyohlala nobani?	*Whom are you going to stay with?* (Lit. *You are going to stay with whom?*)

What size/number?

Finally, the interrogative **ubani?** can also be used to ask questions about numbers. It does this without its initial vowel.

Uqgoke sayizi bani?	*What size do you wear?*
Ngiqgoke usayizi 7	*I wear size 7*
Ufunda standard bani?	*Which standard (at school) are you (studying) in?*
Ngifunda ustandard 7.	*I'm (studying) in standard 7.*
Uhlala kwanamba bani?	*At which number do you stay / Which (room) number are you in?*
Ngihlala kwa-37.	*I stay / I am in room 37.*

3 Unfortunately/fortunately

For *fortunately* you use **ngenhlanhla** (*with luck*) and for *unfortunately* you use **ngeshwa** (*with misfortune*).

Ngeshwa uNobuhle wehluleka ukufika (-ehluleka *be unable to do*)	*Unfortunately Nobuhle couldn't come*
kodwa **ngenhlanhla** uMichael ufikile	*but fortunately Michael came.*

4 It is urgent

To say something is urgent you say:

Indaba iyaphuthuma   *the matter is urgent*

or

Yindaba ephuthumayo   *It is an urgent matter.*

5 Asking someone to convey a message

When asking someone to convey a message you often say *Tell John, Ann, him/her/them ... that ...* followed by the message. To express this in Zulu you say **Mtshele** (< -**tshela** *tell*) **ukuthi ...** (*Tell him/her that ...*) or **Batshele ukuthi ...** (*Tell them that ...*).

Mtshele uJohn ukuthi   *Tell him, John that is,*
 indaba iyaphuthuma.   *that the matter is urgent.*
Mtshele ukuthi nguMary-Ann   *Tell her that (it is) Mary-Ann*
 omfonele.   *(that) has phoned.*
Batshele ukuthi sizohlangana   *Tell them that we will*
 kusasa.   *meet tomorrow.*

To ask the above in a more friendly way (*please*), you begin with **Awu-**.

Awumtshele uJohn ukuthi   *Please tell him, John that is,*
 ngihambile.   *that I have gone/left.*
Awubatshele uJohn noHeather   *Please tell them, John and*
 ukuthi sihambile.   *Heather that is, that we have*
                               gone/left.

You can, of course, leave out the name of the person, provided it is known to whom you are referring.

Mtshele ukuthi sizofika ngo-9.   *Tell him that we will arrive*
                                 at 9 o'clock.

6 Demonstrative pronouns

Demonstrative pronouns are words like *this, that, these, those*. Each noun class has its own demonstrative pronoun. Demonstratives may occur before or after nouns. When they occur before the noun, the noun discards its initial vowel.

Lo (u)muntu	This person
Laba (a)bantu	These people
Leyo (i)mali	That money
Lezo (i)zinkomo	Those cattle

An easy way to remember which demonstrative goes with which noun class is to compare it with the noun class prefix. Noun classes whose noun class prefix has a -mu- in it [classes 1, 1a and 3) take **lo** (*this*) as their demonstrative pronoun, while noun classes with a -**mi**- (class 4) or **in**- (class 9) in their prefix take **le** (*this*) as their demonstrative pronoun. The demonstratives of the other noun classes can easily be derived from their respective noun class prefixes by simply combining **la** with the second syllable of the prefix (not forgetting the rule $a + i > e$, $a + u > o$, and $a + a > a$ – see also Unit 19).

Class 2 **aba- = la + ba > laba**
Class 7 **isi- = la + si > lesi**
Class 11 **ulu- = la + lu > lolu**

The following table contains the *this / these* and *that / those* demonstrative pronouns for the various noun classes. Note how many of the demonstratives overtly agree with the respective noun class prefixes.

		This/These	That/Those
Class 1	um(u)-	lo	lowo
Class 1(a)	u-	lo	lowo
Class 2	aba-	laba	labo
Class 2 (a)	o-	laba	labo
Class 3	um(u-)	lo	lowo
Class 4	imi-	le	leyo
Class 5	i(li)-	leli	lelo
Class 6	ama-	la	lawo
Class 7	isi-	lesi	leso
Class 8	izi-	lezi	lezo
Class 9	in-/im-	le	leyo
Class 10	izin-/izim-	lezi	lezi
Class 11	u(lu)-	lolu	lolo
Class 14	u(bu)-	lobu	lobo
Class 15	uku-	lokhu	lokho

Note that demonstratives of all the **u**-classes take an **o**, while those of the **i**-classes take an **e** and those of the **a**-classes an **a**.

To form *that / those* demonstrative pronouns:

(*a*) monosyllabic demonstratives of the **u**- and **a**-classes add a suffix **-wo** (cf. classes 1 and 6), and those of the **i**-classes a suffix **-yo** (cf. classes 4 and 9);

(*b*) disyllabic demonstratives change their final vowel to **-o** (cf. classes 2 and 5).

Note that demonstratives may function without their co-referent nouns.

Angifuni **le** nto [class 9] ngifuna **leyo** (nto).	*I don't want **this** thing; I want **that one**.*
Asithandi **lezi** (zinto [class 10]).	*We don't like **these** (things).*
Labo (bantu [class 2]) bayahlupheka.	***Those** (people) are suffering.*
Angisho **lo** (muntu [class 1]).	*I don't mean **this one** (person).*

☑ ———————— **Umsebenzi** ————————

1 Write a suitable dialogue based on the information given below.

The telephone rings and you answer it. (*a*) The person asks to speak to your wife Julie. (*b*) You ask who is calling and the caller says that (*c*) she is Yvonne (see Unit 2). You tell her that (*d*) Julie is unfortunately not in and ask whether (*e*) you can take a message (**-thatha umyalezo**). Yvonne says (*f*) 'yes please' (see Unit 4) and asks that you must (*g*) please tell her (Julie) that (*h*) she is unable to come tomorrow (**ngehluleka ukufika kusasa** *I am unable to ...*).

2 Answer in the negative (note that some sentences are in the present tense while others are in the past tense).

(*a*) Unkosikazi [class 1a] Meyer ukhona na?
(*b*) Imali ikhona na?
(*c*) Le ndawo ibiza kakhulu na? (*Is this place very expensive?*)

(d) USusan ukhulume kahle na?
(e) Abantwana bafuna ubisi (*milk*) na?
(f) Liyashisa na? *Is it (the weather) hot?*
(g) Kuyabanda na? *Is it cold?*
(h) Isitimela sifike ngo-10.15 na?
(i) UJohannes ubuyile na? (*returned*)

3 Complete by providing the missing subject concord.

(a) Izitsha (*dishes*) ＿＿ngcolile (*dirty*).
(b) Thina (*we*) ＿＿lahlekile (*lost*).
(c) Uthisha wethu (*our teacher*) ＿＿qinile (*strict*).
(d) Ukudla (*food*) ＿＿phelile (*finished*).
(e) Ingane (*baby*) ＿＿lambile (*hungry*).

4 You are answering a phone call. How will you tell the caller:

(a) to please hold
(b) that you'll put her/him through to the manager (=**umphathi**)
(c) that Mr Smith is not in
(d) that he must please call again within 10 minutes

5 How would you ask someone the following questions?

(a) Whom are you looking for? (Whom do you want?)
(b) Who is crying? (-**khala**)?
(c) Who has not come (-**fikile**)?
(d) Who are you going with?
(e) Who took the bread (**isinkwa**)?
(f) What size do you want?
(g) Which (room) number are you in?

6 How would you ask someone to:

(a) tell Dudu that you are ill (**ngiyagula**)
(b) tell Thandi that you will be late (**ngizophuza ukufika**)
(c) tell Peter and Sally that they must wait (**ilinde**)
(d) tell Muzi that he must not forget to lock the door (**ungakhohlwa ukukhiya umnyango**)
(e) tell Jabulani that he must hurry, please (**makasheshe**)?

7 Supply the missing demonstrative.

(a) Angimazi ＿＿ **mu**ntu (*I don't know this person*)
(b) Singathatha ＿＿ **sinkwa** na? (*May we take this bread?*)

(c) Asithandi ____ ndawo (*We don't like that place*)

(d) Siyabathanda kakhulu ____ bantu (*We like those people very much*)

(e) Angithandi ⸺ (into), ngithanda ____ (into) (*I don't like this one (thing), I prefer that one (thing)*)

17

USIBONGILE VILAKAZI ——— NOMNDENI WAKHE ——— BASEKUDLENI KWANTAMBAMA

Sibongile Vilakazi and his family are having supper

In this unit you will learn how to

- ask for things at the table
- say 'Let us ...'
- say grace
- say that you want some more to eat/drink and how to decline respectfully
- say 'you must not'
- express the concepts 'still' and 'all'

——————————— **Ingxoxo** ———————————

Sibongile Vilakazi, his wife Lindiwe and their two children Sfiso and Doreen are sitting at the dinner table and are about to have their supper.

Sibongile	Masithandaze.
	[after having said grace]
Sfiso	Siziphakele mama?
Lindiwe	Yebo mntanami kodwa ngizoniphakela inyama.
Sibongile	Ngicela usawoti nopelepele Doreen.
Doreen	Nanku. Ngicela amanzi baba.
Sibongile	Nanka. Umasitadi ukhona na?

Lindiwe	Cha, awukho. Sfiso mfana wami, hamba uyosilandela umasitadi. Usefrijini.
Sfiso	Kulungile mama.
Sibongile	Usiphekele ukudla okumnandi kakhulu, Lindi.
Lindiwe	Ngiyabonga baba.
	Sifiso, mntanami, ungaphakamisi izindololwane uma usika inyama. Akungamamenazi amahle.
Sfiso	Ngiyaxolisa mama. [After a little while] Ngisacela inyama mama.
Lindiwe	Ayikho Sfiso. Inyama iphelile.
Sfiso	[a little surprised] Iphelile yonke?
Lindiwe	Yebo, yonke iphelile.
Doreen	Ukhona uphuthini mama?
Lindiwe	Yebo ukhona.
Sibongile	Hawu! usibulele ngokudla okumnandi namhlanje MaNtuli.
	[after everyone has finished his (or her) dessert]
Lindiwe	Nizothanda ukuphinda uphuthini na?
Sibongile	Cha, ngiyabonga. Sengesuthi impela.
Sfiso	Mina ngithanda ukuphinda mama.
Doreen	Nami ngisafuna mama.
Lindiwe	Lethani izitsha zenu ngizoniphakela.

Masithandaze *Let us pray/say grace*

Siziphakele? *Must we dish up for ourselves? (see also Unit 18)*

mntanami *my child (a term often used endearingly)*

Ngizoniphakela *I will dish up for you* (pl.) (=**-ni-**)

-phakela *dish up for*

Ngicela usawoti *Please pass me the salt (Lit. I request the salt, please)*

upelepele *pepper*

Ngicela amanzi *Please pass me the water/Can I have the water please*

Nanka *Here it is (the water)* (see also Unit 8)

Umasitadi ukhona na? *Is there (any) mustard (on the table)?* (see also Unit 8 for **khona**)

umasitadi [class 3] *mustard*

awukho *There isn't any (mustard)* (see also Unit 8)

Mfana wami *My dear boy* (term of endearment for young boys)

Hamba *Go*

uyosilandela umasitadi *(and) go and fetch the mustard for us*

-landela *fetch for*

usefrijini *it is in the fridge* (see also Unit 14)

Kulungile mama *Very well, Mother*

Ungaphakamisi ... *You must not lift ...*

izindololwane *elbows*

uma *when*

-sika *cut*

inyama *meat*

akungamamenazi amahle *It is not good manners*

amamenazi (< Eng. *manners*) manners

Ngiyaxolisa *I am sorry*

Ngisacela inyama *May I please (still) have some more meat*

Inyama iphelile *The meat is finished*

Yonke *All (the meat)*

-phelile *be finished*

Usiphekele ukudla okumnandi kakhulu *You have cooked very nice food for us*

ukudla okumnandi *nice food*

kakhulu *very*

Ukhona uphuthini na? *Is there (any pudding, i.e.) sweets?*

uphuthini [class 3] *sweets*

Usibulele ngokudla okumnandi *You are killing us with the nice food*

ngokudla *with food*

UMaNtuli *Daugher of Ntuli (married women are often addressed as Daughter of so and so)*

Nizothanda ukuphinda uphuthini na? *(Are you (pl.) going to repeat the sweets, i.e.) Do you want some more sweets?*

ukuphinda *to repeat*

Sengesuthi (Se-ng(i)-esuthi) *(I am already satisfied with food, i.e.) I have had enough to eat*

-esuthi *be satisfied with food*

Ngisafuna *I still want (some more)*

Nami *I too*

Lethani *Bring (pl.) (see also Unit 23)*

izitsha zenu *your plates*

Ngizoniphakela *I will dish up for you*

Imibuzo

Phendula imibuzo elandelayo.

(a) Ngubani othandazayo?
(b) USibongile ngubaba kabani?
(c) Ungubani uMaNtuli?
(d) Ngubani opheke ukudla?
(e) Ngubani ofuna ukuphinda uphuthini?
(f) Ngubani isibongo sikaSibongile? (*of Sibongile*)
(g) Ngubani igama lenkosikazi (*wife*) kaSibongile?
(h) USibongile ucelani kuDoreen? (*from Doreen*)

Ulimi

1 Please pass me .../Can I have ...?

When you are having a meal and you want someone at the dinner table to pass you something, you ask **Ngicela** *I politely request* followed by the name of the thing you want.

Ngicela ibhotela.	*Please pass me the butter /* *Can I have the butter please?* (Lit. *I politely request the butter*)
Ngicela ubisi.	*Please pass me the milk.*
Ngicela isinkwa.	*Please pass me the bread.*

2 Let us ...

When you would like people to do something together with you, you can ask them politely by starting the verb with **ma** and letting it end with **-e**.

Masithandaze.	*Let us pray.*
Masihambe.	*Let's go.*
Masidle.	*Let us eat.*
Masiphumule lapha isikhashana, mama.	*Let's rest here for a little while, Mother.*

You use the same structure when asking someone's permission to do something.

Mangikusize baba.	*Let me help you, baba.*
Mangibize udokotela.	*Let me call a doctor.*

Let us say grace

Saying grace before meals is a habit practised by all Zulu people of the Christian faith. Here is an easy example that beginners might find useful.

> **Baba wethu oseZulwini sibonga lokhu kudla esikuphiwa nguwe nezandla ezikwenzile. Konke lokhu sikucela egameni likaJesu Krestu, uMsindisi wethu. Amen.**

(Our Heavenly Father (**Baba wethu oseZulwini**), we thank Thee for this food which Thou has given us (**esikuphiwa nguwe)** and the hands that have prepared it (**ezikwenzile**). All (**konke**) this we ask in the name (**egameni**) of Jesus Christ, our Redeemer (**uMsindisi**). Amen.

3 Asking for more food/drink

To say you want to have some more to eat or drink (of the food/drink you have been consuming), you say **Ngingathanda ukuphinda**. (Lit. *I would like to repeat*) or **Ngisafuna** (Lit. *I still want*), followed (if necessary) by the name of the thing you want.

Ngingathanda ukuphinda itiye, nkosikazi.	*I would like to have some more (i.e. a second cup of) tea, please, ma'am.*
Ngisafuna okuphuzwayo.	*I want another drink, please.*

When asked whether you want anything more to eat or drink, you may politely accept by saying **Ngingajabula** (pl. **Singajabula**) (*Yes please*).

Or you may politely decline by saying *No, I have had enough, thank you*, which is:

- in the case of liquids:

Cha, ngiyabonga. Nganelisiwe.	*No thank you. I am satisfied (i.e. I have had enough).*

- in the case of food:

Cha, ngiyabonga. Sengesuthi.	*No thank you, I have had enough (to eat).*

A very idiomatic way to refuse when asked whether you want anything more to eat is to say **Cha, ngiyabonga. Sengesuthi esentwala**. (Lit. *I'm as full as a louse*) *I have had more than enough to eat.*

4 You must not ...

To tell someone that (s)he *must not* do something, you insert the negative formative **-nga-** in the verb just behind the subject concord and let the verb end with **-i**.

Ungahamb**i** manje Desmond.	*You must not leave now, Desmond.*
Ungakhal**i** ntombi yami, kuzolunga.	*You must not cry, my dear girl, it (things) will be OK.*
Ngi**nga**bhem**i** lapha madoda, akuvunyelwa.	*You must not smoke (in) here guys, it is not allowed.*

Note, however, that the ending of the stem **-khohlwa** (*forget*) does not change in the negative.

Ungakhohlwa Davide.	*You must not forget, David.*
Singakhohlwa madoda!	*We must not forget, guys!*

5 I/we/he/they ... too/also

To say this, you put **na-** in front of the abbreviated emphatic pronoun (i.e. the emphatic pronoun minus its final syllable **-na,** see Unit 12).

1st p. sing.	**Nami** (< mina) ngiyohamba manje.
	I also (I) am going to leave now.
1st p. pl.	**Nathi** (< thina) siyakhala.
	We too (we) are complaining.
2nd p. sing.	**Nawe** (< wena) Josefa uyavilapha!
	You too Joseph (you) are lazy!
Class 1	UThoko **naye** (< yena) ugula namhlanje.
	Thoko too (he) is ill today.
Class 10	Izinja **nazo** (< zona) zomile kakhulu.
	The dogs too (they) are very thirsty.

6 Expressing the concept 'still'

The concept *still*, as in *It is still all right*, *She is still here*, is expressed by the formative **-sa-** (in the case of verbs) or **-se-** (in the case of non-verbs) which appears just after the subject concord.

Ngi**sa**phila.	*(I am still alive, i.e.) I am still fine.*
Awungixolele ngi**sa**bambekile.	*Please excuse me, I am still busy.*
Ilanga li**sa**khanya.	*The sun is still shining.*

In non-verbs **-se-** is used.

UDokotela Bhengu u**se**khona na?	*Is Dr Bhengu still there/here?*
Ku**se**khona isikhathi.	*There is still time.*

Note the change in meaning in the negative.

Ilanga ali**sa**khanyi.	*The sun is not shining anymore.*
Abantu aba**sa**khali.	*The people are not complaining anymore.*
Angi**sa**yi.	*I am not going anymore.*

Note that in the negative with **khona**, **se** implies that the person (or persons) no longer exists, i.e. that (s)he is dead.

> UDokotela Bhengu akasekho.   (*Dr Bhengu does not exist anymore* i.e.) *Dr Bhengu is dead, Dr Bhengu passed away.*

Expressing 'all'

The concept *all* is expressed by means of pronouns. These pronouns are formed by means of a class concord plus the pronominal stem **-onke**. For example:

Class 2	ba - onke > bonke
	bonk'abantu *all the people*
Class 6	a - onke > onke
	onk'amadoda *all the men*
Class 7	si - onke > sonke
	sonk'isinkwa *all the bread*
Class 9	i - onke > yonke
	yonk'imali *all the money*
Class 17	ku- onke > konke
	Ngifuna **konke** *I want all* (indefinite)

Note that these pronouns may also be used to express the concept *every* or *the whole*.

Class 1	wonke umuntu	*every/each person*
Class 5	lonke ilanga	*the whole day*

Note further that the final vowel of these pronouns may be dropped when they occur before a noun, as can be seen in the examples above. This is, however, an optional rule.

7   *The interrogative* ngabe?

This interrogative is used in questions in which there is a certain amount of doubt on the part of the speaker. It usually comes at the beginning of the sentence.

Ngabe uJames uhambile na?	*Has James left perhaps?*
Ngabe usawoti ukhona na?	*Is the salt here perhaps?*
Ngabe uya ebholeni namhlanje na?	*Are you perhaps going to the football today?*

——————— **Umsebenzi** ———————

1   You and your wife Ann have invited your friends Themba and
Florence to your home for dinner. At the dinner table the following
discourse between you and your guests takes place. You (pointing
to a chair) request Florence to (a) please (Unit 6) sit (-**hlala**) here
(**lapha**) and Themba to (b) please sit there (**khona**). After every-
one has been seated you request them (c) to join you in saying
grace. Having said grace you ask your visitors whether (d) they
(perhaps) prefer a red or white wine. They say that (e) they prefer
a red wine. Your wife asks you for the salad (**isaladi**). Themba
hands you the salad and says (f) 'Here it is.' Your wife says, (g)
'Thank you'. You ask your wife to (h) hand you the pepper, which
she does with a (i) 'Here it is'. (j) You thank her. Florence unexpectedly sneezes and immediately (k) apologises. After the meal
you ask your guests whether (k) they would like some coffee (Unit 12)
and they reply (m) (that it would be nice, i.e.) 'Yes, please' (Unit 4).

Use the above data to create a suitable dialogue between the people at the dinner table.

2   Provide the (negative) subject concord.

(a)   (Thina) ____yobonana futhi *We'll see each other again*

(b)   Ubaba nomama ____saphila kahle *My father and mother are
      still fine*

(c)   UMandla a____funi ukuya ekhefini *Mandla does not want to
      go to the café*

(d)   Izandla [class 8] ____yagezana *Hands wash each other* (Zulu
      proverb meaning that one should help another and vice
      versa)

(e)   Amanzi ____yabila *The water is boiling*

(f)   Ikati ____omile [see Unit 13] *The cat is thirsty*

(g)   Le ntombazana [class 9] a____hlakaniphile kakhulu *This girl
      is not very intelligent*

(h)   IsiZulu ____khulunywa yonke indawo *Zulu is spoken every-
      where*

(i)   Abantu ____duba umsebenzi namhlanje *The people are on
      strike today*

3 Answer in the negative and write down full sentences. Note that some of the sentences are in the past tense (Unit 14) while others are in the present (Unit 9).

(a) USimon ubuye mhla ka-12 kuSeptemba na? *Did Simon return on 12 September?*

(b) Ubaba wakho usebenza eThekwini na? *Does your father work in Durban?*

(c) Bahambe ubusuku bonke na? *Have they travelled the entire night?*

(d) Izitolo zivala ngo-6 namhlanje na? *Do the shops close at 6pm today?*

(e) Le nto ibiza kakhulu na? *Is this thing very expensive?*

(f) Nifuna uku-oda manje? *Do you* (pl.) *want to order now?*

4 How would you ask your friend Elizabeth whether she wants:

(a) some more sandwiches (**amasendiwishi**)

(b) some more cake (**ikhekhe**)

(c) some more coffee?

5 How would you decline if a friend asks you whether you want:

(a) some more wine

(b) something more to eat?

6 How would you ask someone with whom you are having lunch:

(a) to please hand you the milk (**ubisi**)

(b) whether there is any salt (**usawoti**) (on the table)?

7 How will you tell someone that:

(a) you are still fine

(b) the shops (**izitolo**) are still open (**-vuliwe**)

(c) the boss (**umakhonya** [class 1]) is still there (**khona**)

(d) he must not hurry (**-shesha**) because (**ngoba**) there is still time (**isikhathi**)

(e) he must not forget (**-khohlwa**)

8 How do you say:

All the people	All the time (**isikhathi**)
All the money	The whole week (**iviki**)
Let us pray (**-thandaza**)	Let us go (**-hamba**)

18
UGAVIN UYA KUDOKOTELA

Gavin goes to the doctor

In this unit you will learn

- what to say when visiting a doctor
- some useful expressions regarding health matters
- how to ask what is the matter with someone
- days of the week
- how to ask permissive questions with 'must'
- how to express wishes and (polite) commands
- how to say you are going to someone/someone's place
- how to ask 'when'?

Ingxoxo

Gavin has not been feeling very well lately and has decided to pay his doctor a visit.

Thoko	Uphi uGavin, Lindi?
Lindi	Uye kudokotela.
Thoko	Unani? Ngabe uyagula?
Lindi	Angazi mina.
	[at the doctor's]
Gavin	Sawubona Dokotela.

Dokotela	Sawubona mnumzana. Unjani?
Gavin	Angizizwa kahle Dokotela.
Dokotela	Unani?
Gavin	Ngiphethwe ngumphimbo Dokotela.
Dokotela	Ubuhlungu na?
Gavin	Yebo.
Dokotela	Ukhwehlela kakhulu?
Gavin	Yebo Dokotela, kodwa hayi kakhulu.
Dokotela	Sicinene na isifuba sakho?
Gavin	Yebo, sicinene.
Dokotela	Unethemperetsha na?
Gavin	Yebo.
Dokotela	Uqale nini ukugula?
Gavin	Ngiqale izolo, Dokotela.
Dokotela	Awulale lapha embhedeni. Ngifuna ukukupopola. ... Awukhumule ihembe. ... Donsa umoya, ... khipha umoya. Donsa futhi ..., khipha futhi ..., Yithi, 'aah'. Ngibona uphethwe yimfuluwenza.
Gavin	Ngingaya emsebenzini na Dokotela?
Dokotela	Cha. Kuhle ulale izinsukwana uze uzizwe ungcono. Ngizokulobela umuthi ozoqeda ukukhwehlela namaphilisi okuqeda ubuhlungu ...
Gavin	Ngibuye futhi Dokotela?
Dokotela	Ngingathanda ukukubona futhi ngoLwesithathu.
Gavin	Ngiyabonga Dokotela. Usale kahle.
Dokotela	Uphole masinya! Hamba kahle.

UGavin uya kudokotela *Gavin goes to the doctor*
Uphi uGavin? *Where's Gavin?* (see also Unit 11)
Uye kudokotela *He went to (see) the doctor*
Unani? *What's the matter with him?*
Ngabe uyagula? *Is he ill perhaps?*
Angizizwa kahle *I don't feel well*
Angazi mina *I don't know* ('I' emphasised) (see also Unit 12)
Unani? *What's the matter with you?*
Ngiphethwe ngumphimbo *My throat is sore* (Lit. *I'm bothered by my throat*)
Umphimbo [class 3] *Throat*
Ubuhlungu na? *Is it* (i.e. *your throat*) *painful?*
Ukhwehlela kakhulu na? *Do you cough a lot?*
khwehlela *cough*
Sicinene na isifuba sakho? *Is your chest congested?*

Unethemperetsha na? *Do you have a temperature?* (Note that Zulu has no word for *temperature*. The expression **Unomkhuhlane na?** *Do you have a cold?* is sometimes used for this purpose.)

Uqale nini ukugula? *When did you start feeling ill?*

Ngiqale izolo *I started yesterday*

Awulale embhedeni *Will you please lie on the bed*

ngifuna ukukupopola *I want to examine you* (=**-ku-**)

ukupopola *to examine*

Awukhumule ihembe *Please take off (your) shirt*

Donsa umoya *Take a (deep) breath*

Khipha umoya *Breathe out*

futhi *again*

Yithi 'aah' *Say* 'aah'

Ngibona uphethwe yimfuluwenza *I think you're suffering from influenza*

Ngingaya emsebenzini na? *May I go to work?* (see also Unit 12)

Kuhle ulale izinsukwana *It's best that you (lie down) stay in bed for a couple of days,* (*stay in bed* is idiomatically expressed in Zulu by the verb **-lala** *lie down*)

izinsukwana *a few days*

uze uzizwe ungcono *until you feel (yourself) (that you are) better*

ungcono *you are better*

Ngizokulobela umuthi *I'll give you a prescription* (Lit. *I will write medicine for you*)

umuthi *medicine*

umuthi ozoqeda ukukhwehlela *medicine that will stop the coughing*

namaphilisi okuqeda ubuhlungu *and tablets to stop the pain*

Ngibuye futhi? *Must I come back (for a check)?*

Ngingathanda ukukubona futhi *I would like to see you again* (see also Unit 12)

ngoLwesithathu *on Wednesday*

Uphole masinya *You must get well soon*

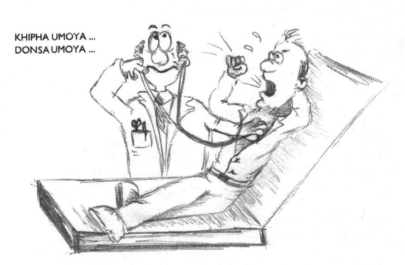

KHIPHA UMOYA ...
DONSA UMOYA ...

Imibuzo

1 Kuyiqiniso noma akusilo? Correct and rewrite the false ones.

(a) UGavin uphethwe yisifuba
(b) UGavin akaguli
(c) UGavin angaya emsebenzini
(d) UGavin uthole (*got*) umuthi kudokotela (*from the doctor*)
(e) UGavin usesibhedlela

2 Phendula imibuzo elandelayo ngemisho egcwele (in full sentences)

(a) UGavin uqale nini ukugula?
(b) UGavin uyakhwehlela na?
(c) UGavin uye kubani?
(d) Sinjani isifuba sikaGavin?
(e) Udokotela uthi (*says*) uGavin uphethwe yini?

3 Phendula imisho elandelayo ngokuyiphikisa. (Answer the following questions in the negative.)

(a) UGavin uye (went) esibhedlela
(b) UGavin ugula kakhulu (very)
(c) Udokotela upopole uLindi
(d) Udokotela ujove uGavin (gave Gavin an injection)
(e) UGavin uya (goes) emsebenzini

Ulimi

---

1 Going to the doctor

It is not very idiomatic to say in Zulu that you are going to see a doctor or that you are going to visit a doctor. In Zulu you say you are going to (=**-ya**) the doctor.

Ngiya kudokotela. *I'm going to the doctor.*

When you want to go and see a medical doctor, you say:

Ngifuna ukuya kudokotela. *I want to go to a doctor.*

To enquire where you can find a doctor, you ask:

Singamthola kuphi udokotela?   *Where can we find a doctor?*
(Lit. *We can find him where the doctor?*)

2   Useful expressions about health matters

Angizizwa kahle. *I'm not feeling well.*	**Uphethwe yini?** *What ails you?*
Unani? *What's the matter with you?*	**Ngiphethwe yikhanda.** *I have a headache.*
Yisikhathi esingakanani ugula? *How long have you been ill?*	**Mangithathe umfutho wegazi lakho.** *Let me take your blood pressure.*
Ngizokulobela umuthi ozokupholisa masinyane. *I will give (=prescribe) you some medicine that will quickly cure (=**pholisa**) you.*	**Kufanele ngikujove.** *I will have to give you an injection.* (Lit. *I'll have to inject you*)
	Uthole umjovo. *He/she got an injection.*

If something ails you, you say **Ngiphethwe ...** followed by the (copulative) noun (beginning with the prefix **ng-** or **y-**) describing the ailment.

Ngiphethwe ngumkhuhlane.	*I have a cold.*
Ngiphethwe yikhanda.	*I have a headache.* (**ikhanda**=*head*)
Ngiphethwe yimfiva.	*I have a fever.*
Ngiphethwe yisisu.	*I've got a stomach ache* (**isisu**=*stomach*).
Ngiphethwe yizinyo.	*I have toothache* (**izinyo**=*tooth*).
Ngiphethwe yisifuba.	*My chest is sore* (**isifuba**=*chest*).
Ngiphethwe ngumlenze.	*My leg is sore.*
Ngiphethwe yindlebe.	*I have an earache* (**indlebe** = *ear*).
Ngiphethwe ngamathonsela.	*I have tonsillitis.*

Nouns whose initial vowel is **u-** or **a-** take the prefix **ng-** while those with an initial **i-** take the prefix **y-**.

Note too that *I have a cold* can also be expressed by means of **Nginomkhuhlane**.

3 What is the matter with you?

When someone is feeling ill and you want to know what is ailing him/her you can ask: **Unani?** To this you can reply by saying either **Ngiphethwe ...** followed by the name of the ailment

Ngiphethwe yisimungumungwane. *I have got measles.*

or **Ngina** + the name of the ailment (see also *and* Unit 23).

Ngi**no**mkhuhlane   *I have got a cold.*
  (**ngina-umkhuhlane**).
Ngi**ne**simungumungwane   *I have got measles.*
  (**ngina-isimungumungwane**).

4 Days of the week

ngomSombuluko	*(on) Monday*	**ngoLwesihlanu**	*(on) Friday*
ngoLwesibili	*(on) Tuesday*	**ngoMgqibelo**	*(on) Saturday*
ngoLwesithathu	*(on) Wednesday*	**ngeSonto**	*(on) Sunday*
ngoLwesine	*(on) Thursday*		

It's important to note that the days of the week are normally used in Zulu in the sense of *on Monday*, *on Tuesday*, ... This is why they all begin with **ngo-** or **nge-** (*on*).

5 Asking (permissive) questions with 'must'

Permissive questions are questions which you ask when you want to gain permission from someone to do something. To ask this kind of question you simply let the (present tense) verb end on **-e**.

Ngibuy**e** kusasa Dokotela?   *Must I come back tomorrow, Doctor?*

Silind**e** noma sihamb**e**?   *Must we wait or must we leave?*
Ngival**e**?   *Must I close (e.g. the door)?*
Ngimbiz**e**?   *Must I call him?*

Important for this kind of question is that the subject concord of classes 1 and 1a is an **a-** in this instance.

ULindiwe **a**ngen**e** na?   *Must Lindiwe come in?*
UCatherine **a**leth**e** itiye na?   *Must Catherine bring the tea?*

6 Expressing a wish/polite command

The structure explained in (5) above may also be used to express wishes and polite commands, which in English are often rendered by means of *must*.

Uphol**e** masinya Emelda.	*You must get well soon, Emelda.*
UN**k**ulunkulu **a**hamb**e** nawe.	*God must (walk=) be with you.*
Usal**e** kahle Geraldine.	*You must stay well, Geraldine.*
Uqed**e** masinyane James.	*You must finish quickly James.*

7 Expressing commands

To express a command (not a polite one!) you use the verbal stem. The verbal stem is that part of the verb that expresses the basic or lexical meaning of the verb. It is also the part of the verb that is listed in Zulu dictionaries. (Do not forget to omit the initial vowel of the noun denoting the person(s) you are addressing.)

Thula (u)Vusi!	*Keep quiet, Vusi!*
Hamba kahle, (u)Themba.	*Go well, Themba.*
Donsa umoya.	*(Draw in air, i.e.) breathe in.*
Khipha umoya.	*(Take out air, i.e.) breathe out.*
Hlala phansi.	*Sit down.*

When a command is addressed to more than one person you simply add **-ni** to the end of the verb stem.

Thula**ni** (a)bantwana!	*Keep quiet, children!*
Hamba**ni** kahle (a)madoda.	*Go ye well, men.*
Sala**ni** kahle.	*Stay ye well.*
Hlala**ni** phansi.	*Sit ye down.*

In the case of monosyllabic verb stems (of which there are only a few in Zulu), **yi-** is added to the front of the stem.

Yima (< -ma) lapha!	*Stand here!*
Yima**ni** lapho!	*Stand ye over there!*
Yithi (< -thi) 'aah'	*Say 'aah'*
Yiza (< -za) lapha!	*Come here!*
Yiza**ni** lapha!	*Come ye here!*

Note the alternative command form of the verb **-za**.

Woza lapha!	*Come here!*
Wozani lapha!	*Come ye here!*

8 Saying you are going to someone/ someone's place

● To say you are going to someone, you use the verb stem **-ya** (*go*) followed (very often) by a noun in classes 1 or 1a to which **ku-** is added.

Ngiya **kuJoan**.	*I'm going to Joan.*
Ugogo uye **kudokotela**.	*Grandma went to see the doctor.*
Sifuna ukuya **kumphathi**.	*We want to go (and speak) to the manager (=**umphathi**).*

● To say you are going to someone's place (for example his home), you replace **ku-** with **kwa-**.

Siya **kwaShirley/kwaSmith**.	*We are going to Shirley's place (i.e. to her home)/to the Smiths' house.*

9 When?

To ask questions with *when* you simply put the interrogative **nini?** (*when?*) after the verb.

Ubuya nini kusasa Fred?	*When are you coming back tomorrow, Fred?*
Sisuka nini isitimela?	*When does the train depart?*
Izikole zivala nini?	*When do the schools close? (for the holidays)*

✔ ——————— **Umsebenzi** ———————

1 Imagine that you are a medical doctor and that you are examining a patient. (*a*) You ask the patient (Mr Khathi) what's wrong with him. (*b*) He says that he doesn't know. You ask (*c*) whether he has a temperature and he replies (*d*) yes. You also enquire (*e*) whether

he suffers from any headaches and he replies (*f*) affirmatively. You ask him (*g*) how long he has been ill and he replies that (*h*) he became ill the day before yesterday (=**kuthangi**). You request him to (*i*) please take off his jacket (**ibhantshi**) because (**ngoba**) (*j*) you want to examine him. After having examined the patient you diagnose that (*k*) he is suffering from tonsillitis and you tell him that you will (*l*) prescribe some medicine.

Write a suitable dialogue based on the information given above. Then re-enact it by performing the role of both doctor and patient.

2 You are not feeling well. You decide to visit a doctor. How will you tell him that you don't feel well and that your stomach bothers you?

3 As a doctor, how will you tell your patient that (s)he needs an injection and that you'll also prescribe some medicine for him/her?

4 Answer the following questions by using the words in brackets.

    (*a*) Uyaphi? (udokotela)
    (*b*) Uvelaphi? (udokotela wamazinyo *dentist*)
    (*c*) Unani? (imfuluwenza)
    (*d*) Uzobuya nini? (ngeSonto)
    (*e*) Ngubani oye kudokotela? (Gavin) (see also Unit 16)

5 Complete the sentences by providing the missing subject concord.

    (*a*) _____enzani Kate? *What are you busy doing Kate?* (see also Unit 13)
    (*b*) Isikhathi _____thini manje? *What is the time now?*
    (*c*) _____njani George? *How is it, George?*
    (*d*) _____yaphi manje? *Where are you* (pl.) *going to now?*
    (*e*) _____ya edolobheni *We are going to town*
    (*f*) _____yaphi abantwana? *Where are the children going?*
    (*g*) _____ngakusiza ngani, mnumzana? *With what can I help you, sir?*
    (*h*) _____omile kakhulu *We are very thirsty*

6 How do you ask/say in Zulu?

    (*a*) What is your name?
    (*b*) Where do you come from?
    (*c*) What price something is?
    (*d*) Smoking is not allowed (see Unit 12)
    (*e*) I'm not feeling well
    (*f*) May I introduce you to ... (see Unit 11)
    (*g*) What someone's occupation is? (see Unit 9)

(h) Ronald is not here (see Unit 8)
(i) Do you have any money (on you)?
(j) Where the Post Office is?
(k) The bread is in the kitchen (see Unit 14)
(l) If there is a telephone somewhere? (see Unit 8)

7 How would you tell Phillip that you wish him to:

(a) get well (**-phola**) soon (=**masinyane**)
(b) go well (**kahle**)
(c) keep (=stay) well
(d) sleep (**-lala**) well (**kamnandi**)

8 Tell Rachel to please (see Unit 6):

(a) turn on (**-vula**) the TV (**iTV** or **umabonwakude**)
(b) switch off (**-vala**) the radio (**umsakazo**)
(c) bring (**-letha**) the sugar (**ushukela**)
(d) call (**-biza**) Jonathan

9 Rewrite in the positive.

(a) Unkosikazi Sibiya akekho
(b) (Thina) asikhali
(c) Ibhasi alifikanga
(d) Umama akalambile
(e) Laba bantu abakhulumi isiZulu

19
UKUGCWALISA AMAFOMU

Filling in forms

In this unit you will learn

- about questions found in registration/other (official) forms and their possible answers
- how to ask someone's (postal) address, telephone number, ID number, age and marital status
- how to ask questions beginning with 'How long ...?'
- how to ask what someone/something is
- how to ask what someone's family relationship is
- how to express possession

———————— Ingxoxo ————————

Menzi Zondo is visiting a doctor. As it is her first visit to this doctor the receptionist (**umamukeli**) requires certain particulars from Menzi.

Umamukeli	Ngubani isibongo sakho?
Menzi	NguZondo.
Umamukeli	Amagama akho aphelele?
Menzi	Elinye nguPatience elinye nguMenzi.
Umamukeli	Ithini i-ID namba yakho?
Menzi	Ithi 5805125082003.

Umamukeli	Ubudala bakho?
Menzi	Ngine-36 ubudala.
Umamukeli	Ushadile na?
Menzi	Yebo.
Umamukeli	Lithini ikheli lakho?
Menzi	Lithi PO Box 468 eSikhawini.
Umamukeli	I-code yakhona?
Menzi	Ithi 3887.
Umamukeli	Usebenza kuphi?
Menzi	Ngisebenza eYunivesithini yaKwaZulu.
Umamukeli	Usebenzani lapho?
Menzi	Ngingumabhalane.
Umamukeli	Lithini ikheli lakhona?
Menzi	Lithi UNIZUL PO Box KwaDlangezwa, 3886.
Umamukeli	Yisikhathi esingakanani ukulo msebenzi?
Menzi	Sekuyiminyaka eyisithupha.
Umamukeli	Ngabe uyilunga le-Medical Aid?
Menzi	Yebo.
Umamukeli	Lithini igama le-Medical Aid yakho?
Menzi	Lithi Profaid Medical Aid.
Umamukeli	Ithini inamba yakho ye-Medical Aid?
Menzi	Ithi 122905.
Umamukeli	Igama nesibongo sesihlobo sakho noma somngane wakho?
Menzi	NguStanley Vusumuzi Gumede.
Umamukeli	Uyini kuwe?
Menzi	Ungumfowethu.
Umamukeli	Ikheli lakhe?
Menzi	Lithi PO Box 58 Mntunzini.
Umamukeli	Ngubani ozokhokha i-akhawundi?
Menzi	Yimina.
Umamukeli	Sekwanele. Awusayine lapha.
	[After Menzi has signed]
	Awuhlale phansi. Udokotela uzokubona masinyane.
Menzi	Ngiyabonga.

Ngubani isibongo sakho? *What is your surname?* (Unit 2)
Amagama akho aphelele? *Your full names?*
amagama *names*

-phelele *be complete*
Elinye ngu... elinye ngu... *The one (name) is ... (and) the other (name) is ...*

Ithini ... (Lit. *What does it* (i.e. *the number*) *say*) *What is ...?*
inamba *number*
Ithi ... *It is* (Lit. It (i.e. *the number*) *says ...*)
ubudala bakho? *your age?*
ubudala *age*
Ushadile na? *Are you married?*
ikheli lakho *your address*
ikheli *address* (comes from English *care of*)
I-code yakhona? *The (postal) code (of) there?*
Usebenza kuphi? *where do you work?*
eYunivesithini yaKwaZulu *University of Zululand*
Usebenzani lapho? *What (kind of) work are you doing there?*
Ngingumabhalane *I am a clerk*
umabhalane *a clerk*
Yisikhathi esingakanani ukulo msebenzi? *How long have you been doing this work?* (i.e. *It is how much time that you are in this work?*)
esingakanani? *how much (time)?*
(**ukulo msebenzi** (=**u-ku-lo msebenzi**) *you-at-this work*)
umsebenzi *job/work*
Sekuyiminyaka eyisithupha *it is six years already* (Unit 24)
iminyaka *years*
isithupha *six*

ngabe *perhaps*
Uyilunga le-Medical Aid? *Are you a member of a Medical Aid?*
ilunga *member*
igama nesibongo sesihlobo *name and surname of relative*
Uyini kuwe? *What (relation) is (s)he to you?*
isihlobo *relative*
noma *or*
somngane wakho *(name and surname) of a friend of yours*
umngane *friend*
Sekwanele *That is all*
Usihloboni nawe? *What kind of relative is he of you?*
Ungumfowethu *He is my brother*
Umfowethu *my brother* (**umfowabo** *His/her brother*)
Ngubani ozokhokha i-akhawundi? *Who is responsible for settling the account?* (i.e. *who will pay the account?*)
-khokha *pay*
Yimina *It is I* ('I' emphasised)
Awusayine lapha *Please sign here*
-sayina *sign*
(**isayini** *signature*)
Awuhlale phansi *Please sit down*
-hlala *sit*
phansi *down*
masinyane *soon*

Imibuzo

Phendula imibuzo elandelayo:

(a) Umamukeli ukhuluma nobani lapha?
(b) Ngubani isibongo sikaMenzi?
(c) Ngubani igama lesihlobo sikaMenzi?
(d) Lithini elinye (*another*) igama likaMenzi?
(e) UMenzi uhlala kuphi?

Dr Joyce & Dr. Hyams / UDkt Joyce noDkt Hyams

DETAILS OF PATIENT / IMININGWANE NGESIGULI
Surname / Isibongo   Full names / Amagama aphelele

Age / Ubudala   Date of birth / Usuku lokuzalwa

DETAILS TO WHOM THE ACCOUNT MUST BE SENT / IMININGWANE NGALOWO OZOTHUNYELWA I-AKHAWUNDI

Surname / Isibongo	Initials / ama-inishiyali
Postal address / Ikheli leposi	Home address / Ikheli lasekhaya
Code / Ikhodi	Code / Ikhodi

Telephone number /   Home / Ekhaya   Work / Emsebenzini
Inombolo yocingo

Friend/relative + name / Igama lomngane / lesihlobo

——————————— **Ulimi** ———————————

1 *Questions with* -thini?

You may use the interrogative **-thini?** (which literally means *says what?*) when you want to find out certain particulars about someone/something, like for instance what the address of a person/company is or what the number of something is. (Do not forget to add the appropriate subject concord referring to the person or thing whose identity is being asked.

● Finding out the (postal) address

Lithini ikheli [class 5] lakho?   *What is your address?*
Lithini ikheli lakho leposi?   *What is your postal address?*

To answer this question you begin with **-thi** (using the same concord as in **-thini?**) followed by the required information.

Lithini ikheli lakho (leposi)? Lithi: 99 Mazibuko Street,
Block E, Umlazi.

● Finding out the number

Ithini inamba [class 9] yocingo   *What is your (work / home)*
[class 11] (lwasemsebenzini/   *telephone number?*
lwasekhaya) lwakho?

Note that **lwa(kho)** refers to **ucingo**, i.e. what is the number of *your telephone.*

Ithini inamba yepasi lokuhamba   *What is your passport number?*
(yepasipoti) lakho?

Note that **la(kho)** refers to **ipasi/ipasipoti**, i.e. what is the number of *your passport.*

Ithini **i**-ID namba yakho?   *What is your ID number?*
Ithini inamba yehhovisi lakho?   *What is your office number?*
Ithini inamba yemoto yakho?   *What is your car registration number?*

This question is answered in the same way as the one with the name and address above.

2 How long have you been ...?

To find out how long someone has been doing something, for example how long (s)he has been employed, you ask:

Yisikhathi esingakanani ukulo msebenzi?	*How long have you been doing this work? / How long have you been in this employment?*
Yisikhathi esingakanani usebenza lapha/lapho?	*How long have you been working here / there?*

Note that **-usebenza** can be replaced by most other words.

Yisikhathi esingakanani **ushadile?**	*How long have you been married?* (note **-shadile** is a stative verb, see Unit 13)
Yisikhathi esingakanani **nihlala** lapha?	*How long have you* (pl.) *been living here?*
Yisikhathi esingakanani **usesibhedlela?**	*How long have you been in hospital?* (see Unit 14 for the pre-locative **s**)

Note that the present tense **-ya-** is never used in the present tense verbs that occur in this environment, for example, you never say, 'Yisikhathi esingakabani **uya**sebenza? (*How long have you been working?*)

Note also that the subject concord of classes 1 and 1a is **e-**, while the subject concord of class 2 is **be-**.

Yisikhathi esingakanani **e**sebenza lapho uJoyce?	*How long has Joyce been working there?*

In the negative **-nga-** is inserted in the verb (just after the subject concord) while the verb ends with **-i**.

Yisikhathi esingakanani u**nga**sebenzi	*How long have you not been working,* (i.e. *How long have you been out of a job?*)
Yisikhathi esingakanani be**nga**sebenzi?	*How long have they been out of work?*

3   Asking someone's age

There are several ways to ask a person how old (s)he is. Here are a few suggestions:

> Uneminyaka emingaki ubudala?   *How old are you?*
> Mingaki iminyaka yakho?

or

> Wazalwa ngamuphi unyaka?   *In what year were you born?*

The answer to this question may for example be given by means of an English numeral preceded by **Ngine-**.

> Uneminyaka emingaki?   Ngine-23   *I am 23*

When the year of birth (date of birth) is asked, the answer may be given by means of **ngonyaka ka-** followed by the year of birth.

> Wazalwa ngamuphi unyaka?   Ngazalwa ngonyaka ka-1962.

4   Saying what someone/something is

To say what someone/something is, like when identifying a person/thing, for example *It is Joe Frazier, It is a cat, It is time,* you put **yi-**, **ngu-** (or **wu-**) or **nga-** before the noun depending on what the initial vowel of the noun is. The following sound rules apply here.

● Nouns beginning with **u-** add **ngu-** to the initial vowel.

> **Ngu**mfowethu   *It is my brother.*
> (< **u**mfowethu *my brother*)
> **Ngu**Jacob (< **u**Jacob) Zuma.   *It is Jacob Zuma.*
> **Ngu**muzi (**u**muzi *homestead*)   *It is the homestead of Cele.*
> kaCele.

● Nouns beginning with **i-** add **yi-** to the initial vowel.

> **Yi**mali (< **i**mali *money*) yami.   *It is my money.*
> **Yi**sikhathi (< **i**sikhathi *time*)   *Now is the time.*
> manje.   (i.e. *It is the time now.*)

● Nouns beginning with **a-** add **nga-** to the initial vowel.

Ngamanzi (< **a**manzi *water*)   *It is cold water.*
  abandayo.
NgamaZulu (< **a**maZulu   *It is the Zulu people who like*
  the Zulu people) athanda   *to preserve (their) traditions.*
  ukugcina amasiko.

In order to say *(S)He etc. is/are ...*, you simply put the appropriate subject concord before the noun beginning with **ngu-**, **nga-** or **yi-**.

Ungumfowethu u-Isaac.   *He is my brother (Isaac that is).*
BangamaZulu labo bantu.   *They are Zulus, those people.*
Uyindodana kababa Madondo.   *He is the son of baba Madondo.*
SingamaNgisi.   *We are English (-speaking) people.*

5   Asking what relation a person is to you/someone else

To ask in what way someone is related to the person you are speaking to, you say:

   Uyini kuwe?   *What (relation) is he/she to you?*

This question is answered by putting **ungu-** in front of the name of the relation:

  Ungudadewethu.   *She is my sister.*
  Ungumfowethu.   *He is my brother.*
  Ungubaba wami.   *He is my father.*

6   Marital status

To find out whether someone is married or not you ask:

   Ushadile yini?   *Are you married **or not** (=**yini**)?*

If you are married you can say:

   Yebo, ngishadile

If you are not (yet) married you can answer:

  Cha, angishadile.   *No, I am not married.*
  Cha, angikashadi.   *No, I am not yet married.*

7 Expressing possession

Possession in Zulu is expressed somewhat differently than it is in English. Where in English you may say *the boy's bicycle, their house, my father's car*, in Zulu you say *the bicycle of the boy, the house of them, the car of my father*.

Possession in Zulu is expressed by means of a possessive concord signifying *of*. Possessive concords look very much like subject concords. This derivation occurs by combining the subject concord with **a-** causing certain sound changes in the form of the subject concords, e.g. **u > w, i > y**, while the vowel of most of the other subject concords is replaced by **a**. Each noun class has its own possessive concord.

Table of possessive concords

		Subject concord		Possessive concord
Class 1	umu-	**u-**	(+ **a** >)	wa-
Class 2	aba-	**ba-**	(+ **a** >)	ba-
Class 1a	u-	**u-**	(+ **a** >)	wa-
Class 2a	o-	**ba-**	(+ **a** >)	ba-
Class 3	umu-	**u-**	(+ **a** >)	wa-
Class 4	imi-	**i-**	(+ **a** >)	ya-
Class 5	i(li)-	**li-**	(+ **a** >)	la-
Class 6	ama-	**a-**	(+ **a** >)	a-
Class 7	isi-	**si-**	(+ **a** >)	sa-
Class 8	izi-	**zi-**	(+ **a** >)	za-
Class 9	in-	**i-**	(+ **a** >)	ya-
Class 10	izin-	**zi-**	(+ **a** >)	za-
Class 11	u(lu)-	**lu-**	(+ **a** >)	lwa-
Class 14	ubu-	**bu-**	(+ **a** >)	ba-
Class 15	uku-	**ku-**	(+ **a** >)	kwa-

Note the form of the possessive concords of especially classes 6, 11 and 15.

Possessive pronouns

Possession is not expressed by the possessive concord only. You also use what is known as possessive pronouns, like when you say in Zulu *the dog of mine* (i.e. my dog), *the car of his* (i.e. his car), *the luggage of theirs* (i.e. their luggage). Just as is the case with the possessive concords, each noun class has its own possessive pronoun. Here are the possessive pronouns for the first, second and third person (i.e. classes 1, 1a, 2 and 2a).

1st p. sing.	**-mi** (*mine*)	1st p. pl.	**-(i)thu** (*our*)
2nd p. sing.	**-kho** (*your*)	2nd p. pl.	**-(i)nu** (*your*)
Class 1/1a	**-khe** (*his*)	Class 2/2a	**-bo** (*their*)

Note that the possessive concord combines with the possessive pronoun and together they form a single word in Zulu.

imoto [class 9] **yami**	*my car*
umbhede [class 3] **wakho**	*your bed*
izikhwama [class 8] **zabo**	*their bags*
igama [class 5] **lakho**	*your name*

When combining with the possessive pronouns of the first and second person plural, all possessive concords change their vowel **a** to **e**.

abantwana [class 2] (ba-inu >) benu	*your children*
itafula [class 5] (la-ithu >) lethu	*our table*
amathikithi [class 6] (a-inu >) enu	*your tickets*

Besides being used with possessive pronouns, the possessive concords may also be used together with nouns. Here too the form of the possessive concord changes in accordance with the form of the initial vowel of the following noun. These sound rules apply:

- **a- + u- > o-**

This rule states that when the vowel **a-** of the possessive concord combines with the initial vowel **u-** of the following noun, then **a- + u- > o-**.

iwashi (**la-u**mfana >) **lo**mfana	*the boy's watch* (i.e. *the watch of the boy*)

isifo (**sa-u**mntwana >)	*the child's illness*
somntwana	(i.e. *the illness of the child*)
amandla (**a-u**mthakathi >)	*the power of the witch doctor*
omthakathi	

- **a- + i- > e-**

When the **a-** of the possessive concord combines with the initial vowel **i-** of the following noun, then **a- + i- > e-**.

amafomu (**a-i**telegilamu>)	*telegram forms (forms of the*
etelegilamu	*telegram)*
ihhovisi (**la-i**meneja >) **le**meneja	*the manager's office*
indlu (**ya-i**khehla >) **ye**khehla	*the old man's house*

- **a- + a- > a-**

When the **a-** of the possessive concord combines with the initial **a-** of the following noun, it remains unchanged.

amandla (**a-a**bantu) **a**bantu	*the power of the people*
ukudla (kw**a-a**madoda)	*the men's food*
kw**a**madoda	

When the possessor is a noun in class 1a (e.g. a noun signifying some-one's name), two important rules concerning the possessive concord apply:

When the noun expressing the possession contains an **m** or an **n** in its prefix, the possessive concord is **ka** throughout.

Imali **ka**Stephen	*Stephen's money*
Umntwana **ka**-Agnes	*Agnes' child*
Umsebenzi **ka**baba	*Father's work*
amandla **ka**Sipho	*Sipho's strength*

When the noun in such instances does not contain an **m** or **n** in its prefix, the possessive concord is equal to: **subject ᐧ oncord** plus **ka**:

Ibhuku li**ka**Margarethe	*Margaret's book*
Abantwana ba**ka**Josefa	*Joseph's children*
Isikhwama samabhuku	*David's bookcase*
si**ka**Davide	
Izibuko zi**ka**mama	*Mother's spectacles*

☑ ─────────── **Umsebenzi** ───────────

1 • You want to enrol for a course at a Technicon. To gain admission you are requested to complete an application form in which the following questions are asked: (*a*) your full name and surname, (*b*) your ID number, (*c*) your date of birth, (*d*) your (postal) address, (*e*) your telephone number, (*f*) your marital status, (*g*) your home language (**ulwimi** [class 11] **lwasekhaya**)

   • Upon your arrival at a hotel you are asked to fill in a registration form. The following information is required: (*a*) your full name and surname, (*b*) your home (=postal) address, (*c*) your nationality, (*d*) your date of birth, (*e*) place of birth, (*f*) coming from, (*g*) going to, (*h*) passport number, (*i*) car registration number, (*j*) date, (*k*) signature

Create an application form or registration form in which the above questions with their answers are given in Zulu.

2 Complete the following sentences by supplying the missing possessive concord.

   • (*a*) Nangu **u**mama ____kho *Here is your mother*
   (*b*) Lesi **yisi**kole ____(i)thu *This is our school*
   (*c*) **Yi**moto ____mi le *It is **my** car this*
   (*d*) Likuphi ikhaya ____kho? *Where is **your** home?*
   (*e*) Bonke **aba**ntwana ____khe bahlakaniphile *All **his** children are intelligent*
   (*f*) Yonke **i**mali ____(i)thu iphelile *All **our** money is finished*
   (*g*) Votela amalungelo ____(i)nu *Vote for **your** rights*
   (*h*) Ngilubonga kakhulu **u**sizo [class 11] ____kho, mnumzane (*I*) *Thank you very much for **your** help, Sir*

   • (*a*) Nanti **i**siko ____(a)maZulu *This is a Zulu custom*
   (*b*) Iphepha ____(i)siZulu belinzima kakhulu *The Zulu examination paper was very difficult*
   (*c*) Sekuyi**si**khathi ____(u)kuhamba manje *It is now time to go*
   (*d*) Nanso **i**moto ____(i)nkosikazi Khumalo *There is Mrs Khumalo's car*
   (*e*) **Izin**dlu ____(a)bantu abakhe lapha zinhle kakhulu *The houses of the people who live here are very beautiful*

(f) Awesule **ama**festele ____(i)moto yami *Please wipe my car's windows*

(g) Votela amalungelo ____abafazi *Vote for women's rights*

(h) Ngilethe **uku**dla ____(i)zingane *I brought the food of the children*

(i) Angikhumbuli i**gama** ____(u)mntwana *I do not remember the child's name*

3 How will you ask someone what is his/her:

(a) hotel's name (**igama lehhotela lenu**)
(b) office number (**inombolo yehhovisi lakho**)
(c) ID number
(d) child's name
(e) age

4 As a nursery school teacher you want to teach your class the names of some animals. How would you tell your pupils what the name of these animals is? Start the sentence with *It is* ...

(a) elephant (**indlovu**)
(b) lion (**ibhubesi**)
(c) black rhinoceros (**ubhejane**)
(d) buffalo (**inyathi**)
(e) tortoise (**ufudu**)
(f) eagle (**ukhozi**)
(g) ingwe (**leopard**)

5 Answer the questions in full sentences. However, do not repeat the underlined noun in your answer. Use its pronoun, i.e. its object concord instead. For example Ubona izilwane na? (*Do you see the animals?*) Yebo, ngiyazibona/Cha, angiziboni. Note that some sentences are in the past tense and others in the present.

(a) Ubona abantu na? Yebo, _____
(b) Ufuna le (i)nto na? Yebo, _____
(c) Ubize uJosefa na? Cha, _____
(d) Uthole (*found*) imali na? Cha, _____
(e) Uthanda isiZulu na? Yebo, _____
(f) Ufuna ikhofi na? Yebo, _____
(g) Ulethe (*brought*) impahla (*goods*) na? Yebo, _____

6 Ask Felicity Khumalo how long she has been:

   (*a*) ill (**-gula**)
   (*b*) married (**-shadile**)
   (*c*) doing this work (**-enza lo msebenzi**)
   (*d*) staying at home (**-hlala ekhaya**)

7 How do we say in Zulu:

   (*a*) Peter's surname (**isi**bongo)
   (*b*) John's house (**in**dlu)
   (*c*) Grandmother's (ugogu) bed (**um**bhede)
   (*d*) Mother's food (**uku**dla)?

20
——— UKUBUKEZA ———
Revision

1 Imagine you are an employer at Carlton Furnishers. You receive a telephone call from someone who wants to speak to the manager (**imeneja**). You begin by first (*a*) stating the name of your firm and then proceed (*b*) to ask the caller who is speaking. She says that (*c*) she is Velaphi. You ask (*d*) Velaphi who? and she says Velaphi Nkosi. You ask (*e*) whether you can help her. (*f*) she asks (politely) to speak to the manager. You inform her that (*g*) the manager is unfortunately not available (=not there). She asks (*h*) when will he be back and you say that (*i*) you don't know. You request her (*j*) to please phone again (**futhi**) tomorrow (**kusasa**).

   Write a suitable dialogue based on the details given above.

2 ● Your name is Terence Anderson. You are at home. The telephone rings and you answer it. How will you:

   (*a*) say that it is your residence
   (*b*) ask who is speaking
   (*c*) say that it is you who are speaking
   (*d*) ask the caller who (s)he wants to talk to
   (*e*) tell the caller (s)he has dialled the wrong number

   ● You are at work. How will you identify your employer (i.e. your company's/firm's name) to the caller?

3 You are working in a shoe store. How will you ask a client what size (shoes) (s)he wears?

4 You want to employ someone as messenger at your office. How will you ask the applicant:

  (a) what his or her (school) qualifications are, i.e. what standard (s)he has completed (**-qede**)

  (b) where (s)he has been employed previously (**phambili**)

5 • Say that you are fond of/like (**-thanda**):

  (a) this place (**indawo**)
  (b) this person
  (c) this store (**isitolo**)
  (d) these people
  (e) this cat (**ikati**)
  (f) this dog (**inja**)

  • But that you do not like:

  (a) that place
  (b) that store
  (c) that hotel
  (d) those people

6 • You are feeling out of sorts and have decided to see your doctor. He asks you some questions. What is the doctor asking you? Answer him appropriately. You may use the words in brackets if necessary.

  (a) Uzizwa njani? (kabi *bad*)
  (b) Uphethwe yini? (ikhanda)
  (c) Libuhlungu na?
  (d) Unethemperetsha na?
  (e) Uqale nini ukugula? (ngeSonto)

  • The doctor tells you:

  (a) Ungayi emsebenzini
  (b) Ulale izinsuku ezintathu (3)
  (c) Ngizokulobela amaphilisi azokusiza
  (d) Ngifuna ukukubona futhi ngoLwesithathu

  What did he tell you?

7 How will you command the people indicated in bold below to do the following:

  (a) come (-za) here (**uNomacala**)

(b) keep quiet (**abantwana**)
(c) close the door (=umnyango) (**ULindiwe**)
(d) switch off (=vala) the lights (=izibane) (**uMenzi**)
(e) hurry up (=shesha) (**amadoda**)

8 You have applied for a loan. You are requested to supply the following information:

(a) Ikheli lakho: ....
(b) Inamba yocingo lwasekhaya ....
(c) Ikheli lalapho usebenza khona ....
(d) Inamba yocingo lwasemsebenzini ....
(e) Yisikhathi esingakanani usebenza lapho? ....
(f) Uhola (*earn*) malini ngonyaka (*annually*)?..............
(g) I-ID namba yakho ....
(h) Uneminyaka emingaki ubudala? ....
(i) Ushadile na?...

Say what information each of the items listed above requires and then give the appropriate answer.

9 By using the interrogative **-thini?** how will you ask someone:

(a) What his/her address is
(b) What his/her telephone number is
(c) What his/her name and surname are
(d) What the time is
(e) What the date is (**idethi**) is today?

21
UKUBHUKA INDAWO
-YOKUHLALA EHHOTELA-
Making a hotel reservation

In this unit you will learn how to

- make a (hotel) reservation
- to say 'from ... to ...'
- ask 'how many?'
- say that you are sorry
- form and use adjectives
- express some more numbers

Ingxoxo

Simon Hlongwane and his family plan to spend their next holiday in Durban. In the past they have always rented a holiday flat. This time, however, they have decided to stay in a hotel. As advance booking is essential during high season, Simon has decided to telephone a hotel and make his booking in good time.

Simon   Sawubona mnumzana, ngithanda ukubhuka indawo yokuhlala.

Umamukeli   Uyidinga nini?

Simon   Ngifuna indawo kusuka kumhla ka-10 kuya kumhla ka-21 kuDisemba.

Umamukeli   Ubhukela abantu abangaki?

Simon	Sibathathu, yimina, nenkosikazi yami nomntwana.
Umamukeli	Ufuna ikamelo elihlalisa ababili nekamelo elihlalisa oyedwa.
Simon	Cha, sifuna ikamelo elihlalisa ababili.
Umamukeli	Uneminyaka emingaki umntanakho?
Simon	Uneminyaka emihlanu. Singathanda uma ehlala kanye nathi.
Umamukeli	Kulungile, akunkinga. Awubambe kancane ngizoku-tshela masinyane uma kunendawo.
Simon	Ngiyabonga.
Umamukeli	Ngiyaxolisa, sesigcwele ngomhla ka-10 no-11 kodwa kusuka kumhla ka-12 indawo izoba khona.
Simon	Ngiyajabula. Yimalini ngosuku?
Umamukeli	Ikamelo yi-R250 ngosuku lapho nihlalisana.
Simon	Le mali ihlangene nemali yebhulakufesi?
Umamukeli	Yebo.
Simon	Kulungile, ngizoyithatha.
Umamukeli	Kulungile. Usithumele idiphozithi elingu-R300.
Simon	Kulungile.

Ukubhuka *to book* (*to reserve*)
indawo yokuhlala *a place to stay, accommodation* (see Possession, Unit 19)
indawo *place*
Uyidinga (=u-yi-dinga) nini? (*When do you need it* (*the place*), i.e.) *for when?*
-dinga *need*
nini? *when?*
kusuka kumhla ka-10 *from the 10th*
kuya kumhla ka-21 *to the 21st*
kuDisemba *in December*
-bhukela *book for*
abantu abangaki? *how many people?*
-ngaki? *how many?*
Sibathathu *We are three* (*people*)
yimina *It is I*
inkosikazi yami *my wife*
nomntwana *and a child*
ikamelo elihlalisa ababili (*a room accommodating two* (*people*), i.e.) *a double room*

ikamelo *room*
elihlalisa (*which let stay, i.e.*) *accommodate*
ababili *two* (*people*)
ikamelo elihlalisa oyedwa *a room accommodating only one* (*person*)
oyedwa *only one* (*person*)
Uneminyaka emingaki? *How old is he* (*i.e. your child*)?
umntanakho *your child*
Uneminyaka emihlanu *He is 5 years* (*old*)
uma ehlala kanye nathi *if he stays with us*
uma *if*
kanye *together*
nathi(na) *with us*
akunkinga *there is no problem*
Awubambe kancane *Please hold a little*
ngizokutshela *I will tell you*
masinyane *soon, quickly*
uma kunendawo *if there is place,* i.e. *accommodation*
Ngiyaxolisa *I am sorry*

sesigcwele ngomhla ka-10 no-11
*we are already full, i.e. fully booked,
(on) the 10th and the 11th*
-gcwele *be full*
ngomhla ka- *on the day of*
indawo izoba khona (*place will be
there, i.e.*) *there will be room*
izoba *it* (i.e. *place*) *will be*
khona *there*
Ngiyajabula *I am glad*
Yimalini ngosuku? *What is the
price per day?*
Ikamelo yi-R250 ngosuku *The
room is R250 per day*

ngosuku *per day*
lapho *if*
nihlalisana *you (pl.)* (*staying
together, i.e.*) *sharing*
le mali *this money*
ihlangene? *does it include?*
imali yebhulakufesi? *money for
breakfast?*
ngizoyithatha *I will take it*
Usithumele *You must send us* (see
also Unit 18)
idiphozithi elingu-R300 *a deposit
of R300*

Imibuzo

Phendula imibuzo elandelayo.

(a) USimon nomuzi wakhe (*his family*) bafuna ukuyovakashela (*to go on holiday*) kuphi?
(b) USimon ufuna ikamelo elihlalisa abantu abangaki?
(c) Ikamelo yimalini ngosuku?
(d) Umntwana kaSimon uneminyaka emingaki ubudala?
(e) USimon uthanda ukubhuka indawo yokuhlala kusuka nini kufikela nini?
(f) Imali yekamelo ihlangene nemali yani?
(g) Bafuna idiphozithi eliyimalini?

———————————— **Ulimi** ————————————

1 Making a reservation

When you want to book accommodation you say **Ngithanda uku-bhuka** (from English *book*) **indawo yokuhlala** or **Ngithanda ukubhalisa indawo yokuhlala**. (*I want to (book accommodation, i.e.) make a reservation.*

When you want to reserve a seat for a show/concert/film, you say:

Ngithanda ukubhukela (ukubhalisela) ikhonsathi/ ifilimu lika-8pm.	*I would like to make a reservation for the 8pm show/picture.*

The response from the ticket officer is usually: *(For) How many tickets?* **Ufuna amathikithi amangaki?**). To this you can reply **Amathikithi angu-** or **abe ngu-** plus the number (in English) of tickets you want.

Ngifuna (amathikithi) **angu-3/abe ngu-3**

To make an air booking you say:

Ngifisa ukubhalisa/ukubhuka indawo endizeni. (Lit. *I desire to a book to place on an aeroplane.*)

2 From ... to ...

- If it is a *date*, you say **kusuka** or **kusukela kumhla ka-** plus day of the month, **kuya kumhla ka-** plus day of the month:.

Kusuka kumhla ka-5 kuya   *From the 5th to the 8th*
  kumhla ka-8

If you want to mention the month you add **ku-** (plus name of the month)

Kusuka kumhla ka-14   *From the 14th to the 18th of*
  kuya kumhla ka-18   *April, May, February...*
  ku-Apreli, kuMeyi, kuFebruwari...

- If it is *time* you say **kusuka ku-** plus time (in English), **kuya ku-** plus time:

Kusuka ku-8 kuya ku-12   *From 8 to 12*

- If it is *numbers*, you say **kusuka ku-** plus number (in English)

Kusuka ku-50 kuya ku-60   *From 50 to 60*
Kusuka ku-R10,000 kuya   *From R10,000 to R20,000*
  ku- 20,000

If it is *days of the week* you use **kuze kube** plus name of the day:

kusuka (or kusukela)   *From Monday to Friday*
  ngoMsombuluko kuze kube
  ngoLwesihlanu

- To ask *distances between places* (see also Unit 11) you say **ukusuka ... kuya ...**

Kungamakhilomitha amangaki   *How (many kilometres=) far is*
  ukusuka eGoli kuya   *it from Johannesburg to the*
  eKruger Park?   *Kruger Park?*
Kungu-350 khilomitha.   *It is 350 km.*
Kungamakhilomitha amangaki   *How far is it from here to*
  ukusuka lapha kuya eMtuba?   *Mtubatuba (a place in*
                                  northern KwaZulu-Natal)?
Kungu-400 khilomitha.   *It is 400 km.*

3 How many?

You use the stem **-ngaki?** to express *how many?* in Zulu. Important about **-ngaki?** is that it is one of the so-called adjectival stems in Zulu (see 5 below) and consequently must combine with an adjectival concord (referring to the preceding noun).

Nibone **izin**dlovu **ezin**gaki?	*How many elephants did you see?*
Ufuna **ama**dazini **ama**ngaki?	*How many dozen do you want?*
Ufuna ukuqasha **aba**ntu **aba**ngaki?	*How many people do you want to hire?*

When the answer to a question with **-ngaki?** is a numeral from 2 to 5, many speakers are inclined to make use of the adjectival numerals.

Ufuna **ama**thikithi **ama**ngaki?	*How many tickets do you want?*
Ngifuna **ama**thikithi **ama**hlanu.	*I want five tickets.*
Uyohlala **izin**suku **ezin**gaki?	*How many days are you going to stay?*

Ngiyohlala **izin**suku **ezin**tathu. *I am going to stay three days.*

Note that it is not necessary to repeat the noun in your answer if you do not want to. You can simply omit it.

Uyohlala **izinsuku** ezingaki?	*How many days are you going to stay?*
Ngiyohlala **ezintathu**.	*I am going to stay three (days).*
Ufuna **amarandi** amangaki?	*How many Rands do you want?*
Ngifuna **amabili**.	*I want two (Rands).*

They are 20

To say how many something is you put a subject concord plus **ngu-** before the English numeral.

Bangaki abantu?	*How many are the people?*
(Abantu) **Bangu**-9.	*They (the people) are 9.*
Zingaki izinsuku ku-Oktoba?	*How many days are in October?*
(Izinsuku) **Zingu**-31.	*They (the days) are 31.*
Mangaki amantombazana ekilasini?	*How many are the girls in the class?*
(Amantombazana) **Angu**-16.	*They (the girls) are 16.*

How many are you?

To ask this, you say **Nibangaki?** If your answer is any number from 2 to 5, you say **siba-** plus the appropriate adjective.

Sibabili.	*We are two.*
Sibathathu.	*We are three.*

When you are more than five, you may say **singu-** plus a numeral (in English).

Singu-10, Singu-12 . . .

To say *it is only I*, you say **Yimina kuphela**.

4 Saying you are sorry

To say you are sorry you can either say **Ngiyaxolisa** (*I am sorry*) or simply (interjectively) **Uxolo** (*Sorry*).

Ngiyaxolisa kodwa angikwazi ukukusiza.	*I am sorry but I cannot help you.*
Uxolo! Sicela ukwedlula lapha.	*Sorry! We please want to pass here.*

5 Adjectives

Adjectives are words that tell us something about the quality of a person or a thing. Stated differently, adjectives are words that qualify other words, especially nouns. For example in: a *big* apple, a *wicked* man, a *beautiful* girl.

An important difference between adjectives in English and their counterparts in Zulu is that in English, adjectives normally occur before the noun they describe (a *small* child, a *big* dog), while in Zulu they usually follow the noun: **umntwana** *omncane*, **inja** *enkulu* ...

Adjectives in Zulu consist of a prefix and a stem. There are only a few adjectival stems in Zulu, so it may be useful to memorise these stems as they are all used frequently. Note how many of the adjectival stems form contrasting pairs. Note also that four numerals occur as adjectival stems.

Adjectival stems			
-hle	*good, beautiful*	**-bi**	*bad, ugly, evil*
-de	*long, tall, high*	**-fishane**	*short*
-khulu	*big, large*	**-ncane**	*small, few, young*
-dala	*old*	**-sha**	*new, young*
-ngaki?	*how many?*	**-ningi**	*many*
-bili	*two*	**-thathu**	*three*
-ne	*four*	**-hlanu**	*five*

Adjectival stems operate with what are known as adjectival concords. The form of this concord is very similar to that of the class prefix of the noun that is described by the adjective.

All adjectival concords begin with a vowel. The following rules of thumb apply here:

- If the class prefix contains a **u**, the concord starts with an **o**. (Cf. classes 1, 3, 11, 14 and 15.)

- If the class prefix contains an **i**, the concord starts with an **e**. (Cf. classes 4, 5, 7, 8, 9 and 10.)

- If the class prefix contains an **a**, the concord starts with an **a**. (Cf. classes 2 and 6.)

Adjectival concords		
Class 1	um(u)-	**om(u)-**
Class 1a	u-	**om(u)-**
Class 2	aba-	**aba-**
Class 2a	o-	**aba-**
Class 3	um(u)-	**om(u)-**
Class 4	imi-	**emi-**
Class 5	i(li)-	**eli-**
Class 6	ama-	**ama-**
Class 7	isi-	**esi-**
Class 8	izi-	**ezin-**
Class 9	in-	**en-**
Class 10	izin-	**ezin-**
Class 11	u(lu)-	**olu-**
Class 14	u(bu)-	**obu-**
Class 15	uku-	**oku-**

Compare the following examples of adjectives in Zulu:

Class 1:   u**mu**ntu o**mu**bi *a bad / evil person*
Class 2:   a**ba**ntu a**ba**dala *old people*
Class 5:   i(**li**)lokwe e**li**hle *a nice / beautiful dress*
Class 6:   a**ma**kati a**ma**bili *two cats*
Class 10: i**zin**taba e**zin**kulu *big mountains*

See whether you can supply the missing adjectival concord in the following examples. Don't forget to note the form of the noun class prefix.

U(lu) suku ____hle! *(Have) a nice day!*
Si**naba**ntwana ____bili. *We have two children.*
Une**mi**nyaka ____hlanu. *He is five years old.*
Kubiza **amar**andi ——hlanu. *It costs 5 Rands (R5).*
Sicela i**zin**komishi zetiye ____tathu. *We like three cups of tea, please.*
Sifuna i(**li**)kamelo ____khulu. *We want a big room.*
Kung**ama**mayela ____ngaki? *How many miles is it?*
Ng**ama**mayela ____bili. *It is 2 miles.*
Ukhuluma **isi**Zulu ____hle! *You speak a beautiful Zulu!*
Ung**umu**ntu ____hle Stephen. *You are a good person, Stephen.*
Asifuni **uku**dla ____ningi. *We don't want much food.*

Adjectives used predicatively

The only difference in Zulu between expressions such as *an old man* and *the man is old, a beautiful girl* and *the girl is beautiful* lies in the form of the adjectival concord. When you want to say someone/something *is old, is ugly, is beautiful, is small,* you simply omit the initial vowel of the adjectival concord.

Abantu **aba**ningi	*Many people*
Abantu **ba**ningi.	*The people are many.*
Isitolo **esi**khulu	*A big store*
Isitolo **si**khulu.	*The store is big.*
Umuntu **om**dala	*An old person*
Umuntu **m**dala.	*The person is old.*
Amarandi **ama**hlanu	*Five Rand*
Amarandi **ma**hlanu.	*The Rands are five.*
Izinsuku **ezi**ngaki?	*How many days?*
Izinsuku **zi**ngaki?	*The days are how many?*

Questions that often have adjectives as answers are those with the question words (interrogatives) **njani?** (*how?/of what kind?/of what sort?*) and **ngaki?** (*how many?*).

Linjani izulu namhlanje?	***How is*** *the weather today?*
Lihle/Libi.	*It is fine / It is bad.*
Injani intombi yakhe?	***How is*** *his girlfriend,*
	i.e. *How does she look like?*
Inhle kakhulu.	*She is very beautiful.*
Ulethe indaba **enjani**?	*What kind of news did you bring?*
Ngilethe indaba **embi**.	*I have brought bad news.*
Usho abantu **abanjani**?	*What kind of people do you mean?*
Ngisho abantu **abadala**.	*I mean old people.*

6 Numerals

● The numeral *one* is expressed by means of the stem **-nye** (*one*). To say, for example, *one person, one dozen, one day*, you do two things: you delete the initial vowel of the noun and you add the second part of the noun prefix to **-nye**.

Kufike muntu (< u**mu**ntu) **mu**nye	*Only one person came*
Ngifuna dazini (< i(**li**)dazini) **linye**	*I want one dozen*
Khipha randi (< i(**li**)randi) **linye**	*Take out R1*
Siyohlala suku (u(**lu**)suku, **lunye**)	*We are going to stay one day*

● Many speakers prefer to use English numerals for the numerals from 6 upwards. Such numerals must, however, be preceded by the following structure:

abangu- with **aba-** nouns (class 2), e.g. Baqashe abantu abangu-12.
  They hired 12 people.
angu- with **ama-** nouns (class 6), e.g. Ngikhokhe amarandi angu-20.
  I payed R20.
ezingu- with **izi(n)-** nouns (classes 8 and 10),
  e.g. Ngisebenze izinsuku ezingu-8. *I worked 8 days.*

☑ ——————————— **Umsebenzi** ———————————

1   You and your family are planning to spend a holiday on the North
    Coast of KwaZulu-Natal. As you prefer to stay in a hotel and early
    reservation is essential you telephone a hotel to enquire about
    accommodation.

    The receptionist (**umamukeli**) who answers your call says that (*a*)
    it is the Elangeni Hotel (see Unit 16) and asks whether (*b*) she can
    help you. You say that (*c*) you want to make a reservation and she
    says that (*d*) she will put you through to (see Unit 16) Reservations
    (**kwabaseReservations**). The person answering says: (*e*)
    'Reservations (**eReservations**) here, Sally speaking' (Unit 16). You
    tell her that (*f*) you would like to make a reservation (*g*) from the
    3rd to the 12th of July (**uJulayi**). Sally wants to know (*h*) how
    many you are and you reply that (*i*) you are four (people). Sally
    asks (*j*) how many rooms do you want and you reply that (*k*) you
    want two rooms. You ask (*l*) what the price per day is and she says
    that (*m*) it is R225 per day sharing (=**lapho nihlalisana** *when
    you stay together*, i.e. *you are sharing*).

    Use the above information to create a suitable dialogue between
    you, the receptionist and Sally.

2   Say in Zulu that you want:

    (*a*) 2 eggs (**amaqanda**)   (*h*) 1 egg
    (*b*) 3 chairs (**izihlalo**)   (*i*) 1 chair
    (*c*) 2 tomatoes (**otamatisi**   (*j*) 1 tomato
           [class 2a]
    (*d*) 5 people   (*k*) 1 person
    (*e*) 2 Rand   (*l*) 1 Rand
    (*f*) 3 Rand   (*m*) 4 Rand
    (*g*) 5 Rand   (*n*) 15 Rand

3   ●   Ask Vusi how many of the following he wants:

        (*a*) glasses (**izingilazi**)
        (*b*) knives (**imimese** [class 4])
        (*c*) spoons (**izipunu**)
        (*d*) dishes (**amapuleti**)
        (*e*) tickets (**amathikithi**)
        (*f*) people

- Also ask him how many of the following there are. For example **Bangaki abantu?** *How many are the people?* Then give the answer to each question by using the total given in brackets.

  (a) children in the school (**esikoleni**), (650)
  (b) dogs (**izinja**) on the farm (**epulazini**), (2)
  (c) months (**izinyanga**) in a year (**onyakeni**), (12)
  (d) days (**izinsuku**) in June (**kuJuni**), (30)
  (e) cups (**izinkomishi**) on the table (**etafuleni**), (5)
  (f) boys in the class (**ekilasini**), (9)
  (g) weeks (**amaviki**) in a month (**enyangeni**), (4)
  (h) you (pl.), (2)

4 Answer the following **njani?** (*how?*) questions by using the adjective stems given in brackets:

  (a) Unjani uMavis? : (-hle) kakhulu *She is very pretty*
  (b) Sinjani isiZulu?: (-hle) kakhulu *It is very beautiful*
  (c) Injani imoto yakho? (*your car*) : (-dala) kakhulu *It is very old*
  (d) Anjani amawolintshi (*oranges*)? (-bi) *They are bad*

5 Describe the nouns by making use of the adjective stems given in brackets. For example: umuntu (-dala) = umuntu **omdala**).

  (a) abantu (-dala)   (f) indawo (*place*) (-hle)
  (b) umuntu (-khulu)   (g) abantwana (-ningi)
  (c) imali (-ningi)   (h) umfana (-de)
  (d) ikati (*cat*) (-ncane)   (i) ukudla (-bi)
  (e) intombi (*girl*) (-hle)   (j) amantombazane (*girls*)
                                     (-ncane)

6 Answer the questions by making use of the adjectives given in brackets.

  (a) Unjani u-anti (*aunty*) Lisbethe? (-hle)
  (b) Uthole umsebenzi onjani? (-ncane)
  (c) Kunjani namhlanje? (-bi)
  (d) Umakhelwane (*neighbour*) wakho ngumuntu onjani? (-dala)
  (e) Anjani la mantombazana? (-hle)

7 You are asked something. How will you tell the person that you are sorry but (**kodwa**) you do not know.

8 You and your partner want to go to the cinema tonight. Tell the ticket officer that you want to reserve two seats for the 9 o'clock show.

9 How will you say:

    (*a*) From 9 (am = **ekuseni**) to 5 (pm = **ntambama**)
    (*b*) From 100 to 200
    (*c*) From the 12th to the 15th of March (**uMashi**)
    (*d*) From Monday to Saturday?

22

— ESITOLO SEFENISHA —

In the furniture store

In this unit you will learn

- what to say when buying household appliances
- how to ask about the cash price, instalments, discounts, the guarantee and delivery
- how to express 'if' and 'when'
- more about adjectives and how to use them

──────────── Ingxoxo ────────────

Celani Mthethwa and his wife Sarah are interested in buying a new refrigerator. They visit one of their local discount stores and talk to one of the salesmen in the household appliance section.

Umthengisi	Nginganisiza ngani?
Celani	Sicela ukubona amafriji.
Umthengisi	Wozani ngizonikhombisa amafriji esinawo
	[In the domestic appliances department]
	Nanka. Nifuna sayizi bani?
Celani	Sifuna usayizi ongaka [pointing to a fridge].
Umthengisi	Kulungile. Linjani leli?
Sarah	Usayizi ulungile kodwa angithandi umbala walo.
Umthengisi	Ufuna elimbala muni?

Sarah	Ngithanda elinombala omhloshana.
Umthengisi	Siyaxolisa nkosikazi, okwamanje asinalo (ifriji) elinombala onjalo. Kodwa akunkinga, sizoli-oda efektrini.
Celani	Lizofika nini?
Umthengisi	Ngiqinisile ukuthi leli viki elizayo lizofika.
Celani	Singakhokha ngamancozuncozu noma sithenge ngokheshe?
Umthengisi	Kokubili, kodwa uma ukhokha ngamancozuncozu sizofaka inzalo.
Celani	Sithola isephulelo uma sithenga ngokheshe?
Umthengisi	Yebo, sizonephulela u-10%.
Celani	Niyadiliva na?
Umthengisi	Yebo kodwa lokhu kufuna enye imali.
Sarah	Linegaranti?
Umthengisi	Yebo, nkosikazi. Linalo.
Celani	Liyisikhathi esingakanani?
Umthengisi	Lingunyaka.
Celani	Siyabonga.

Umthengisi *Salesman*
Nginganisiza ngani? *With what can I help you* (pl.)*?/What can I do for you* (pl.)*?*
Sicela ukubona amafriji *We would like to see the refrigerators please*
amafriji *refrigerators*
Wozani *Come!* (pl.)
ngizonikhombisa *I will show you* (pl.)
amafriji esinawo *the refrigerators* (*which =*) *that we have*
Nanka *Here they are* (*the refrigerators*)
Nifuna sayizi bani? *What size do you want?*
usayizi ongaka *a size like this* (*one*)
-ngaka *as big as this*
Linjani leli? *What do you think of this one?* (i.e. *How is this one* (*refrigerator*)*?*)
-njani? *how?*
umbala walo *the colour of it* (*the refrigerator*)
umbala *colour*

elimbala muni? *one* (*refrigerator*) *that is* (*of*) *what colour?*
elinombala omhloshana *one that is off-white*
-mhloshana *off-white*
Siyaxolisa *We are sorry/we regret*
okwamanje *at present*
asinalo *we do not have one* (i.e. *refrigerator*)
elinombala onjalo *one which is of that colour*
-njalo *like that*
kodwa *but*
akunkinga *that is no problem*
sizoli-oda (=**si-zo-li-oda**) *we will order it*
efektrini *at* (=*from*) *the factory*
Lizofika nini? *When will it come* (=*be here*)*?*
Ngiqinisile *I am certain*
ukuthi (*so*) *that*
leli viki elizayo *this coming week*
iviki *week*
elizayo *that comes*
-za *come*

Singakhokha ngamancozuncozu?	**Niyadiliva?** (from English *deliver*)
Can we pay in instalments?	*Do you deliver?*
-khokha *pay*	**lokho kufuna enye imali** (*that*
ngamancozuncozu *by way of*	*seeks other money, i.e.) that is*
instalments	*extra (money)*
noma *or*	**Linegaranti (Li-na-igaranti)** *Does*
sithenge *must we pay* (see Unit 18	*it have a guarantee?* (from English
for *must*)	*guarantee*; note the alternative pro-
ngokheshe *(with) cash*	nunciation of this word: **igalanti**
ukheshe *cash*	**(=i-ga-lan-tee)**
kokubili *both*	**linalo** *it has one (guarantee)*
sizofaka *we will include*	**Liyisikhathi esingakanani?** *How*
inzalo *interest*	*long is it* (*the guarantee*)*?*
Sithola *Do we get*	**-ngakanani?** *how long?*
isephulelo *a discount*	**Linguyaka** *It* (*the guarantee*) *is*
uma *if*	*(for) a year*
sizonephulela (si-zo-n(i)-ephulela)	**unyaka** *year*
we will give you (pl.) *a discount*	

Imibuzo

Phendula imibuzo elandelayo.

(*a*) UCelani noSarah bafuna ukuthengani?
(*b*) USarah uthanda ifriji elimbala muni?
(*c*) Igalanti lefriji liyisikhathi esingakanani?
(*d*) Bayoli-oda kuphi ifriji?
(*e*) Umthengisi uthe (*said*) lizofika nini ifriji?
(*f*) UCelani uzotholani uma ethenga ngokheshe?

--- **Ulimi** ---

1 Is that the cash price?

To find out whether the price of something is the cash price, you ask
Yintengo kakheshe leyo? *Is that* (leyo) *the cash price?* or **Yintengo kakheshe le?** *Is this* (le) *the cash price?*

To this the salesman might reply:

Yebo yiyo. (intengo)	*Yes, that is (it).* (*the cash price*)
Cha, akusiyo.	*No, it is not (it).*

2 Can I pay in instalments?

To find out whether you may pay in instalments you can say **Ngingakhokha ngamancozuncozu na?** (If you find **ngaman-cozuncozu** a bit difficult to pronounce try to master its pronunciation by saying it several times over in isolation.)

To find out how many instalments, i.e. over how many months, you have to pay, you can ask:

Ngikhokha izinyanga ezingaki? *How many instalments?*
(How many months do I
(have to) pay off?)

If it is over six months: **Ukhokha izinyanga eziyisithupha** (or **ezingu-6**) – (**isithupha** *six*). Over 24 months: **Ukhokha izinyanga ezingu-24**.

If you have payed a deposit and you want to know over how many months the balance must be paid, you ask:

Ngikhokhe imali eseleyo *Over how many months do I*
(*the balance*) ezinyangeni *pay the balance?*
ezingaki?

or

Imali eseleyo ikhokhwa *The balance is paid over how*
ezinyangeni ezingaki? *how many months?*

To which the salesman may for instance reply:

Imali eseleyo uyikhokha *The balance* (lit. the remaining
ezinyangeni ezingu-12. money) *you pay (off) over*
12 months.

3 Asking for a discount

When you pay cash and you want to know (as many South Africans often do) whether you are going to get any discount, you can ask:

Ngithola (Sithola) isephulelo na? *Do I / we get a discount?*
Sizothola isephulelo uma *Do we get a discount for*
sithenga ngokheshe? *paying cash? (do we get a*
discount if we buy cash?)

Yintengo kakheshe leyo noma *Is that the cash price or are you*
uzongephulela na? *going to give me a discount?*

Simalini isephulelo uma
  sithenga ngokheshe?

How much is the discount
if we pay cash?

4   No problem!

When someone asks you a favour and you are willing to oblige you can reply: **Akunkinga.** *It is no problem*.

5   Is it guaranteed?

To ask whether the thing you want to buy is guaranteed, you say: **Inegaranti?**, where the initial **i-** refers to **into** *the thing* you are interested in buying. Otherwise you can use the subject concord of the name of the thing you are buying.

(Ifriji) Linegalanti?   *Does it (the refrigerator)*
                                        have a guarantee?

If you are interested in the time of the guarantee, you can make use of the stem **-ngakanani?** (*how long?, how many?*) and ask: **Yisikhathi esingakanani igaranti?** (*How long is the guarantee?*). To this the answer may be:

Siyizinyanga ezingu-6.   *It (the time) is six months.*
Singunyaka.   *It is one year.*

(Note: The **si-** refers here to the noun **isikhathi**.)

In the case of cars, where distance as a rule is also guaranteed, you say **Inegaranti elingu-** plus number of kilometres.

Inegaranti elingu-10000 km.   *It (the car) has a guarantee*
                                      (which is=) for 10,000 km.

6   If

The concept *if* is expressed in Zulu by means of the word **uma**. What is important about the use of this word is that the subject concord of classes 1 (**umu-**) and 1a (**u-**) changes from **u-** to **e-**, that of class 2 (**aba-**) and 2a(**o-**) from **ba-** to **be-**, whilst that of class 6 (**ama-**) changes from **a-** to **e-**. The rest of the subject concords remain unchanged.

Sizojabula kakhulu   *We will be (very glad=)*
 uma uvuma.   *delighted if you agree.*

| Uzothola isephulelo **uma** uthenga ngokheshe. | *You will get a discount if you pay cash.* |

Uma may also be used to express *when*.

| **Uma** uJosua [class 1a] **efika** mtshele ukuthi ngiyamfuna. | *When Josua comes tell him that I want (to see) him.* |
| **Uma be**fika batshele ukuthi siyabafuna. | *When they come tell them that we want (to see) them.* |

7 More about adjectives

In Unit 21 you have learned how a small number of adjectives are formed and used. All the other adjectives in Zulu (known as *relatives*) are formed slightly differently. The main difference between these relative adjectives and the ones you studied in Unit 21 lies in the form of the concords they use (as can be seen in the following table). Notice once again the similarity in form between the concords and the noun class prefixes from which they have been derived.

Table of adjectival and relative concords

		Adjectival concords	Relative concords
1st p. sing.		engim-	engi-
1st p. pl.		esiba-	esi-
2nd p. sing.		om-	o-
2nd p. pl.		eniba-	eni-
Class 1	um(u)	om(u)-	o-
Class 2	aba-	aba-	aba-
Class 3	um(u)	om(u)-	o-
Class 4	imi-	emi-	e-
Class 5	i(li)-	eli-	eli
Class 6	ama-	ama-	a-
Class 7	isi-	esi-	esi-
Class 8	izi-	ezin-	ezi-
Class 9	in-/im-	en-	e-
Class 10	izin-/izim-	ezin-	ezi-
Class 11	u(lu)-	olu-	olu-
Class 14	u(bu)-	obu-	obu-
Class 15	uku-	oku-	oku-

Note the following differences between the adjectival and relative concords:

- The relative concords of the first and second person (excluding the 2nd p. sing.) are formed by placing an **e-** before the subject concord.

- Adjectival concords of the so-called nasal classes (i.e. noun classes containing a nasal in their class prefix) retain their initial vowel only when used as relative concords, (cf. classes 1, 3, 4, 6, 9 and 10).

- In the case of all the other noun classes (except class 8), the adjectival and relative concords are identical.

Meaning of relative concords

You make use of relative concords when you want to say *who* (as in: people *who* smoke), *that* (as in: the dog *that* barks) and so on. Unlike the adjectival concords that occur with only a limited number of (adjectival) stems, the relative concords may combine with most other words and stems.

(a) Verb stems
All verbal stems may be used with the relative concord.

Ngifuna umuntu **o**khuthele.	*I want a person **who** is diligent.*
Ngithanda abantu **aba**kwazi ukukhuluma isiZulu kahle.	*I like people **who** know (how to speak) Zulu well.*
Sizobuya ngeviki **eli**zayo (< -za *comes*).	*We shall return (on) the week **that** comes.*
Sicela amanzi **aba**nda**yo** (< -banda *be cold*).	*We want water that is cold, please.*

When nothing follows on the verbal relative stem **-yo** is sometimes added to the end of the stem (see e.g. the last two examples above).

The negative of relatives formed with verb stems:

Insert **-nga-** just after the relative concord and let the verb end on the negative ending **-i** (in the present tense) or **-anga** (in the past tense).

Asifuni umuntu **o**nga**thand**i ukusebenza.	*We do not want a person who does not like to work.*
Baphi abantu aba**nga**khulumi isiZulu?	*Where are the people who do not speak Zulu?*

Ingane engakhali ifela embelekweni.	*The child who does not cry dies in the carrying-skin.* (Zulu proberb meaning that if one refrains from voicing one's grievances it may be assumed one is satisfied)

(*b*) Relative stems

There are a small number of non-verbal stems in Zulu which are often used with relative concords. Some of these stems denote colours.

-mnandi	*pleasant, tasty*
ukudla okumnandi	*food that is tasty*, i.e. *tasty food*
-bukhali	*sharp*
ummese obukhali	*a knife that is sharp,* i.e. *a sharp knife*
-manzi	*wet*
indwangu emanzi	*a cloth that is wet,* i.e. *a wet cloth*
-ngcono	*better*
indawo engcono	*a place that is better,* i.e. *a better place*
-lula	*light*
umsebenzi olula	*work that is light*, i.e. *light work*
-qotho	*honest*
Nangu umuntu oqotho	*Here is an honest person*
-njalo	*like that*
Angithandi umuntu onjalo	*I do not like a person who is like that*
-nje	*like this*
Ngihlonipha intombi enje	*I respect a girl who is like this*

● Relative stems denoting colours.

-mnyama	*black*
ihhashi elimnyama	*a black horse*
-mhlophe	*white*
isinkwa esimhlophe	*white bread*
-nsundu	*brown*
amakhethini abomvu	*brown curtains*
-luhlaza	*blue/green*
ingubo eluhlaza	*a blue/green dress*

Position of relatives in sentences

Finally, it must be noted that while the equivalents of the Zulu relatives may appear before the noun in English, they usually follow the noun in Zulu.

amanzi **abandayo**	*cold* water
abantu **abavilaphayo**	*lazy* people
umuntu **oqotho**	an *honest* person
umsebenzi **onzima**	a *difficult* task

● Questions that have relatives as answers

Just like adjectives, relatives too are often the answer to questions with **njani?** (*how?, of what kind?*).

Kunjani ukudla namhlanje?	*How is the food today?*
Kumnandi.	*It is nice.*
Unjani umama wakho?	*How is your mother?*
Ungcono namhlanje.	*She is better today.*
Ufuna umsebenzi onjani?	*What kind of work are you looking for?*
Angifuni umsebenzi onzima.	*I do not want heavy work.*

--- **Umsebenzi** ---

1 Sibusiso and Nonhlanhla Mbhele are interested in buying a new washing machine (**umshini wokuwasha**). They visit a local store where they are welcomed by one of the salesmen. Sibusiso tells him that (*a*) they are interested in buying a washing machine. The salesman asks them (*b*) what kind (of washing machine) they have in mind (i.e. what kind they want) and Nonhlanhla says that (*c*) they are interested in an automatic washing machine (**umshini wokuwasha ozenzelayo**). The salesman shows them the washing machines they have in stock and Nonhlanhla finds one that she likes. She asks the salesman (*d*) what price it is. He tells her and she wants to know (*e*) what the quality (**-njani?**) of the machine is. He says that (*f*) it is very strong (**-qinile**). Sibusiso asks whether (*g*) they may pay in instalments. The salesman says (*h*) yes, over six months. Sibusiso wants to know whether (*i*) they do deliveries, to which the salesman replies that (*j*) they will deliver (the machine) tomorrow or on Thursday (**ngoLwesine**).

Use the above information to create a suitable dialogue between the people concerned.

2 Complete the sentences by providing the missing relative concord.

(a) **Abantu** ____**hlala** lapha bampofu (*poor*) kakhulu. *The people who live here are very poor.*

(b) Niboqaphela bane**zinja** ____**nolaka** labo bantu. *You must be careful, they have vicious dogs, those people.*

(c) Wenze **umsebenzi** ____**nzima** Jonathan. *You have done a difficult job, Jonathan.*

(d) Sicela **amanzi** ____**bandayo**. *We want some cold water, please.*

(e) Sifuna **u(lu)bisi** ____**shisayo**. *We want some hot milk.*

(f) Letha **amapuleti** ____**setafuleni**, Velaphi. *Bring the dishes that are on the table, Velaphi.*

(g) Nanti **ilokwe** ____**luhlaza** olifunayo. *Here is the blue dress that you are looking for.*

(h) Asifuni **abantu** ____**ngasazi** isiNgisi. *We do not want people who do not know English.*

(i) Nangu **umuntu** ____**ngakwazi** ukukhuluma isiBhunu. *Here is the person who cannot speak Afrikaans.*

(j) Iphi **insizwa** ____**funa** umsebenzi? *Where is the young man who is looking for a job?*

3 You are interested in buying a new stove (**isitofu**). How would you ask the salesman:

(a) whether it has a guarantee

(b) (if it has) for how long the guarantee lasts

(c) whether they give a discount for cash

(d) whether you can pay off over six months

(e) whether it will cost extra if (**uma**) they deliver

23
NGIFUNA UKUBIKA
— UKUGQEKEZWA —
I want to report a burglary

In this unit you will learn how to

- report a crime
- say that you possess/do not possess something
- express the continuous near past tense
- ask 'When?'-questions
- ask questions with 'at what time?'
- say 'turn right' and 'turn left'
- express commands

————— Ingxoxo —————

Ivor van Rensburg's house has been burgled. As is required by law he has to report the incident at the local police station.

Ivor   Uxolo Phoyisa, ngibuza ishantshi.
Iphoyisa   Yenyuka ngalezi zitebhisi bese uqhubeka ngephaseji.
                Ekugcineni kwephaseji ujikela ngakwesokudla.
                Ishantshi lingakwesobunxele.
[Eshantshini   *in the charge office*]
Ivor   Ngifuna ukubika ukugqekezwa kwendlu yami.
Iphoyisa   Kwenzeke nini?
Ivor   Kwenzeke izolo ebusuku.

Iphoyisa	Benikuphi izolo ebusuku?
Ivor	Besivakashele abangane bethu.
Iphoyisa	Bebile na?
Ivor	Yebo. Bebe imoto yenkosikazi yami, izingubo, nevideo recorder.
Iphoyisa	Bangene kanjani endlini abagqekezi?
Ivor	Baphule ifasitele ekamelweni lokuhlala.
Iphoyisa	Ibikuphi imoto?
Ivor	Ibisegalajini.
Iphoyisa	Belikhiyiwe na igalaji?
Ivor	Yebo, belikhiyiwe.
Iphoyisa	Baphule ingide na?
Ivor	Yebo.
Iphoyisa	Inesihlabamkhosi le moto?
Ivor	Yebo, inaso.
Iphoyisa	Inhloboni?
Ivor	IyiToyota Corolla 1600.
Iphoyisa	Imbala muni?
Ivor	Iluhlaza.
Iphoyisa	Ingeyamuphi unyaka?
Ivor	Ingeka-1992.
Iphoyisa	Kusekhona okunye na?
Ivor	Cha, yilokho kuphela.

Uxolo Phoyisa *Pardon Mr Policeman*
ngibuza ishantshi *I ask (where) the charge office (is)* (see also Unit 14)
ishantshi *(from English charge) charge office*
Yenyuka *Go upward, ascend*
ngalezi zitebhisi *with these steps* (see Unit 16 for demonstratives)
bese *and then*
uqhubeka ngephaseji *continue with the passage*
-qhubeka *proceed, continue*
iphaseji *passage*
Ekugcineni kwephaseji *At the end of the passage*
ujikela ngakwesokudla *you turn to your right*

ngakwesokudla *right-hand side*
lingakwesobunxele *it (the charge office) is on your left*
ngakwesobunxele *left-hand side*
ngifuna ukubika *I want to report*
ukugqekezwa kwendlu yami *the burglary of my house* (see Unit 19 for possessives)
-gqekeza *burgle* (e.g. **Bagqekeze indlu yethu** *they have burgled our house*)
Kwenzeke nini? *When did it happen?*
-enzeka *happen*
nini? *when?*
izolo *yesterday*
ebusuku *in the (late) evening, at night*
Besivakashele *We were visiting*

abangane *friends*
Bebile (ba-ebile) na? *Have they stolen (anything)? (*see also Unit 13 for vowel verbs)
Bebe (ba-ebe) *They have stolen*
-eba *steal*
imoto yenkosikazi yami *the car of my wife*
inkosikazi yami *my wife*
izingubo *clothes*
ne-video recorder *and a video recorder* (see also Unit 4 for *and*)
Bangene kanjani? *How did they (*enter=) *gain access?*
-ngena *enter*
kanjani? *how?*
endlini *in the house*
abagqekezi *burglars*
Baphule ifasitele *They broke a window*
-phula *break (something)*
ekamelweni lokuhlala *in the lounge*
ikamelo lokuhlala *lounge*

ibikuphi imoto? *where was the car?*
ibisegalajini *it was in the garage*
igalaji *garage*
Belikhiyiwe na igalaji? *Was the garage locked?*
Baphule ingide na? *Did they break the lock?*
ingide *lock*
Inesihlabamkhosi *Does it (the car) have a burglar alarm?*
Isihlabamkhosi *burglar alarm*
Yebo inaso *Yes, it (the car) has one*
Inhloboni? *What kind is it (the car)?*
IyiToyota *It is a Toyota*
Imbala muni? *What colour is it?*
Iluhlaza *It is blue*
Ingeyamuphi unyaka? *What model is it?* (i.e. *it is (a car) of which year)*
Ingeka-1992 *It is (a car) of 1992*
Kusekhona okunye na? *Is there anything else?*
Yilokho kuphela *That is all*

Imibuzo

Phendula imibuzo elandelayo.

(*a*) U-Ivor ubike**ni** emaphoyiseni?
(*b*) Abagqekezi bebe**ni** endlini ka-Ivor?
(*c*) Inhloboni imoto yenkosikazi ka-Ivor?
(*d*) Abagqekezi bangene kanjani egalajini?
(*e*) Abagqekezi bayithole kuphi endlini i-video recorder?
(*f*) U-Ivor ubike kuphi ukugqekezwa kwendlu yakhe?

Ulimi

1 I have/I have not

Have or *has*, as in *I have a dog, she has a car*, is expressed by means of subject concord plus **na-** plus noun.

When the noun starts with **u-**, **na-** changes to **no-**; when it starts with **i-**, **na-** changes to **ne-**. In all other instances **na-** remains unchanged.

U**ne**mali (u-**na-i**mali) na?	*Do you **have** money?*
U**no**msebenzi (u-**na-u**msebenzi) na?	*Do you **have** work / a job?*
U**ne**nhlanhla Margaret ngoba imoto yakho i**ne**nshuwarensi.	*You are lucky (**have** luck) Margaret because your car **has** got insurance.*
U**na**bantwana na Thandi?	*Do you **have** any children, Thandi?*

In the negative, **na-** remains unchanged.

Angi**na**mali.	*I do not have any money.*
Asi**na**mali.	*We do not have any money.*
Aba**na**mali.	*They do not have any money.*

2 Yes, I have/No, I have not

When someone asks you whether you have a certain thing and you want to say that *you have* or that *you have not*, you make use of an abbreviated version of the so-called emphatic pronouns (see Unit 12) which you use in the place of the noun that you have omitted and which (in this instance) signifies *one*. (Remember to replace the noun with the abbreviated pronoun of the same person or class.)

Une**moto** [class 9], Nomusa?	*Do you have a car, Nomusa?*
Cha, angina**yo** [class 9].	*No, (I do not have **one**=) I haven't.*
Uno**msebenzi** [class 3] na, Sonja?	*Do you have a job, Sonja?*
Yebo, ngina**wo** [class 3].	*Yes, I have (**one**).*
USolmon une**laysense** [class 5] lokushayela imoto na?	*Does Solmon have a driving licence?*
Cha, akana**lo** [class 5].	*No, he does not have **one**.*
UThoko une**sithuthuthu** [class 7] na?	*Does Thoko have a motor bike?*
Yebo, una**so** [class 7].	*Yes, he has **one**.*

3 I want to report ...

If you want to report a matter at the police station you say **Ngifuna ukubika ...** (*I want to report ...*).

ingozi yemoto *a car accident*	**ukugqekezwa kwendlu yami**
ukwebiwa kwemoto yami *the theft*	*a burglary of my house*
of my car	

4   Left and right

To say *Turn right* or *Turn left* you say **jikela ngakwesokudla** or **jikela ngakwesobunxele**.

> Hamba ngalo mgwaqo bese   *Go with this road and then*
> **ujikela** (*turn to*) **ngakwesokudla**   *turn to your right (left) there*
> **(ngakwesobunxele)** lapho   *at the stop street*
> esitobhini

To say something is on the left or on the right you put the subject concord of the thing in question before the word **ngakwesokudla** (*right-hand side*) or **ngakwesobunxele** (*left-hand side*). As these are rather long words it is perhaps a good idea to exercise their pronunciation by repeating them several times in isolation.

> Jikela ngakwesobunxele.   *Turn to the left. You will see*
> Uzobona i-Sales House   *the Sales House is on the right.*
> ingakwesokudla.

5   Asking questions with 'when?'

You use **nini?** to express *when?* This interrogative normally occurs immediately after the verb.

> Ufike nini Lisbethe?   *When did you come Lisbeth?*
> Bahambe nini?   *When did they leave?*
> Kwenzeke nini?   *When did it happen?*

When you want to ask when something is taking place, you put the appropriate subject concord before **nini?**

> Linini ikhonsathi lakhe?   *When is her concert?*
> Unini umhlangano?   *When is the meeting?*

● If the answer to a 'when?'-question is a time, you say **ngo-** plus the time (which may be given in English).

Niyohamba nini?	*When are you leaving?*
Siyohamba ngo-10.	*We are leaving at 10 o'clock.*

If the answer is a day, you say **ngeSonto** (*Sunday*), **ngoMsombuluko** (*Monday*), **ngoLwesibili** (*Tuesday*), and so on.

● If the answer is a certain date, you say **ngomhla ka-** followed by the date (which may be given in English).

Niyohamba nini?	*When are you leaving?*
Siyohamba ngomhla ka-14 March.	*We are leaving on 14 March.*

● If the answer is a certain year, you say **ngonyaka ka-** followed by the year (which may be given in English).

Uyoqeda nini?	*When are you going to finish (e.g. with your studies)?*
Ngiyoqeda ngonyaka ka-1997.	*I am going to finish in (the year of) 1997.*

6 At what time?

To ask the time at which something happened or will happen, you use **ngasiphi isikhathi?**

Ufike ngasiphi isikhathi Johanna?	*(At) What time did you come, Johanna?*
Ngifike ngo-9, nkosikazi.	*I came (at) 9 o'clock, madam.*
Izitolo zivula ngasiphi isikhathi?	*(At) What time do the shops open?*
Zivula ngo-9.	*They open at 9 o'clock.*

7 Expressing commands in Zulu

Zulu distinguishes between commands given to a single person and commands given to more than one person. In case of the latter, **-ni** is added to the verb.

Thula!	*Be quiet!*	[but]	Thula**ni**!	*Be quiet!* (pl.)
Suka!	*Go away!*	[but]	Suka**ni**!	*Be gone!* (pl.)
Sukuma!	*Stand up!*	[but]	Sukuma**ni**!	*Stand up!* (pl.)

Monosyllabic verbs take a **yi-** in front, and vowel verb stems a **y-**.

Yima (< -ma) lapha!		*Stand / Wait here!*
	[but]	**Y**ima**ni** lapha! (pl.)

Yiza (< -za) lapha!	*Come here!*
[but]	**Yizani** lapha! (pl.)
Yenyuka (< -enyuka) lapha!	*Go up here!*

Note the variant form for *come here!*

Woza lapha Themba!	*Come here, Themba!* (sing.)
Wozani lapha madoda!	*Come here, men!* (pl.)

Remember to omit the initial vowel of the noun denoting the person(s) to whom the command is directed.

Vuka (**u**)Philemon!	*Wake up Philemon!*
Wozani (**a**)madoda!	*Come here, men!*

8 Expressing 'was/were' in the near past tense

To express a completed action (in the past tense) we use the verbal ending **-ile** (see Unit 14).

-hamba	*walk*	-hambile	*walked*
-bona	*see*	-bonile	*saw*

To express an action or process that was taking place at a certain point in time in the near past, as in *he was ill (at the time), they were asleep (at the time), I was in hospital (at the time)*, you use the stem **be-**. The following rules apply here:

Subject concords consisting of more than a vowel

(e.g. the subject concord of the 1st p. sing., 1st p. pl., 2nd p. pl., classes 2, 5, 7, 8, 10, etc.): **be-** plus subject concord.

1st p. sing.	Bengi-	**Bengi**gula izolo. *I was sick yesterday.*
1st p. pl.	Besi-	**Besi**vakashela abangane ngaleso sikhathi.
		We were visiting friends at that time.
class 5	Beli-	**Beli**khiyiwe na igalaji?
		Was it (i.e. *the garage), locked?*
class 17	Beku-	**Beku**shisa kakhulu izolo.
		It was very hot yesterday.

Note that the subject concord of class 2 is **be-** in this instance.

class 2	Bebe-	Abadlali bethu **bebe**dlala kahle kakhulu.
		Our players were playing very well.

Subject concords consisting of a vowel only

(e.g. the subject concord of the 2nd p. sing., class 1, 3, 4, 6 and 9): subject concord plus **b-** plus subject concord.

2nd p. sing.	Ubu- (< ub(e)-u)	**Ubu**kuphi izolo Pearl? *Where were you yesterday, Pearl?*
class 9	Ibi- (< ib(e)-i)	**Ibi**pakwa kuphi imoto yakho? *Where was your car parked?*

Note that the subject concord of classes 1, 1a and 6 is **e-** in this instance.

class 1a	Ube-	**Ube**kuphi uRosalina? *Where was Rosalina?*
class 6	Abe-	Amantombazana **abe**sekhaya *The girls were at home*

Do not forget to insert **-s-** between the subject concord and the following locative noun (see also Unit 14 in this regard).

Ubukuphi Moses?	*Where were you Moses?*
Bengisekhaya, mnumzana.	*I was at home, sir.*
Ibikuphi inja yakho Pamela?	*Where was your dog, Pamela?*
Ibisejaladini.	*He was in the yard.*
Bebekuphi abantwana?	*Where were the children?*
Bebesekamelweni labo.	*They were in their room.*

If you do not want to repeat the locative noun, you can use the pronoun **khona** instead.

Ubu**sekhonsathini** lika- Bruce Springsteen, Craig?	*Were you at Bruce Springsteen's concert, Craig?*
Yebo, bengi**khona**.	*Yes, I was **there**.*
Ube**khona** na uMatthew?	*Was Matthew **there**?*
Yebo, ube**khona**.	*Yes, he was **there**.*

To say that you (or someone else) were not there, you insert **-nge-** before **khona** while omitting the final **-na**.

Ubukhona na, Lindi?	*Were you there, Lindi?*
Cha, **bengingekho**.	*No, I was not there.*
Ubekhona na uNonhlanhla?	*Was Nonhlanhla there?*
Cha, **ubengekho**.	*No, she was not there.*

———— Umsebenzi ————

1 Your car radio (**irediyo** [class 9] **yemoto**) has been stolen. You are at your local police station to report the theft. The police sergeant (**usayitsheni**) on duty asks if (*a*) he can help you. You answer (*b*) 'Yes, please'. You tell him that (*c*) you want to report the theft of your car radio (**ukwebiwa kwerediyo yemoto yami**). He enquires (*d*) when did it happen and you inform him that (*e*) it happened last night (**izolo ebusuku**). He also wants to know (*f*) where the theft took place and you tell him that (*g*) it took place at home (**ekhaya**). (*h*) He asks whether anything else was stolen (**kukhona okunye okwebiwe na?**) and you reply (*i*) 'No, that is all'.

Create a suitable dialogue between you (=**mina** *I*) and the police sergeant based on the information given above.

2 Ask Maria:

   (*a*) what time did she leave (-**hambe**) yesterday (**izolo**)
   (*b*) what time does she finish work for the day (=-**shayisa** *knock off work*)
   (*c*) what time does she start (-**qala**) to work (**ukusebenza**) in the morning (**ekuseni**)
   (*d*) where she was yesterday
   (*e*) where Jonathan was yesterday
   (*f*) where the car keys (**izikhiye zemoto**) were (that you were looking for)
   (*g*) whether she has a driver's licence (**ilayisense lokushayela imoto**)
   (*h*) whether she has a cold (**umkhuhlane**)
   (*i*) whether she has flu (**imfuluwenza**)

3 Answer the questions. Do not repeat the bold-faced nouns. Use each one's (abbreviated) pronoun instead.

   (*a*) Une**ntombi** James? Yebo, ____
        Do you have a girlfriend, James?
   (*b*) Indlu yenu ine**sihlabamkhosi** na? Cha, ____
        Does your house have a (burglar) alarm?
   (*c*) Une**mali** George? Cha, ____
        Do you have any money, George?

(d) USolmon uno**msebenzi** na? Cha, ___
Does Solmon have a job?

(e) Une**sikhashana** manje Mandla? Yebo, ___
Do you have (a little time, i.e.) a moment to spare now, Mandla?

(f) Unelayisense na? Yebo, ___
Do you have a licence?

(g) Nine-TV na? Cha, ___
Do you (pl.) have a TV?

(h) Unabantwana na, Bheki? Yebo, ___
Do you have children, Bheki?

(i) Unebhayisikili na, mfana? Cha, ___
Do you have a bicycle, boy?

4 Answer in the negative.

(a) Ubaba **ubekhona** na? *Was father there?*
(b) Wena **ubukhona** na? *Were you there?*
(c) Nina **benikhona** na? *Were you (pl.) there?*
(d) Amaphoyisa **abekhona** na? *Were the police there?*
(e) **Belikhona** ibhasi na? *Was there a bus?*

5 How do you tell someone that you were:

(a) ill (**-gula**)
(b) in hospital (**isibhedlela**)
(c) at work (**umsebenzi**)
(d) at home (**ikhaya**)
(e) John's place (**kwaJohn**)?

6 Complete the text by providing the missing subject and object concords (referring to the nouns given in bold face).

(a) **Umama** ___yashanela (*is sweeping*). ___shanela izibi (*dirt*) namaphepha (*and papers*). **Umama** aka___funi **izibi** ekhaya. **Umama** ___wola (*gather*) izibi. U___thela (*throw*) (**izibi**) ebhaleni (*in the wheelbarrow*).

(b) **UNana** ___yakhala (*is crying*). **UNana** ___khalela (*cry for*) iswidi (*a sweet*). U___bonile (*saw it*) (**amaswidi**) kubaba (*at her father*). **Umama** ___thi (*says*): Thatha (*take*) iswidi Nana. **UNana** uya___thatha (**iswidi**). UNana uya___thanda (**ubaba**). Nobaba uya___thanda (**uNana**).

7 You are a teacher. Give the following commands to the pupils in your class. (Use the noun **abantwana** to address them and do not forget to apply the rule of the intial vowel.)

    (a)   Sit down! (**hlala phansi**)
    (b)   Stand up! (**sukuma**)
    (c)   Keep quiet!
    (d)   Take out (**khipha**) your books (**izincwadi zenu**)
    (e)   Close (**vala**) your eyes (**amehlo**)

24
UMNUMZANE MAPHUMULO USEPOSIHHOVISI
Mr Maphumulo at the Post Office

In this unit you will learn

- what to say when doing business at the Post Office
- some popular expressions concerning postal matters
- about different kinds of telegram messages
- how to use the preposition **nga-** (*by/with*)
- about verbs beginning with **uku-**
- how to express the concept 'already'

Ingxoxo

Mr Maphumulo has several things to do at the Post Office this morning. He speaks to the Post Office official (owascposini).

Maphumulo	Sawubona mnumzana. Ngifuna ukuthumela le ncwadi eMelika. Yimalini?
Owaseposini	Ihambe ngesikebhe noma ngendiza?
Maphumulo	Ngendiza.
Owaseposini	Mangiyikale. [After having weighed the letter] Yi-R5.50.
Maphumulo	Ngithanda ukuposa leli phasela.
Owaseposini	Gcwalisa leli fomu [Handing Mr Maphumulo the required form]

Maphumulo	Ngiyabonga.
Owaseposini	Yilokho kuphela?
Maphumulo	Cha, ngisathanda ukurejista le ncwadi.
Owaseposini	Kulungile [After having registered the letter] Yi-R3.75. Nanti irisidi lakho.
Maphumulo	Ngiyabonga. Amathelegilamu ashaywa kuphi?
Owaseposini	Ashaywa ekhawunda 7.
Maphumulo	Ngiyabonga.
	[At counter 7]
Maphumulo	Ngicela ukushaya ithelegilamu.
Owaseposini	Usugcwalise ifomu na?
Maphumulo	Cha, akuphi amafomu ethelegilamu?
Owaseposini	Asemashalofini emuva kwakho. Amafomu amhlophe asebenza kwelakithi, aluhlaza aya phesheya. Ungakhohlwa ukubhala igama nekheli lakho enzansi kwethelegilamu.
Maphumulo	Kulungile.

---

useposihhovisi   *(Mr Maphumulo) he is at the Post Office* (Unit 14)
ukuthumela   *to send (to)*
le ncwadi   *this letter*
eMelika   *America*
ihambe   *must it go* (Unit 18)
ngesikebhe   *by (ship, i.e.) overseas mail*
noma   *or*
ngendiza   *by (aeroplane, i.e.) airmail*
mangiyikale (ma-ngi-yi-kale)   *Let me weigh it* (Unit 17)
ukuposa   *to post*
leli phasela   *this parcel*
Gcwalisa   *Complete*
leli fomu   *this form*
yilokho kuphela?   *is it all?*
ngisathanda   *I still like to*
ukurejista   *(from English register) to register*
nanti irisidi lakho   *here is your receipt*
irisidi   *receipt*

amathelegilamu ashaywa kuphi?   (Lit. *Telegrams are (hit=) sent (off) where?) Where is the telegram counter?*
amathelegilamu   *telegrams*
ekhawunda 7   *at counter 7*
ukushaya ithelegilamu   *to send a telegram*
usugcwalise ifomu?   *have you already completed/filled in a form?*
ifomu   *form*
amafomu ethelegilamu   *telegram forms* (Lit. *forms of a telegram*)
nanko   *there they are (i.e. the telegram forms)*
Asemashalofini   *They are on the shelves* (Unit 14)
amashalofu   *shelves*
emuva kwakho   *behind you*
emuva   *behind*
amafomu amhlophe   *white forms*
-mhlophe   *white*
-sebenza   *work, function*
kwelakithi   *in ours (country), inland*
aluhlaza   *the blue ones (forms)*

-ya *go*	**ukubhala** *write (down)*
phesheya *overseas*	**igama nekheli** *name and address*
ungakhohlwa *you must not forget*	**ikheli** *address*
(Unit 17)	**enzansi** *below, at the bottom*

Imibuzo

Phendula imibuzo elandelayo.

(*a*) UMaphumulo **ukuphi** lapha?

(*b*) UMaphumulo ufuna ukuthumela kuphi incwadi yakhe? (*his letter*)

(*c*) Incwadi kaMaphumulo (*of Maphumulo*) izohamba ngendiza noma ngesikebhe?

(*d*) Amathelegilamu ashaywa kuphi?

(*e*) Amafomu ethelegilamu agcinwa (*kept*) kuphi?

(*f*) Amafomu ethelegilamu amhlophe asebenza kuphi?

Ulimi

1 Expressions concerning postal matters

Ngithanda ukurejista le ncwadi.
I want to register this letter.

Ngithanda ukufaka leli phasela entshuwalensini. *I want to (put in =) insure this parcel.*

faka *put in*

Ngicela amaposikadi angu-4.
I need 4 postcards please.

Amalayisense e-TV akhokhwa kuphi? *Where are TV licences paid?* i.e. *Where can I pay* (=-**khokha**) *my TV licence?*

Ngithanda ukufaka amarandi anguR100 e-akhawuntini yami yaseposini. *I want to deposit*

(=-**faka**) *R100 in my Post Office Savings Account.*

Ngifuna ukukhipha amarandi angu-R50 e-akhawuntini yami yaseposini. *I want to withdraw* (=-**khipha**) *R50 from my Post Office Savings Account.*

Ngibuza ikhawunda lamaphasela?
Where is the parcel counter please?

I-akhawunti yocingo ikhokhwa kuphi? *Where is the telephone account paid?* i.e. *Where do I pay my telephone account?*

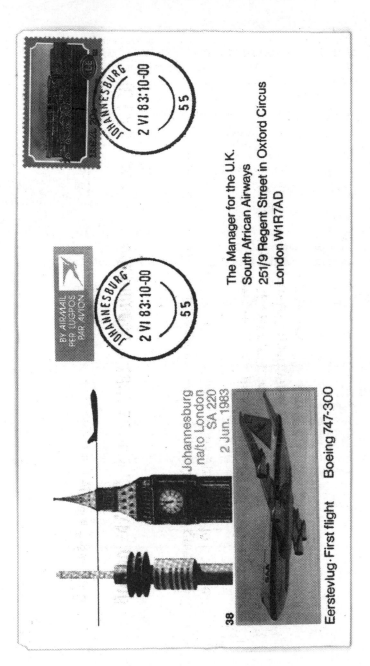

2   Buying stamps

Stamps can be bought at the Post Office as well as (in booklet form of 10 each) at selected stores. To ask for stamps you say:

Ngicela izitembu.   *I want some stamps, please.*

To this the clerk or attendant can respond by asking:

Ufuna izitembu ezingaki?   *How many stamps do you want?*

You can reply **Ngifuna ezingu-** ... plus the English numeral (*I want ... (stamps)*). (See also numerals, Unit 21.)

To ask for overseas stamps (e.g. stamps for Germany, Britain, and so on) you add **zase-** plus the name of the country.

Ngifuna izitembu ezingu-   *I want ... stamps for Germany.*
    zaseGermany.
Ngifuna izitembu zaseNgilandi.   *I want stamps for England.*

3   Telegram messages

Birthday wishes

- **Ngikufisela okuhle kodwa ngosuku lokuzalwa kwakho.**
  I wish you only the best on your birthday.

- **Halala ngosuku lokuzalwa. Ngikufisela unwele olude!**
  Congratulations on your birthday. I wish you long hair,
  i.e. *a long life!*

- **Halala ngosuku lokuzalwa kwakho. Ngikufisela impilo-ntle nempilonde.**
  Congratulations on your birthday. I wish you a pleasant life and a long life.

Note: in the plural **ngi-** (*I*) is replaced by **si-** (*we*)

Funeral/death notices

- **Ugogo ushone izolo. Umngcwabo ungomGqibelo ngo-10 eMadadeni.**
  Grandma passed away yesterday. Funeral Saturday at 10 o'clock in Madadeni.

- **UJames Skosana ushone engozini yemoto ngoLwesibili.**
  James Skosana died in car accident on Tuesday.

Sympathy

- **Sizwelana nani ngokushona kukababa wenu.**
  We sympathise with you (pl.) concerning the passing away of your father.

Emergency

- **Ubaba ugula kakhulu. Buya ekhaya ngokushesha.**
  Father seriously ill. Come home as soon as possible.

Congratulations!

- **Halala! Uwine umklomelo wokuqala emncintiswaneni wethu!**
  Congratulations! You have won first prize in our competition.

Wedding

- **Halala ngomshado wenu. Sinifisela okuhle kodwa. UNkulunkulu makanibusise.**
  Congratulations on your wedding. We wish you everything of the best. God bless you (pl.).

4 The preposition nga-

nga- (by)

To say *by* as in *by plane*, *by car*, *by train*, you use the preposition **nga-** (*with*) followed by the means of transport. The usual sound rules apply here: **nga-** changes to **ngo-** when followed by a noun beginning with **u-**, and to **nge-** when followed by a noun beginning with **i-**.

nga-imoto > ngemoto	*by car*
nga-indiza > ngendiza	*by plane*
nga-umkhumbi > ngomkhumbi	*by boat*

Note that this **nga-** is also used in the interrogative **ngani?** (*with what (means)?*).

Uhambe ngani Paulina?	*(With =) By what (means) did you travel, Paulina?*
Ngihambe ngethekisi (<nga-ithekisi).	*I travelled by taxi.*
Nifike ngani?	*(With =) By what (means) did you (pl.) come?*
Sifike ngebhasi.	*We came by bus.*
Sihamba ngendiza (<nga-indiza) lapho siya eThekwini.	*We travel by plane when we go to Durban.*

nga- (with/on)

The preposition **nga-** is also used to mean *with*.

Sibhala ngepensele (nga-ipensele).	*We write with a pencil.*
Halala ngosuku (< nga-usuku) lokuzalwa kwakho.	*Congratulations on your birthday.*

5 Means of transport

indiza	*plane*	**imoto**	*car*
isitimela	*train*	**ibhasi**	*bus*
ikhumbi	*combi (car)*	**ithekisi**	*taxi*
ibhayisikili	*bicycle*	**isithuthuthu**	*motorbike*

6 To

To say *to* as in *to work*, *to read*, you put **uku-** before the verb stem.

ukusebenza	*to work*
ukuthumela	*to send*
ukuposa	*to post*
ukuhamba	*to walk, to travel*
ukwazi (< uku-azi)	*to know*

Ngifuna **uku**hamba	*I want to* (*walk* =) *go.*
Ngithanda **ukw**azi	*I would like to know* (= **-azi**)
Ukubona kanye **ngukubona** kabili.	*To see once is to see twice* (Zulu proberb meaning 'Once bitten twice shy').
Ngicela **uku**shaya itelegilamu.	*I would like to send a telegram please.*

7 Already

The concept *already* is basically expressed by an auxiliary verb with the stem **se-**. The following rules apply here:

(*a*) **se-** with subject concords consisting of *more than a vowel only*, for example **ngi-, si-, ba-, li-, ku-**, and so on. Place the subject concord immediately after **se-**.

Sengimtshelile uJonathan.	*I have **already** told (him) Jonathan.*
Ibhasi **seli**hambile.	*The bus has **already** departed.*
Sekungu-6 na?	*Is it already 6 o'clock?*
Izitolo **sezi**valiwe na?	*Are the shops closed **already**?*
Isikhathi **sesi**fikile na?	*Is it time **already**?* (i.e. *Has the time already arrived?*)

Note that the subject concord of class 2 is **be-** in this instance.

Abantu **sebe**hambile na?	*Have the people **already** left?*
Abantwana **sebe**khathele, bafuna ukuphumula.	*The children are **already** tired, they want to rest.*

(*b*) **-se** with subject concords consisting of *a vowel only*, for example **u-, i-, a-** and so on. Attach the subject concord to the front of **-se** and repeat it immediately after **-se** in the place of the **-e** of **-se**.

2nd p. sing.	**Usu**gcwalisile (< u-s(e)-ugcwalisile) ifomu na? *Have you **already** filled in a form?*
	Usumtshelile (< u-s(e)-umtshelile) na ubaba? *Have you **already** told father?*
class 9	Inyanga **isi**phumile (< i-s(e)-iphumile) *The moon has **already** (come out, i.e.) risen*

Note that the subject concords of classes 1, 1a and 6 are **-e** when following **-se**.

class 1a	UJason **use**hambile (< u-s(e)-ehambile). *Jason has **already** left.*
	Umama **use**lele (< u-s(e)-elele). *Mother is **already** asleep.*
class 6	Amanzi **ase**bilile (< a-s(e)-ebilile). *The water has **already** boiled.*
	Amadoda **ase**buyile (a-s(e)-ebuyile). *The men have **already** returned.*

8 The verb stem -shaya

The verb stem **-shaya** (*hit*) has a variety of idiomatic usages, some of which are very useful.

Sishaya isiZulu ekhaya.	*We speak Zulu at home.*
Shayani izandla. (*hands*)	*Clap your hands!* (pl.)
Bashaye phansi. (*the ground*)	*They refused.*
Ngizomshayela ithelegilamu.	*I will send (for) her a telegram.*
Shaya ikhefu. (*period of rest*)	*Rest for a while.*
Sishaye idamu. (*dam*)	*We swam.*
Ushaye utshani. (*grass*)	*He ran away.*
Ukushayela umuntu ucingo.	*To phone someone.*

———————— **Umsebenzi** ————————

1 You need to pop into the Post Office.

(a) How would you ask a passer-by where the Post Office is?

(b) You are told **iposihhovisi isePick and Pay Shopping Centre**. What did the passer-by tell you?

(c) You need to buy some stamps at the Post Office. How do you ask for them?

(d) The Post Office clerk asks you **Ufuna (izitembu) ezingaki?** What did she ask you and what will your answer be?

(e) You also want to register a letter. How do you tell the clerk what you want to do?

2 You are asked **uhambe ngani?** How do you say *I went* (**-hambe**) *by*:

(a) plane
(b) train
(c) car
(d) taxi
(e) bus?

3 You are asked **Uthanda ukwenzani (=uku-enzani) namhlanje?** (*What would you like to do today?*) Say that you would like to:

(a) rest (**-shaya ikhefu**)
(b) go (=**-ya**) to town (**edolobheni**)
(c) do some shopping (=**-yokuthenga ezitolo**)
(d) do nothing in particular (=**-zenzela umathanda**)
(e) work in the garden (=**-sebenza engadini**)

4 Provide the missing subject concords of the 1st p. sing., 1st p. pl., classes 1, 1a and 2 in the following text.

Igama lami nguThemba. (*I*) ____hlala kubazali bami (*at = with my parents*) nodadewethu (*and (with) my sister*). Igama likadadewethu (*of my sister*) nguThandi. (*We*) ____hlala eDandi. UThandi nami ____sahamba isikole (*we still attend school*). Mina (*I*) ____funda ibanga lesibili (Std. 2). UThandi yena ____funda ibanga lesine (Std. 4). Ubaba ____sebenza eGoli. Umama ____ sebenzi. ____bheka (*look after*) ugogo (*grandma*) nathi (*and us*). Ubaba a____yi emsebenzini (*to work*) namhlanje ngoba kuyiholide (*because it is a holiday*). Bonke abantu baseDandi (*All the people of Dundee*) ____yajabula (*are happy*).

5 How would you ask someone whether:

(a) the train has already left
(b) the plane from Durban (**indiza yaseThekwini**) has already landed (=**-fikile**)
(c) he has already recovered (from illness) (=**-pholile**)
(d) uMaDlamini has already returned (=**-buyile**)
(e) the men have already completed (**-qede**) the work (**umsebenzi**)

6 Send a telegram to:

(a) a friend of yours in which you congratulate him on his birthday

(b) a colleague of yours in which you wish him well with his forthcoming marriage.

Use the following words and expressions (if possible in addition to your own) in your telegrams:

usuku lokuzalwa kwakho, umshado (*marriage*), uNkulunkulu makabusise (*God bless*), halala, impilontle nempilonde, nina nobabili (*both of you*), sikufisela/sinifisela

25

UKUBUKEZA

Revision

1 You have to attend a business meeting in Johannesburg. You go to a local Travel Agency to make the necessary flight arrangements and you speak to one of the consultants. She asks (*a*) what she can do for you and you tell her that (*b*) you want to make a reservation (**-bhalisa/-bhuka**) on the 7 am flight to Johannesburg (**endizeni eya eGoli isuka ngo-7 ekuseni**). She asks (*c*) for how many people (you want to book) and you tell her (*d*) it is only for yourself. She asks (*e*) when your return flight is (=when are you returning **buya**) and you say that (*f*) you would like to return on (=**nga**) Thursday on the 5 pm flight (**indiza esuka ngo-5 kusihlwa**). (*g*) She asks how you would like to pay, cash or by credit card. You answer that (*h*) you will pay by credit card.

Create a suitable dialogue based on the information given above.

2 You are interested in buying a second-hand car. You visit a second-hand car dealer and speak to one of the salesmen. He asks you (*a*) what kind of car (**nhloboni yemoto**) you have in mind. You say that (*b*) you are interested in a Toyota Corolla. The salesman asks (*c*) what price class you are interested in (what are you willing to pay) and you tell him (*d*) (anything) from R20,000 to R30,000. He says (*e*) he has a white Toyota Corolla for (=costing **ebiza**) R29,000. You ask to see it and he shows you the car. You ask (*f*) how big (**-ngakanani?**) a deposit (**idiphozithi**) is needed and he replies (*g*) R6,000 and that (*h*) the rest (**imali eseleyo**) you

pay over 24 months. You ask whether (*i*) the vehicle is guaranteed and he tells you that (*j*) it is guaranteed for 10,000 km or (**noma**) 6 months.

Use the above information to create a suitable dialogue between you and the salesman.

3   The grandmother of a close friend of yours has passed away. Send him/her a telegram in which you sympathise with his/her bereavement.

4   Say that you have travelled by:

(*u*)   car
(*b*)   bus
(*c*)   train
(*d*)   plane

5   Say that the following people have already left:

(*a*)   Emma
(*b*)   the White person (**umlungu**)
(*c*)   baba Sithole
(*d*)   abantwana

6   Someone wanted to see you yesterday but could not find you at home. How will you tell him that you were:

(*a*)   in town (**idolobha**)
(*b*)   at work (**umsebenzi**)
(*c*)   visiting (**-vakashela**) a friend
(*d*)   playing golf (**-dlala igalofu**)

7   You are going away on holiday. How will you tell a friend that you:

(*a*)   are going to return (**-buya**) on 14 April
(*b*)   will be arriving at **Johannesburg** Airport (**eJohannesburg airport**) at 9 am
(*c*)   are coming back on Sunday (**iSonto**)

8   Say that you have (possess) the following:

(*a*)   money
(*b*)   two children
(*c*)   a light vehicle (**bakkie 'iveni'**)
(*d*)   two cars
(*e*)   a job
(*f*)   a radio (**umsakazo**)

How will you say that you do not have these things?

9 Complete the sentences by filling in the missing relative concord:

   (a) Ufuna umsebenzi ____njani? *What kind of work do you want?*

   (b) Abantu ____**duba umsebenzi** bazoxoshwa *People who strike will be dismissed*

   (c) UNkosikazi Zuma ungumuntu ____**qinile** kakhulu *Mrs Zuma is a very strict person*

   (d) Ingane ____ngakhali ifela embelekweni *A child who does not cry dies on its mother's back* (Zulu proverb meaning that it is unwise to refrain from voicing one's complaints and grievances)

   (e) Ngiyohamba ngesitimela ____suka ngo-8 am *I am leaving (with=) on the 8 o'clock train*

   (f) Lo muntu usebenze izinsuku ____ngu-13 *This person worked for 13 days*

   (g) Udadewethu uneminyaka ____ngu-16 *My sister is 16 years old*

10 You want to buy an expensive article. How will you ask the salesman:

   (a) whether the listed price is the cash price

   (b) whether you can pay off over six months

   (c) what is the discount for cash?

11 Give the Zulu version for the following:

   (a) amounts: R1–R10

   (b) numbers: 2–5 people
                 5–10 days (**izinsuku**)

12 Complete the sentences by filling in the missing adjectival concords.

Ngikufisela *I wish (for) you*:

   (a) usuku ____hle *a nice day*

   (b) unyaka ____hle *a (beautiful, i.e.) prosperous year*

   (c) impilo ____de *a long life*

   (d) izulu ____hle *nice weather*

Lowo muntu *That person (is)*:

   (a) ____dala

   (b) ____hle

(c) ____ncane

(d) ____bi

13 How do you say in Zulu you work from:

    (a) 8 am to 5 pm

    (b) Monday to Friday

    (c) the 10th to the 20th?

14 Answer the sentences first in the positive and then in the negative. Do not, however, use the words written in bold in your answer. Use their respective object concords instead.

    (a) Ukhuluma **isiZulu** na? *Do you speak Zulu?*

    (b) Uyasazi **isiTswana** na? *Do you know Tswana?*

    (c) Uyamazi **uThuli Gamede** na? *Do you know Thuli Gamede?*

    (d) Ufonele **abantu baseposini** na? *Have you called the Post Office people?*

    (e) Ufunde **iSowetan** namhlanje? *Have you read the Sowetan (newspaper) today?*

    (f) Ubone **ubaba Madiba** ku-TV izolo? *Have you seen **baba Madiba** (President Nelson Mandela) on TV yesterday?*

    (g) Ufake **imali** na? *Have you put (the) money in?*

    (h) Uthanda **inyama yengulube** na? *Do you like pork?*

15 Complete the sentences by providing the missing subject concord.

Namuhla nguKhisimuzi. Thina (*we*) ____yajabula. Sizogqoka (*wear*) izingubo (*clothes*) zethu. Izingubo zethu ____lingana (*fit*) kahle (*nicely*). Nezicathulo zethu (*Also our shoes*) ____lingana kahle. Ubaba nomama ____thenge izingubo zethu edolobheni. Umama ____thenge ukudla okuningi. Ubaba -sebenzi namuhla (*today*). (Abantu) ____valile (*closed*) ehhovisi.

KEY TO THE EXERCISES

Unit 1

Umsebenzi 1 (*a*) Yebo, sawubona Fikile. (*b*) Ngikhona. Wena unjani? (*c*) Hamba kahle. **2** (*a*) Sanibona/ Sanibonani madoda. (*b*) Ninjani? (*c*) Nami ngikhona. **3** (*a*) Sawubona mnumzana. (*b*) Sawubona Mandla/ Bhuti Mandla/Sawubona mfowethu. (*c*) Sawubona nkosikazi. (*d*) Sawubona mnumzana/ndoda. (*e*) Sawubona dade/sisi. (*f*) Sawubona baba/mnumzana. **4** (*a*) Sala kahle Raymond. (*b*) Salani kahle. **5** Ninjani?/Niphila njani?/Nisaphila na?/Ngikhona Ngiyaphila/Ngisaphila kahle. **6** (*a*) Banjani? (*b*) Ukhona/Uyaphila. (*c*) Bakhona/Bayaphila. (*d*) Siyaphila. (*e*) Ninjani? (*f*) Kulungile. **7** (*a*) Sakubona/Sawubona mfowethu. (*b*) Salani kahle bafana. (*c*) Ngiyaphila.

Unit 2

Umsebenzi 1 (*a*) Yebo/Yebo-ke. (*b*) Ngikhona/Ngiyaphila. (*c*) Yebo, ngisaphila. (*d*) Ngingu- (plus your name). (*e*) Ningu- (plus your surname). (*f*) Sala kahle. (*g*) Ngingu- (plus your name or surname). **2** (*a*) NginguJoseph Gumede igama lami. (*b*) Ngubani igama lakho?/Lithini igama lakho? (*c*) Ngubani isibongo sakho?/Sithini isibongo sakho? (*d*) Uphumaphi? (*e*) Ngiphuma (plus place name). (*f*) Sala kahle/Hamba kahle. **3** abafazi/imizi/ amabhasikidi/amawashi/izitolo/ amadoda/abantwana/imikhonto/ izimoto/obaba **4** umuntu/ isinkwa/irandi/inkomo/ummese/ umSuthu/ikamelo/intombazana **5.** Hamba kahle Simon. Ngubani igama lakho? Igama lami nguSally. Isibongo sami nguPeters. Sawubona baba. Uphila njani? Ngiyaphila/ Ngiphila kahle. Ungubani wena? **6.** Sithini isithakazelo sakho Desmond?

Unit 3

Umsebenzi 1 (*a*) Ungumhlobo/ Uphuma/Sikhuluma/Ngiyasazi **2** Uyakwazi ukukhuluma isiFulentshi/isiBhunu/isiXhosa/ isiZulu? **3** Ngiyasazi isiNgisi/ isiZulu/isiSuthu/kodwa angisazi isiJalimani/isiVenda/isiBhunu. **4** Ngiyaxolisa kodwa angiqondi kahle usho ukuthini. **5** (*a*) Ngubani igama lakho, mfowethu? (*b*) NginguMzilikazi igama lami, mnumzana. (*c*) Uphumaphi? (*d*) Ngiphuma eGoli. (*e*) Ungumhlobo muni/Ungowasiphi isizwe baba Mzilikazi? (*f*) NgingumZulu, mnumzana. (*g*) Uphumaphi? (*h*) Ngiphuma eMlazi, mnumzana.

Unit 4

Umsebenzi 1 (*a*) Sawubona mnumzana. Yebo. (*b*) Ngingakusiza ngani? (*c*) Ngifuna uhlaza (imifino) nezithelo. (*d*) Ufunani? (*e*) Ngifuna amazambane nobhontshisi nobhanana. (*f*) Yimalini amawolintshi? (*g*) Yi-R10 usakazana. (*h*) Kukhona okunye na? (*i*) Yilokho kuphela. 2 nebothela/noFikile/namaXhosa/nekhofi/nopelepele 3 Ngingajabula./Cha, ngiyabonga. 4 (*a*) Ngibonga usizo lwakho, mnumzana. (*b*) Ngibonga isinkwa esithosiwe. (*c*) Ngibonga impatho efudumele. 5 (*a*) abelungu (*b*) amathikithi (*c*) amarande (*d*) abafundisi (*e*) izitolo (*f*) izinkomo (*g*) izintaba (*a*) umuntu (*b*) inja (*c*) isikolo (*d*) umntwana (*e*) indoda (*f*) iqanda (*g*) umfula (*h*) ibhodlela (*i*) indawo (*j*) intombazana

Unit 5 (Revision)

1 (*a*) Sawubona mnumzana (or your own name). (*b*) Mehlomadala Ray!? (*c*) Yebo. Unjani? (*d*) Ngiyaphila/Ngikhona. (*e*) Unjani wena? (*f*) Nami ngiyaphila/Ngikhona. 2 (*a*) Ngingu- (plus your name). (*b*) Ngubani igama lakho?/Lithini igama lakho. (*c*) Sithini isibongo sakho?/Sithini isibongo sakho? (*d*) Ngiphuma (plus place name). (*e*) Wena uphumaphi? (*f*) Uhlalaphi? 3 -kusiza ngani?/jabula/ibhotela/noshizi/Yimalini/Yi-/ Kukhona okunye na?/sekwanele 4 (*a*) abantwana (*b*) izindlovu (*c*) omalume (*d*) izitimela (*e*) amatafula (*f*) izimemo (*g*) imizi (*h*) amaphinifo 5 (*a*) umlungu (*b*) isilwane (*c*) umZulu (*d*) iNgisi (*e*) iBhunu (*f*) ingane (*g*) umkhonto

(*h*) uphopho 6 (*a*) isiZulu (*b*) isiNgisi (*c*) obhanana (*d*) o-anyanisi (*e*) igama (*f*) isiBhunu (*g*) isiXhosa (*h*) ophayinaphu (*i*) otamatisi (j) isibongo (*a*) I do not know (to speak) Zulu. (*b*) Do you know how to speak English?/Do you speak English? (*c*) What is your name? (*d*) Is that all (you want)? (*e*) Can I help you? (*f*) Are you still OK? (*g*) Who are you? (*h*) I am a Dutchman/I am Dutch. (*i*) I am an Englishman/I am English. (j) I am a German/I am German. 7 (*a*) Sawubona Denise. (*b*) Sawubona nkosikazi/mama. (*c*) Sawubona baba. (*d*) Sawubona ndoda/baba. (*e*) Sanibonani madoda. (*f*) Sawubona mnumzane (*g*) Sawubona mfana. 8 (*a*) Salani kahle bafowethu. (*b*) Hamba kahle baba. (*c*) Igama lami nguNorman. (*d*) Isibongo sami nguNyembezi. (*e*) Ngiyasazi isiZulu. (*f*) Angisazi isiBhunu. (*g*) UDavid ungumZulu. (*h*) Ngiyabonga. (*i*) Yimalini? Yi-R5. (j) Ngikhuluma isiNgisi nesiZulu. 9 (*a*) Ngiyabonga. (*b*) Ngingajabula. (*c*) Unjani? (*d*) Cha, ngiyabonga. (*e*) Yimalini?/Kubiza malini? (*f*) Ngubani igama lakho?/Lithini igama lakho? 10 (*a*) Awuphinde. Angiqondi kahle usho ukuthini. (*b*) Awukhulume kancane angiqondi kahle. 11 (*a*) Uyasazi nesiTswana na? (*b*) Uyakwazi ukukhuluma nesiXhosa na? (*c*) Ngiyasazi isiTswana kodwa hayi kakhulu. (*d*) Usifundephi? (*e*) Ngisifunde emalokishini.

Unit 6

Imibuzo (*a*) Yebo, uyasazi. (*b*) Cha, akafuni uwoyela. (*c*) Ukhokha amarandi angu-85. (*d*) NguKepisi.

Umsebenzi 1 (a) Ngingakusiza ngani, mnumzana? (b) Ngifuna uphetroli. (c) Wamalini? (d) Awuthele uphetroli we-R80. (e) Awuhlole amanzi nowoyela. (f) Ngihlole amasondo? (g) Ngingajabula/ Ngingathanda. (h) Kukhona okunye na? (i) Cha, yilokho kuphela. (j) Nasi isipho sakho, ndoda. **2** (a) ba (b) i (c) si (d) lu (e) li (f) i (g) a (h) ku (i) si (j) a (k) ba (l) li **3** Unjani?/ Ngikhona/unjani/ngikhona/ **Ba**njani/ Bayaphila **4** (a) Yimalini ubhanana?/Ubhanana ubiza malini? (b) Yimalini uphayinaphu?/Uphayinaphu ubiza malini? Ngizothatha munye. **5** (a) Ngicela usawoti. (b) Ngicela amanzi. (c) Ngicela upelepele. (d) Ngicela ubisi. (e) Ngicela ushizi.

Unit 7

Imibuzo 1 (a) Kuyiqiniso. (b) Cha, akusilo iqiniso. U-Edith noKen bajabula kakhulu. (c) Kuyiqiniso. (d) Cha, akusilo iqiniso. Ngu-Edith ofisela uNcamsile. impilontle nempilonde. **2** (a) U-Edith ufisela uNcamsile impilontle nempilonde. (b) UKen ufisela uNcamsile unwele olude. (c) U-Edith noKen balethele uNcamsile isipho esincane. (d) UNcamsile ukhumbula usuku lokuzalwa kwakhe.

Umsebenzi p.64: -m-; -si-; -li-; -ku-; -m-; -yi-; -ngi-; -ku- **1** Mary othandekayo, Halala ngokukhumbula usuku lokushada kwenu (of you (pl.). Nginifisela impilontle nempilonde. Yimi Umngane wakho (Your name) **2** (a) Mehlomadala! (b) We (c) Hhayibo!/Hhayi! (d) Nxephe!

3 (a) Uyangifuna (b) ngiyakufuna (c) Bayasibiza (d) bayanibiza (e) Uyangazi (f) ngiyakwazi (g) Uyasikhumbula (h) ngiyanikhumbula (i) Uyangikhumbula (j) ngiyakukhumbula (k) Ngingakusiza (l) Ngizokufonela **4** (a) Angimazi. (b) Ngizomtshela. (c) Awumbize (d) Awumtshele **5** Ngikufisela uKhisimuzi omuhle nonyaka omusha omuhle. **6** Mzilikazi umgane wami (my friend), ngikuhalalisela/halala! ngokukhumbula usuku lokuzalwa kwakho. Ngikufisela unwele olude/ impilontle nempilonde. **7** (a) Awungilethele itiye, Jacob. (b) Awungivulele isango, Jacob. (c) Awungibizele uJoseph, Jacob. (a) Ngizokulethela itiye, Jacob. (b) Ngizokuvulela isango, Jacob. (c) Ngizokubizela uJoseph, Jacob.

Unit 8

Imibuzo (a) Kuyiqiniso. (b) Cha, uNomsa ufuna ushintshi we-R50. (c) Cha, uNomsa ucela i-cooldrinki/ iStoney. (d) Kuyiqiniso. (e) Cha, uNomsa ukhokhe R2.00.

Umsebenzi 1 malini/phethe/ ukhona/akekho/Ukhona **2** (a) Ngiyasebenza. (b) Ngisebenza namhlanje. (c) Ngiyagula. (d) Ngiyaya. (e) Ngiya edolobheni. **3** (a) Lukhona ucingo lapha?/Ukhona udokotela lapha?/Likhona irestouranti elibizayo lapha na? (b) Ngicela ubhiya. (c) Uphethe ushintshi we-R20 na? **4** (a) Cha, alukho. (b) Cha, alikho. (c) Cha, awekho. (d) Cha, asikho. (e) Cha, ayikho. **5** (a) Uphi umnumzana Clayton? (b) Siphi isikhwama semali sami? (c) Iphi inja kaLeonard? (d) Liphi i-oda lethu? (e) Iphi imeneja?

(f) Uphi umama? (g) Uphi uDavid? (h) Baphi abantwana? **6** Nango/Naso/Nanso/Nanto/Nanso/Nango/Nango/Nampo **7** (a) Izitolo zivaliwe namhlanje. (b) Amasupamakethe avuliwe namhlanje.

Unit 9

Imibuzo (a) Cha, nguGodfrey ocele uwiski onamanzi. (b) Cha, nguGodfrey osebenza eThekwini. (c) Kuyiqiniso. (d) Cha, nguGodfrey ongumthengisi wezimoto. (e) Kuyiqiniso.
Umsebenzi 1 (a) Awuhlale phansi, Sally. (b) Mangikwazise kumngane wami u-Emelda. (c) Ungathanda okuphuzwayo na? (d) Ngingajabula. (e) Uthanda ukuphuzani? (f) Itiye elinobisi lizolunga. (g) Usebenzani, Sally? (h) Ngingamamukeli. (i) Usebenza kuphi? (j) Ngisebenza kwa-Arthur Jones and Associates. (k)Wena usebenzani? (l) Ngiyafundisa/Nginguthishela. (m) Kuhle lokho. (n) Awungixolele. (o) Ngifanele ngihambe. (p) Ngibonga itiye. (q) Nisale kahle. **2** (a) Ngiyabonga. (b) Ngibonga kakhulu. (c) Ngibonga usizo lwakho. **3** (a) Ngiyabonga (b) Siyabona (c) Ufunani? (d) Ufuna imali? **4** (a) Cha, uGodfrey akaphuzi ubhiya. (b) Cha, uJames akasebenzi eGoli. (c) Cha, uMartin akafuni iCoca Cola. (d) Cha, asikhulumi isiZulu. (e) Cha, abafuni ukubaleka. (f) Cha, alishisi kakhulu. (g) Cha, akubizi. **5** (a) Ngifuna i-akhawundi. (b) Ngifuna ukulala (c) Ngifuna ukudla. (d) Ngifuna ukulalela umsakazo/irediyo. (e) Ngifuna udokotela. **6** (a) Laba bantu basebenza edolobheni. (b) Lo

muntu usebenza epulazini. (c) Lesi sikole siphume phambili. (d) Izingane ziyahlabelela. (e) Amaposikadi ayabiza. (f) Amaphephandaba athengiswa ekhefini. (g) Ilanga likhipha inhlanzi emanzini. **7** (a) Nginguthisha. (b) Ngingumabhalane. (c) Ngingunjiniyela. (d) Ngingummeli. (e) Ngingunesi. **8** (a) NguSolmon ofuna u-ayisikhrimu. (b) NguMary ocele itiye. (c) Yimi engi-ode ubhiya. (d) NguKevin ongudokotela.

Unit 10 (Revision)

1 Baba nomama othandekayo. Ngiyanihalalisela ngokukhumbula usuku lokushada kwenu. Nginifisela impilontle nempilonde. **2 You:** Uphethe ushintshi na mfana? **Vendor:** Wamalini. **You:** We-R50. **3** Sifiso othandekayo. Ngikufisela uKhisimuzi omuhle nonyaka omusha omuhle. **4** (a) Ngifuna uphetroli. (b) Wamalini? (c) We-R80. (d) Likhona ithoyilethe lapha na? (e) Yebo, likhona. (f) Likuphi? (g) Nanto. (h) Livuliwe na? (i) Cha. Livaliwe. (j) Uphethe ukhiye na? (k) Yebo. **5** (a) UNohlanhla ukhona na? (b) Ucingo lukhona na? (c) U(bu)tshwala bukhona na? (d) Uweta ukhona na? (e) Akhona amanzi abandayo? (f) Inyuziphepha likhona na? (g) Likhona ikhemisi na? (h) Abelungu bakhona na? (i) Sikhona isikole esincane? (j) Likhona iyunivesithi? **6** (a) Yebo, ukhona./Cha, akekho. (b) Yebo, lukhona./Cha, alukho. (c) Yebo, bukhona./Cha, abukho. (d) Yebo, ukhona./Cha, akekho. (e) Yebo, akhona./Cha, awekho. (f) Yebo, likhona./Cha, alikho. (g) Yebo, likhona./Cha, alikho. (h) Yebo, bakhona./Cha, abekho. (i) Yebo, sikhona./Cha, asikho. (j) Yebo, likhona./Cha, alikho. **7** (a) Yebo, ngiyasikhuluma./Cha, angisikhulumi. (b) Yebo, ngiyamazi./Cha, angimazi. (c) Yebo, ngiyawuthanda./Cha, angiwuthandi. (d) Yebo, ngiyayidla./Cha, angiyidli. (e) Yebo, ngiyayibhema. Cha, angiyibhemi. (f) Yebo, ngiyayifuna. Cha, angiyifuni. (g) Yebo, ngiyamthanda. Cha, angimthandi. (h) Yebo, ngiyawuthanda,/Cha, angiwuthandi. (i) Yebo, ngiyazesaba./Cha, angizesabi. (j) Yebo, ngiyalifunda./Cha, angilifundi. **8** (a) Angisebenzi namhlanje. (b) Angiyi edolobheni. (c) Angihlali eGoli. (d) UNomusa akahlali eThekwini. (e) ULizzie akasebenzi kwa-du Toit. (f) Ugogo akaguli namhlanje. (g) Abantwana abayi esikoleni namhlanje. (h) Amadoda awasebenzi kakhulu. (i) Ibhantshi lakhe alibizi. (j) Angizwa. **9** (a) Ngikhuluma isiNgisi. (b) Ngiyafuna, (c) U-Esther usebenza edolobheni. (d) UJohannes ulalela irediyo. (e) Imoto yakhe iyabiza. (f) Ngiyezwa. (g) Ngizwa kahle (Alt. Ngiyazwisisa). (h) Abantwana bayagula. (i) Ugogo uphila kahle namhlanje. (j) Sithanda ibhola. **10** (a) Ngicela usoso katamatisi. (b) Ngicela umasitadi. **11** (a) Umfowethu uyisisebenzi sikaHulumeni. (b) Ubaba unguprofesa. (c) Umama ungumabhalana. (d) ULindiwe ungunesi. (e) UTitus uyisitshudeni. **12** (a) person (b) dog (c) village/kraal (d) money (e) meat (f) store (g) school (h) work/job (i) help/ assistance (j) water (k) The Swazi language (l) newspaper (m) jam (n) bread (o) change **13** (a) That's all.

(b) May I have the milk, please / Pass the milk, please. (c) Here is Jabulani. (d) Thank you very much. (e) What is Sharon's job? (f) What time is it now? (g) Sorry/ I beg your pardon. (h) What are you doing now? (i) Cheers! (j) Good heavens!

Unit 11

Imibuzo 1 (a) Akusilo iqiniso. URon uphuma eMelika. (b) Akusilo iqiniso. EMnambithi kuseLadysmith eNatali. (c) Kuyiqiniso. (d) Kuyiqiniso. **2** (a) NguBob noRon. (b) USam uphuma eMnambithi. (c) EMnambithi kuseNatali. (d) UNeil wethule uRon noBob kuSam.

Umsebenzi 1 (a) Kevin, mangikwazise/mangikwethule ku-Oscar. (b) Uphumaphi, Oscar? (c) Ngiphuma ePitoli (Pretoria). (d) UKevin uphuma esiKotilandi. (e) Likuphi ithoyilethe? (f) IFirst National Bank ikude kangakanani (how much) ukusuka lapha? (g) IKruger National Park ingamakhilomitha amangaki ukusuka ePitoli? (h) Ngikhokhe R100/ Amarandi angu-100. (i) Uphi uKevin? (j) Ihhotela lethu liseduze naseCity Hall. **2** (a) Ngiphuma esiKotilandi/ eSoweto/eThekwini/eFilidi/(eVryheid (pronounced e-fry-hight)). (b) Siya KwaZulu. (c) EMalitzboko kungamamayela angu-90 ukusuka eThekwini. (d) NginguJessica. Sihlala eLandani. (e) IStandard Bank iseWest Street. (f) Cha, isiteshi siseduze. (g) Ngifuna R150/Amarandi angu-R150. (h) I-O K Bazaars iseSmith Street. (i) Wamalini? **3** (a) Sawubona, mama. Sawubona Vincent, mfowethu. (b) Mama, mangikwazise kuSheila. (c) Ngijabulela ukukwazi, nkosikazi. (d) Nangu umfowethu, uVincent. (e)

Kumnandi ukukwazi, Vincent. (*f*)
Uphumaphi mntanami (*my child*)? (*g*)
NgiseThekwini/Ngiphuma eThekwini.
4 (*a*) UMoses ukhona na?/Cha,
akekho. (*b*) Umlungu ukhona?/Cha,
akekho. (*c*) Abelungu bakhona?/Cha,
abekho. (*d*) Ikhemisi likhona?/ Cha,
alikho. (*e*) Isibhedlela sikhona?/Cha,
asikho. (*f*) Udokotela ukhona?/Cha,
akekho. **5** (*a*) mother (*b*) may I/let
me introduce you (*c*) It is nearby (*d*)
Johannesburg (*e*) Where are you going?
(*f*) money (*g*) Do you know how to
speak Zulu? (*h*) father (*i*) I am
glad/delighted (*j*) post office (*k*) Durban
(*l*) Where do you stay? (*m*) Englishman
(*n*) my brother (*o*) Where do you come
from? (*p*) station (*q*) Pretoria (*r*) How
much does it cost? (*s*) A Zulu person
6 izinto/amaBhunu/ izibane/izinyoni/
abelungu/ophayinaphu/
amabhayisikili/imizi **7** (*a*)
Awungene. (*b*) Awuvale umnyango. (*c*)
Awubize uweta. (*d*) Awusilethele
amanzi. (*e*) Awungisize. **8** (*a*)
Uyaphi? (*b*) Uphumaphi? (*c*)
Uhlalaphi? (*d*) Likuphi ikamelo
lokudlela? (*e*) Uphethe ushintshi na?
(*f*) Uyakwazi ukukhuluma isiZulu na?

Unit 12

Imibuzo **1** (*a*) Akusilo iqiniso.
Banesipesheli senhlanzi namhlanje. (*b*)
Akusilo iqiniso. USipho uthanda
iwayini. (*c*) Kuyiqiniso. (*d*) Akusilo
iqiniso. Akubhenywa lapho. **2** (*a*)
Uweta uphakamisa ipepper steak. (*b*)
USipho nekosikazi yakhe bafuna
ukuphuza iwayini. (*c*) Isipesheli
yinhlanzi namhlanje (*d*) Yinkosikazi
kaSipho efuna izambane elithosiwe. (*e*)
Ipepper steak ivuthwe kancane kodwa
ingavuzi igazi.
Umsebenzi **1** Sawubona

ntombazana/dade. / Sicela imeniyu/
Awusilethele imeniyu. Uphakamisani
namhlanje, dade/ntombazane? /
Ngizolithatha (i-T bone steak). /
Ngithanda livuthwe kakhudlwana. /
Ngingajabula. / Ngingathanda/Ngicela/
Ngifuna ubhiya. **2** (*a*) abathengisi
(*b*) izitolo (*c*) izinja (*d*) imishini (*e*)
amahhashi (*f*) izinyoni (*g*) amakati (*h*)
otamatisi **3** (*a*) indoda (*b*) into (*c*)
isikole (*d*) umntwana (*e*) umuntu (*f*)
umuzi (*g*) inkosi (*h*) inkomo **4** (*a*)
ucingo (*b*) isinkwa (*c*) umama (*d*)
isiNgisi (*e*) ubisi (*f*) ibhotela (*g*) igama
lami (*h*) isiZulu (*i*) imali (*j*) inyama (*k*)
isibongo sami (*l*) isiBhunu (*m*) amanzi
(*n*) ubaba (*o*) kakhulu **5** (*a*)
Ngingathanda ukukhuluma isiZulu.
(*b*) Ngingathanda ukufunda izincwadi.
(*c*) Ngingathanda ukubukela iTV. (*d*)
Ngingathanda ukudlala ibhola. **6**
(*a*) Ngifuna ukulalela umsakazo. (*b*)
Ngifuna ukuphumula. (*c*) Ngifuna
ukushaya ucingo. (*d*) Ngifuna
icooldrinki.

Unit 13

Imibuzo (*a*) Akusilo iqiniso. USipho
akaceli imeniyu. (*b*) Akusilo iqiniso.
Sipho uthanda iwayini emhlophe. (*c*)
Akusilo iqiniso. ULindiwe uthanda
newayini emhlophe. (na- = *also*) (*d*)
Kuyiqiniso. ULindiwe wanelisiwe. (*e*)
Akusilo iqiniso. NguSipho okhala
ngokudla.
Umsebenzi **1** (*a*) Awungiphathele
(*b*) Ngizokubizela (*c*) Ngizokuvalela (*d*)
Ngizokubhekela (*e*) Ngizokwenzela (*f*)
Awusilethele **2** (*a*) Amahitha
akhona na? (*b*) (Ihitha) Limalini?/
Libiza malini? (*c*) Ngingakhokha
ngeCredit Card noma: ... (*d*) Namukela
amasheke na? **3** (*a*) Laba bantu
benze umsebenzi omkhulu. (*b*)

Isalukazi samukele imali. (c) i(li)hembe lami lomile. (d) Izicathulo zami azomile. (e) UMark akazi lutho. (f) Amadoda ejwayele le ndawo. (g) Ubaba akanelisiwe. (h) (Thina) Asazi. (i) (Mina) Angazi. (j) Le ndaba yehlukile. 4 (a) Ngikhathele. (b) Sidiniwe. (c) Ligcwele. (d) Kulungile. (e) Balele. (f) Iphelile. (g) Bathokozile. (h) Ngisuthi/e. (i) Sanelisiwe. (j) Sikhathazekile.

Unit 14

Imibuzo 1 (a) Kuyiqiniso. (b) Akusilo iqiniso. UThemba ufuna ukuposa incwadi. (c) Akusilo iqiniso. UThemba upose incwadi yakhe esigxotsheni seposi. (d) Akusilo iqiniso. Ngumfana osize uThemba. (e) Kuyiqiniso.

Umsebenzi 1 (a) Qonda ngqo (*straight*) ngalo mgwaqo uze (*until*) ufike kuBoshoff Street. KuBoshoff Street ujikele ngakwesokudla uqhubeke (*continue*) uze ufike eChurch Street. EChurch Street ujikele ngakwesokudla. Uzobona iSonto LesiVumelwano lilapho. **Or:** Hamba ngalo mgwaqo uze ufike eChurch Street. Lapho eChurch Street ujikele ngakwesobunxele emarobhothini. Uqonda ngqo ngeChurch Street uze ufike eSontweni LesiVumelwano. (b) Qonda ngqo ngalo mgwaqo uze ufike eLoop Street. Ekhoneni leLoop Street neComercial Road ujikele ngakwesobunxele emarobothini. Uqonde ngqo ngeLoop Street uze ufike epolisiteshini. 2 Uxolo, mnumzana (nkosikazi, etc.), ngibuza isiteshi/ ngicela umgwaqo oya esiteshini. 3 (a) U-Emma akekho. (b) Inyama ayikho. (c) Asifuni uweta. (d) UNkosazana Zwane akakhulumi iqiniso. (e) Abelungu abathandi

utshwala. (f) Akushisi kakhulu. (g) Iwayini ayibandi. (h) Inyuziphepha ayifikanga. (i) UJohannes akamtshelanga. (j) Amadoda awazamanga kakhulu. 4 (a) ziphuza (b) silahlekile (c) unamandla (d) lingcolile (e) sivaliwe 5 (a) ushizi usefrijini (b) ibhotela lisetafuleni (c) ummese usediloweni (d) uJason ukudokotela (e) izitsha zisosinkini (f) abantwana bakunina (g) uMarjorie usekamelweni lakhe (h) Imali isesikhwameni sakho (i) IMalibu Hotel iseMarine Parade. (j) ICapitol Towers Hotel isekhoneni le-Longmarket ne-Church Street 6 (a) Likuphi iMalibu Hotel?/Ngibuza iMalibu Hotel? (b) Isiteshi sikuphi?/Ngibuza isiteshi? (c) Likuphi ipolisiteshi?/Ngibuza ipolisiteshi? (d) Ikuphi inkundla yezindiza?/Ngibuza inkundla yezindiza? (e) Iphi inkosikazi Dlamini?/Uphi umemu Dlamini? 7 (a) Uxolo (*pardon*), mnumzana (nkosikazi, etc.), lo mgwaqo uya eSandlwana na? (b) Sikuphi iSandlwana, mnumzana (nkosikazi, etc.)? 8 (a) Ubaba uye emsebenzini. (b) Sivuke ngo-7. (c) Ibhasi lifike ngo-10. (d) USharon uphuze i-cooldrink. (e) UWilliam uhambile. (f) Ngisebenze eGoli.

Unit 15 (Revision)

1 (a) Moses, mangikwazise kubangane bami. /Moses, mangikwethule kubangane bami. NguMark lo, nguJudy lo. (b) **Mark** Ngijabulela ukukwazi. **Judy** Nami ngijabulela ukukwazi. **Moses** Ngijabulela (ukuni-azi =) ukunazi. (-ni- = *you* (pl.)) 2 (a) Ngicela imeniyu. Ngifuna (Ngingathanda) i-rump steki evuthwe kancane (e-

(*which*) = relative concord, see Unit 22). Ngifuna ukuphuza iwayini/icooldrinki/itiye, etc. (*b*) Ngingakhokha ngeCredit Card? **3** (*a*) Uxolo (*pardon*) nkosikazi, ngibuza iStandard Bank /iStandard Bank ikuphi? (*b*) Uxolo mnumzana, ngibuza i-Elangeni Hotel/i-Elangeni Hotel ikuphi? (*c*) Uxolo dade (*sister*), ngibuza i-Aquarium/I-Aquarium ikuphi? (*d*) Mangibuze (*may I please ask*) mfowethu, amalisho akuphi?/Uxolo mfowethu, ngibuza amalisho? (*e*) Uxolo ndoda, ukuphi umgwaqo oya ekundleni yezindiza? **4** (*a*) Yebo, ngilivalile. (*b*) Yebo, ngimbonile. (*c*) Yebo, ngiyasazi. (*d*) Yebo, ngilithengile. (*e*) Yebo, ngimtshelile. (*a*) Cha, angilivalanga. (*b*) Cha, angimbonanga. (*c*) Cha, angisazi, (*d*) Cha, angilithenganga. (*e*) Cha, angimtshelanga. **5** (*a*) EHluhluwe kungamakhilomitha amangaki ukusuka lapha? (*b*) Kungamakhilomitha angu-250. **6** (*a*) Ngifuna ukudla. (*b*) Ngifuna ukuhamba. (*c*) Ngifuna ukuphumula. (*d*) Ngifuna ukulala. **7** (*a*) No smoking (*allowed here*). (*b*) No entrance (here). **8** (*a*) Ningathanda itiye noma ikhofi? **9** (*a*) Uqonde ngqo ngalo mgwaqo bese. (*b*) ujikela ngokwesokudla ekhoneni le-Church Street ne-New Market Street. **10** (*a*) Ngiye emsebenzini. (*b*) Ngibatshelile. (*c*) Ngenze isiphosiso. (*d*) Ngikhulume nobaba Mkhize. **11** (*a*) Ngiyasebenza. (*b*) Ubaba Mabuya uqamba amanga. (*c*) UMaDlamini ukhalile. **12** (*a*) UThobile ukudokotela (*b*) Ubaba wami usemsebenzini (*c*) Umama wami usedolobheni (*d*) UNomacala ukuMenzi (*e*) Impahla isemotweni (*f*) Incwadi iseposini (*g*) Abantwana

baphandle (*h*) Izinja zisendlini

Unit 16

Imibuzo **1** (*a*) Cha, uMark uhlala ePitoli. (*b*) Cha, umnumzana Thwala akekho ehhovisi lakhe. (*c*) Kuyiqiniso. (*d*) Mhlawumbe (*maybe*) uyayazi, mhlawumbe akayazi. Asazi. (*e*) Akusilo iqiniso. Umnumzana Thwala uzobuya emva kwelantshi. **2** (*a*) UMark ufonela uMnumzana Thwala. (*b*) Uye elantshini. (*c*) Ithi 420 2493. (*d*) UMark uhlala ePitoli. (*e*) Uzobuya emva kwelantshi. **Umsebenzi** **1** (*a*) Ngicela ukukhuluma noJulie. (*b*) Ngubani okhulumayo. (*c*) Ngingu-Yvonne. (*d*) Ngeshwa uJulie akekho. (*e*) Ngingathatha umyalezo na? (*f*) Ngingajabula. (*g*) Mtshele ukuthi. (*h*) Ngehluleka ukufika kusasa. **2** (*a*) Unkosikazi Meyer akekho. (*b*) Imali ayikho. (*c*) Le ndawo ayibizi kakhulu. (*d*) USusan akakhulumanga kahle. (*e*) Abantwana abafuni ubisi. (*f*) Alishisi. (*g*) Akubandi. (*h*) Isitimela asifikanga ngo-10.15. (*i*) UJohannes akabuyanga. **3** (*a*) zingcolile (*b*) silahlekile (*c*) uqinile (*d*) kuphelile (*e*) ilambile **4** (*a*) Awubambe kancane. (*b*) Ngizokwedlulisela kumphathi. (*c*) Umnumzana Smith akekho. (*d*) Awufone futhi emva kwemizuzwana eyishumi (= 10). **5** (*a*) Ufuna ubani? (*b*) Kukhala ubani? (*c*) Ngubani ongafikanga? (*d*) Uyohamba nobani? (*e*) Ngubani othathe isinkwa? (*f*) Ufuna sayizi bani? (*g*) Uhlala kwanamba bani?/Ukwanamba bani? **6** (*a*) Mtshele uDudu ukuthi ngiyagula. (*b*) Mtshele uThandi ukuthi ngizophuza ukufika. (*c*) Batshele uPeter noSally ukuthi balinde/mabalinde. (*d*) Mtshele uMuzi ukuthi angakhohlwa ukukhiya (umnyango). (*e*) Mtshele uJabulani ukuthi makasheshe. **7** (*a*) lo (*b*) lesi (*c*) le (*d*) labo (*e*) le, leyo

Unit 17

Imibuzo (*a*) NguSibongile. (*b*) USibongile ngubaba kaSifiso noDoreen. (*c*) UMaNtuli nguLindiwe. (*d*) NguLindiwe. (*e*) NguSifiso noDoreen. (*f*) Isibongo sikaSibongile nguVilakazi. (*g*) Igama lenkosikazi kaSibongile nguLindiwe. (*h*) USibongile ucela usawoti nopelepele kuDoreen.
Umsebenzi **1** (*a*) Awuhlale lapha, Florence. (*b*) Themba, awuhlale lapho. (*c*) Masithandaze. (*d*) Ningathanda iwayini ebomvu noma (iwayini) emhlophe? (*e*) Singathanda iwayini ebomvu. (*f*) Nanti. (*g*) Ngiyabonga. (*h*) Ngicela upelepele, Ann. (*i*) Nanku. (*j*) Ngiyabonga. (*k*) Ngiyaxolisa. (*l*) Ningathanda ikhofi na? (*m*) Yebo, singajabula. **2** (*a*) Siyobonana (*b*) basaphila (*c*) akafuni (*d*) ziyagezana (*e*) ayabila (*f*) lomile (*g*) ayihlakaniphile (*h*) sikhulunywa (*i*) baduba **3** (*a*) Cha, uSimon akabuyanga mhla ka-12 kuSeptemba. (*b*) Cha, ubaba wami akasebenzi eThekwini. (*c*) Cha, abahambanga ubusuku bonke. (*d*) Cha, izitolo azivali ngo-6 namhlanje. (*e*) Cha, le nto ayibizi kakhulu. (*f*) Cha, asifuni uku-oda manje. **4** (*a*) Usafuna amasendiwishi, Lisbethe? (*b*) Usafuna ikhekhe, Lisbethe? (*c*) Usafuna ikhofi, Lisbethe? **5** (*a*) Cha, ngiyabonga. (Nganelisiwe) (*b*) Cha, ngiyabonga. (Sengesuthe) **6** (*a*) Ngicela ubisi. (*b*) Ukhona usawoti na?/Usawoti ukhona na? **7** (*a*) Ngisaphila. (*b*) Izitolo zisavuliwe. (*c*) Umakhonya usekhona. (*d*) Ungasheshi ngoba kusekhona isikhathi/isikhathi sisekhona. (*e*) Ungakhohlwa. **8**

Bonke abantu/Sonke isikhathi/Yonke imali/Lonke iviki/Masithandaze/ Masihambe

Unit 18

Imibuzo **1** (*a*) Cha, akusilo iqiniso. UGavin uphethwe ngumphimbo. (*b*) Cha, akusilo iqiniso. UGavin uyagula. (*c*) Cha, akusilo iqiniso. UGavin angeye (*he may not go*) emsebenzini. (*d*) Kuyiqiniso. (*e*) Cha, akusilo iqiniso. UGavin akekho esibhedlela. **2** (*a*) UGavin uqale izolo ukugula. (*b*) Yebo, uyakhwehlela. (*c*) UGavin uye kudokotela. (*d*) Isifuba sikaGavin sicinene. (*e*) Udokotela uthi uGavin uphethwe yimfuluwenza. **3** (*a*) UGavin akayanga esibhedlela. (*b*) UGavin akaguli kakhulu. (*c*) Udokotela akapopolanga uLindi. (*d*) Udokotela akajovanga uGavin. (*e*) UGavin akayi emsebenzini.
Umsebenzi **1** (*a*) Uphethwe yini, mnumzane Khathi? (*b*) Angazi, Dokotela. (*c*) Unethemperetsha na? (*d*) Yebo, Dokotela. (*e*) Uphethwe yikhanda na? (*f*) Yebo, Dokotela. (*g*) Uqale nini ukugula? (*h*) Ngiqale kuthangi, Dokotela. (*i*) Awukhumule ibhantshi ngoba. (*j*) ngifuna ukukupopola. (*k*) Ngibona uphethwe ngamathonsela. (*l*) Ngizokulobela umuthi. **2** Angizizwa kahle, Dokotela. Ngiphethwe yisisu. **3** Udinga (*need*) uᵣ jovo/Kufanele uthole (*get*) umjovo. Ngizokukulobela umuthi (-ku- = *you*). **4** (*a*) Ngiya kudokotela. (*b*) Ngivela kudokotela wamazinyo. (*c*) Ngiphethwe yimfuluwenza/ Nginemfuluwenza. (*d*) Ngizobuya ngeSonto. (*e*) NguGavin oye kudokotela. **5** (*a*) Wenzani (*b*) sithini (*c*) Kunjani (*d*) Niyaphi (*e*) Siya (*f*) Bayaphi (*g*) Ngingakusiza (*h*) Somile

6 (*a*) Ngubani igama lakho? (*b*) Uphumaphi?/Uvelaphi? (*c*) Yimalini? (*d*) Ukubhema akuvunyelwa. (*e*) Angizizwa kahle. (*f*) Mangikwazise ku... (*g*) Usebenzani? (*h*) URonald akekho. (*i*) Uphethe imali na?/Ngabe uphethe imali? (*j*) Ngibuza iposihhovisi/Likuphi iposihhovisi? (*k*) Isinkwa sisekhishini (*l*) Lukhona ucingo na? **7** (*a*) Uphole masinyane. (*b*) Uhambe kahle. (*c*) Usale kahle. (*d*) Ulale kamnandi. **8** (*a*) Awuvule iTV/umabonwakude, Rachel. (*b*) Awuvale umsakazo, Rachel. (*c*) Awulethe ushukela, Rachel. (*d*) Awubize uJonathan, Rachel. **9** (*a*) Unkosikazi Sibiya ukhona. (*b*) Siyakhala. (*c*) Ibhasi lifikile. (*d*) Umama ulambile. (*e*) Laba bantu bakhuluma isiZulu.

Unit 19

Imibuzo (*a*) Umamukeli ukhuluma noMenzi lapha. (*b*) Isibongo sikaMenzi nguZondo. (*c*) Igama lesihlobo sikaMenzi nguStanley. (*d*) Elinye igama likaMenzi nguPatience. (*e*) UMenzi uhlala eSikhawini.

Umsebenzi 1 (*a*) Igama nesibongo: Philemon Dladla (*b*) I-ID namba: 72070125082003 (*c*) Idethi lokuzalwa: 1-07-72 (*d*) Ikheli: 67 South Street Hatfield (*e*) Inombolo yocingo: 368 4376 (*f*) Ushadile na?: Angishadile (*g*) Ulwimi lwasekhaya: SiSwati *Example*: (*a*) Igama nesibongo: Lisa Nonhlanhla Kunene (*b*) Ikheli: Claim Street 101, Hillbrow (*c*) Isizwe: South African (*d*) Idethi lokuzalwa: 62-05-11 (*e*) Indawo yokuzalwa: EShowe (*f*) Uvelaphi?: EMgungundlovu (*g*) Lapho uya khona?: Ekhaya (*h*) Inombolo yepaspoti: P00844896 (*i*) Inombolo yemoto: KHF993T (*j*) Idethi: 08-04-95

(*k*) Isayini: (*your signature*) **2** (*a*) wakho (*b*) sethu (*c*) yami (*d*) lakho (*e*) bakhe (*f*) yethu (*g*) enu (*h*) lwakho (*a*) lamaZulu (*b*) lesiZulu (*c*) sokuhamba (*d*) yenkosikazi (*e*) zabantu (*f*) emoto (*g*) abafazi (*h*) kwezingane (*i*) lomntwana **3** (*a*) Lithini igama lehhotela lenu? (*b*) Ithini inombolo yehhovisi lakho? (*c*) Ithini I D number yakho? (*d*) Ngubani igama lomntanakho (lomntwana wakho)? (*e*) Uneminyaka emingaki ubudala? **4** (*a*) Yindlovu. (*b*) Yibhubesi (*or* Libhubesi). (*c*) Ngubhejane. (*d*) Yinyathi. (*e*) Ngufudu (*or* Lufudu). (*f*) Ngukhozi (*or* Lukhozi). (*g*) Yingwe. **5** (*a*) Yebo, ngiyababona. (*b*) Yebo, ngiyayifuna. (*c*) Cha, angimbizanga. (*d*) Cha, angiyitholanga. (*e*) Yebo, ngiyasithanda. (*f*) Yebo, ngiyalifuna. (*g*) Yebo, ngiyilethile. **6** (*a*) Yisikhathi esingakanani ugula, Felicity? (*b*) Yisikhathi esingakanani ushadile, Felicity? (*c*) Yisikhathi esingakanani wenza lo msebenzi, Felicity? (*d*) Yisikhathi esingakanani uhlala ekhaya, Felicity? **7** (*a*) isibongo sikaPeter (*b*) indlu kaJohn (*c*) umbhede kagogo (*d*) ukudla kukamama

Unit 20 (Revision)

1 (*a*) KuseCarlton Furnishers lapha. (*b*) Ngubani okhulumayo? (*c*) NguVelaphi okhulumayo. (*d*) Velaphi bani? Ngingakusiza ngani? (*f*) Ngicela ukukhuluma nemeneja. (*g*) Ngeshwa imeneja alikho. (*h*) Lizobuya nini? (*i*) Angazi. (*j*) Awufone futhi kusasa. **2** (*a*) Kukwa-Anderson lapha. (*b*) Ngubani okhulumayo? (*c*) NguTerence okhulumayo. (*d*) Ufuna ukukhuluma nobani? (*e*) Uxolo, wedukile. *Example:* KuseSilverton Engineering lapha, KuseJones, McMillan and Associates

lapha, Kuse-O K Bazaars lapha, etc.
3 Ugqoka sayizi bani? **4** (*a*) Uqede
standard bani esikoleni? (*b*) Usebenze
kuphi phambili? **5** (*a*) Ngithanda le
ndawo. (*b*) Ngithanda lo muntu. (*c*)
Ngithanda lesi sitolo. (*d*) Ngithanda
laba bantu. (*e*) Ngithanda leli kati.
(*f*) Ngithanda le nja. (*a*) Angithandi
leyo ndawo. (*b*) Angithandi leso sitolo.
(*c*) Angithandi lelo hhotela. (*d*)
Angithandi labo bantu. **6** (*a*) How
do you feel? /Ngizizwa kabi. (*b*) What's
the matter? Ngiphethwe yikhanda. (*c*)
Does it hurt? Yebo, libuhlungu. (*d*) Do
you have a temperature? Ngicabanga
kanjalo (*I think so*). (*e*) When did you
start feeling ill? Ngiqale ngeSonto. (*a*)
You must not go to work/to your office.
(*b*) You must stay in bed for three days.
(*c*) I will prescribe (some) tablets/pills
that will help you. (*d*) I want to see you
again on Wednesday. **7** (*a*) Woza
lapha Nomacala. (*b*) Thulani
bantwana. (*c*) Vula umnyango Lindiwe.
(*d*) Vala izibane Menzi. (*e*) Sheshani
madoda. **8** (*a*) Address (*b*)
Telephone number at home (*c*)
Business address (*d*) Telephone
number at work (*e*) How long in
present employment (*f*) Annual income/
salary (*g*) I D Number (*h*) Age (*i*)
Marital status **9** (*a*) Lithini ikheli
lakho? (*b*) Ithini inombolo yocingo
lwakho? (*c*) Lithini igama lakho?/Sithini
isibongo sakho? (*d*) Sithini isikhathi?
(*e*) Lithini idethi namhlanje?

Unit 21

Imibuzo (*a*) USimon nomuzi wakhe
bafuna ukuyovakashela eThekwini. (*b*)
USimon ufuna ikamelo elihlalisa
abantu ababili. (*c*) Ikamelo yi-R250
ngosuku. (*d*) Umntwana kaSimon
uneminyaka emihlanu ubudala. (*e*)

USimon uthanda ukubhuka indawo
yokuhlala kusuka kumhla ka-10
kufika kumhla ka-21 kuDisemba. (*f*)
Imali yekamelo ihlangene nemali
yebhulakufesi. (*g*) Bafuna idiphozithi
elingu-R300.
Umsebenzi 1 (*a*) KuseLangeni
Hotel lapha. (*b*) Ngingakusiza ngani?
(*c*) Ngithanda ukubuka indawo
yokuhlala. (*d*) Awubambe kancane
(*Please hold a while*). Ngizokwedlulisela
kwabaseReservations. (*e*)
Kusereservations lapha. NguSally
okhulumayo. (*f*) Ngithanda ukubhuka
indawo yokuhlala. (*g*) Kusuka kumhla
ka-3 kufika kumhla ka-12 kuJulayi. (*h*)
Nibangaki? (*i*) Sibane. (*j*) Ufuna
amakamelo amangaki? (*k*) Sifuna
amakamelo amabili. (*l*) Ikamelo
yimalini ngosuku? (*m*) Yi-R225
ngosuku lapho nihlalisana. **2**
Ngifuna: (*a*) amaqanda amabili (*b*)
izihlalo ezintathu (*c*) otamatisi ababili
(*d*) abantu abahlanu (*e*) amarandi
amabili (*f*) amarandi amathathu (*g*)
amarandi amahlanu (*h*) qanda linye (*i*)
sihlalo sinye (*j*) tamatisi munye (*k*)
muntu munye (*l*) randi linye (*m*)
amarandi amane (*n*) amarandi angu-15
3 Vusi, ufuna: (*a*) izingilazi
ezingaki? (*b*) imimese emingaki? (*c*)
izipunu ezingaki? (*d*) amapuleti
amangaki? (*e*) amathikithi amangaki?
(*f*) abantu abangaki? Vusi: (*a*)
bangaki abantwana esikoleni? Bangu-
650. (*b*) zingaki izinja epulazini?
Zimbili. (*c*) zingaki izinyanga
onyakeni? Zingu-12. (*d*) zingaki
izinsuku kuJuni? Zingu-30. (*e*) zingaki
izinkomishi etafuleni? Zinhlanu. (*f*)
bangaki abafana ekilasini? Bangu-9.
(*g*) mangaki amaviki enyangeni?
Mane. (*h*) Nibangaki? Sibabili **4** (*a*)
Unjani uMavis? Muhle kakhulu. (*b*)
Sinjani isiZulu? Sihle kakhulu. (*c*)

Injani imoto yakho? Indala kakhulu. (d) Anjani amawolintshi? Mabi. **5** (a) abantu abadala (b) umuntu omkhulu (c) imali eningi (d) ikati elincane (e) intombi enhle (f) indawo enhle (g) abantwana abaningi (h) umfana omude (i) ukudla okubi (j) amantombazane amancane **6** (a) U-anti Lisbethe muhle. (b) Ngithole umsebenzi omncane. (c) Kubi namhlanje. (d) Umakhelwane wami ngumuntu omdala. (e) La mantombazana mahle. **7** Ngiyaxolisa/ Uxolo kodwa angazi. **8** Ngithanda ukubhukela ifilimu lika-9 izihlalo ezimbili. **9** (a) Kusuka ku-9 ekuseni kuya ku-5 ntambama. (b) Kusuka ku-100 kuya ku-200. (c) kusuka kumhla ka-12 kuya kumhla ka-15 kuMashi. (d) Kusuka ngoMsombuluko kuze kube ngoMgqibelo.

Unit 22

Imibuzo (a) Bafuna ukuthenga ifriji. (b) USarah uthanda ifriji elinombala omhloshana. (c) Igalanti lingunyaka. (d) Bayoli-oda efektrini. (e) Uthe lizofika iviki elizayo. (f) UCelani uzothola isephulelo.
Umsebenzi 1 (a) Sithanda ukuthenga umshini wokuwasha. (b) Nifuna umshini onjani? (c) Sifuna umshini wokuwasha ozenzelayo. (d) Yimalini lo mshini? (e) Unjani lo mshini? (f) Uqinile kakhulu. (g) Singakhokha ngamancozuncozu na? (h) Yebo. Ungakhokha izinyanga ezingu-6. (i) Niyadiliva na? (j) Sizodiliva kusasa noma ngoLwesine. **2** (a) abahlala (b) ezinolaka (c) onzima (d) abandayo (e) olushisayo (f) asetafuleni (g) eliluhlaza (h) abangasazi (i) ongakwazi (j) efuna **3** (a) (Isitofu) Sinegaranti na? (b)

(Igaranti) Liyisikhathi esingakanani? (c) Sithola isephulelo uma sithenga ngokheshe na? (d) Ngingakhokha izinyanga eziyisithupha/ezingu-6 na? (e) Nifuna enye imali uma nidiliva na?

Unit 23

Imibuzo (a) U-Ivor ubike ukugqekezwa kwendlu yakhe emaphoyiseni. (b) Abagqekezi bebe imoto, izingubo ne-video recorder. (c) IyiToyota Corolla imoto yenkosikazi ka-Ivor. (d) Abagqekezi baphule ingide yegalaji (= ya-igalaji *of the garage*). (e) Abagqekezi bathole i-video recorder ekamelweni lokuhlala. (f) U-Ivor ubike ukugqekezwa kwendlu yakhe emaphoyiseni.
Umsebenzi 1 (a) Ngingakusiza ngani? (b) Yebo, ngingajabula. (c) Ngifuna ukubika ukwebiwa kweridiyo yemoto yami. (d) Kwenzeke nini? (e) Kwenzeke izolo ebusuku. (f) Kwenzeke kuphi? (g) Kwenzeke ekhaya. (h) Kukhona okunye okwebiwe na?/ Bantshonthe (*stole*) okunye (*anything else*?) na? (i) Cha, yilokho kuphela. **2** (a) Uhambe nini izolo, Maria? (b) Ushayisa nini, Maria? (c) Uqala nini ukusebenza ekuseni, Maria? (d) Ubukuphi izolo, Maria? (e) UJonathan ubekuphi izolo, Maria? (f) Izikhiye zemoto bezikuphi, Maria? (g) Unelayisense lokushayela imoto, Maria? (h) Unomkhuhlane, Maria?/ Ngabe unomkhuhlane, Maria? (i) Unemfuluwenza, Maria?/Ngabe unemfuluwenza, Maria? **3** (a) Yebo, nginayo. (b) Cha, ayinaso. (c) Cha, anginayo. (d) Cha, akanawo. (e) Yebo, nginaso. (f) Yebo, nginalo. (g) Cha, asinayo. (h) Yebo nginabo. (i) Cha, anginalo. **4** (a) Cha, ubaba ubengekho. (b) Cha, bengingekho. (c)

Cha, besingekho. (*d*) Cha, abengekho.
(*e*) Cha, belingekho. **5** (*a*) Bengigula
(*b*) Bengisesibhedlela (*c*)
Bengisemsebenzini (*d*) Bengisekhaya
(*e*) BengikwaJohn **6** (*a*) Umama
uyashanela. Ushanela izibi
namaphepha. Umama akazifuni izibi
ekhaya. Umama uwola izibi. Uzithela
(izibi) ebhaleni. (*b*) UNana uyakhala.
UNana ukhalela iswidi. Uwabonile
(amaswidi) kubaba. Umama uthi:
Thatha iswidi Nana. UNana
uyalithatha (iswidi). UNana
uyamthanda (ubaba). Nobaba
uyamthanda (uNana). **7** (*a*) Hlalani
phansi bantwana! (*b*) Sukumani
bantwana! (*c*) Thulani bantwana! (*d*)
Khiphani izincwadi zenu, bantwana!
(*e*) Valani amehlo bantwana!

Unit 24

Imibuzo (*a*) UMaphumulo
useposihhovisi lapha. (*b*) UMaphumulo
ufuna ukuthumela incwadi yakhe
eMelika. (*c*) Incwadi kaMaphumulo
izohamba ngendiza. (*d*)
Amathelegilamu ashaywa ekhawunda
7. (*e*) Amafomu ethelegilamu agcinwa
emashalofini. (*f*) Amafomu ethelegilamu
amhlophe asebenza kwelakithi.
Umsebenzi 1 (*a*) Ngibuza
iposihhovisi, Mnumzana/Mangibuze,
Mnumzane. Iposihhovisi likuphi? (*b*)
The Post Office is in the Pick and Pay
Shopping Centre. (*c*) Ngicela izitembu.
(*d*) How many stamps do you want?
Ngifuna (eg) izitembu ezinhlanu/
eziyishumi, etc. (*e*) Ngifuna ukubhalisa
incwadi. **2** Ngihambe: (*a*)
ngendiza (*b*) ngesitimela (*c*) ngemoto
(*d*) ngeteksi (*e*) ngebhasi **3** Ngithanda:
(*a*) ukushaya ikhefu (*b*) ukuya
edolobheni (*c*) ukuyokuthenga ezitolo
(*d*) ukuzenzela umathanda (*e*)

ukusebenza engadini **4** Igama lami
nguThemba. Ngihlala kubazali bami
nodadewethu. Igama likadadewethu
nguThandi. Sihlala eDandi. UThandi
nami sisahamba isikole. Mina
ngifunda ibanga lesibili (Std. 2).
UThandi yena ufunda ibanga lesine
(Std. 4). Ubaba usebenza eGoli.
Umama akasebenzi. Ubheka ugogo
nathi. Ubaba akayi emsebenzini
namhlanje ngoba kuyiholide. Bonke
abantu baseDandi bayajabula. **5** (*a*)
Isitimela sesihambile na? (*b*) Indiza
isifilkile na? (*c*) Usupholile na? (*d*)
UMaDlamini usebuyile na? (*e*)
Amadoda aseqede umsebenzi na? **6**
(*a*) Sifiso, mngane wami (*my friend*).
Halala ngosuku lokuzalwa kwakho.
Impilontle nempilonde! (*b*) Mzilikazi
ohloniphekileyo. Ngikufisela okuhle
kodwa ngomshado wakho.
UNkulunkulu makabusise nina
nobabili.

Unit 25 (Revision)

1 (*a*) Ngingakusiza ngani,
mnumzana? (*b*) Ngithanda ukubhalisa
indawo endizeni eya eGoli esuka ngo-7
ekuseni. (*c*) Ufuna ukubhukela
(ukubhalisela) abantu abangaki? (*or*:
Nibangaki? *How many are you?*) (*d*)
Yimina kuphela. (*e*) Ubuya nini? (*f*)
Ngithanda ukubuya ngoLwesine
ngendiza esuka ngo-5 kusihlwa. (*g*)
Uthanda ukukhokha kanjani?
Ngokheshe noma ngeCredit Card? (*h*)
Ngizokhokha ngeCredit Card. **2** (*a*)
Ufuna nhloboni yemoto, mnumzana?
(*b*) Ngifuna iToyota Corolla. (*c*)
Ungathanda ukukhokha malini,
mnumzana? (*d*) Kusuka ku-R20 000
kuya ku-R30 000. (*e*) NgineToyota
Corolla emhlophe ebiza R29 000. (*f*)
Idipozithi lingakanani? (*g*) Lingu-

R6000. (h) Imali eseleyo uyikhokha ngezinyanga ezingu-24. (i) (Imoto) Inegaranti? (j) Yebo. Yi-10 000 km noma izinyanga ezingu-6.
3 Ngizwelana nani ngokushona kukagogo. **4** Ngihambe: (a) ngemoto (b) ngebhasi (c) ngesitimela (d) ngendiza **5** (a) U-Emma usehambile. (b) Umlungu usehambile. (c) Ubaba Sithole usehambile. (d) Abantwana sebehambile. **6** (a) Bengisedolobheni. (b) Bengisemsebenzini. (c) Bengivakashela umngane wami. (d) Bengidlala igalofu. **7** (a) Ngiyobuya ngomhla ka-14 ku-Apreli. (b) Ngiyofika eJohannesburg airport ngo-9. (c) Ngiyobuya ngeSonto. **8** (a) Nginemali. (b) Nginabantwana ababili. (c) Ngineveni. (d) Nginezimoto ezimbili. (e) Nginomsebenzi. (f) Nginomsakazo. (a) Anginamali. (b) Anginabantwana ababili. (c) Anginaveni. (d) Anginazimoto ezimbili. (e) Anginamsebenzi. (f) Anginamsakazo. **9** (a) onjani (b) abaduba (c) oqinile (d) engakhali (e) esisuka (f) ezingu-13 (g) engu-16 **10** (a) Yintengo kakheshe le? (b) Ngingakhokha izinyanga ezingu-6 na? (c) Simalini isephulelo (imalini 'idiscount') uma ngikhokha ngokokheshe? **11** (a) randi linye (R1); amarandi amabili (R2); amarandi amathathu (R3); amarandi amane (R4); amarandi amahlanu (R5); amarandi angu-6; amarandi angu-7; amarandi angu-8; amarandi angu-9; amarandi ayishumi or: amarandi angu-10 (b) abantu ababili; abantu abathathu; abantu abane; abantu abahlanu izinsuku ezinhlanu (or: ezingu-5); izinsuku ezingu-6; izinsuku

ezingu-7; izinsuku ezingu-8; izinsuku ezingu-9; izinsuku ezingu-10 **12** Ngikufisela: (a) usuku oluhle (b) unyaka omuhle (c) impilo ende (d) izulu elihle Lowo muntu: (a) mdala (b) muhle (c) mncane (d) mubi **13** Ngisebenza: (a) kusuka ku-8 ekuseni (= am) kuya ku-5 ntambama (= pm). (b) kusuka ngoMsombuluko kuze kube ngoLwesihlanu. (c) kusuka kumhla ka-10 kuya kumhla ka-20. **14** (a) Ukhuluma isiZulu na? Yebo, ngiyasikhuluma./Cha, angisikhulumi. (b) Uyasazi isiTswana na? Yebo, ngiyasazi./Cha, angisazi (c) Uyamazi uThuli Gamede na? Yebo, ngiyamazi./Cha, angimazi. (d) Ufonele abantu baseposini na? Yebo, ngibafonele./Cha, angibafonelanga. (e) Ufunde iSowetan namhlanje? Yebo, ngiyifundile./Cha, angiyifundanga. (f) Ubone ubaba Madiba ku-TV izolo? Yebo, ngimbonile./Cha, angimbonanga. (g) Ufake imali na? Yebo, ngiyifakile./Cha, angiyifakanga. (h) Uthanda inyama yengulube na? Yebo, ngiyayithanda./Cha, angiyithandi. **15** Namuhla nguKhisimuzi. Thina siyajabula. Sizogqoka izingubo zethu. Izingubo zethu zilingana kahle Nezicathulo zethu zilingana kahle. Ubaba nomama bathenge izingubo zethu edolobheni. Umama uthenge ukudla okuningi. Ubaba akasebenzi namuhla. (Abantu) Bavalile ehhovisi.

FURTHER READING

Doke, C M *Textbook of Zulu Grammar* Maskew Millar/Wits University Press, Johannesburg

Nyembezi, C L S *Learn More Zulu* Shuter & Shooter, Pietermaritzburg

Dent, G R & Nyembezi, C L S *Scholar's Zulu Dictionary (English – Zulu, Zulu – English)* Shuter & Shooter, Pietermaritzburg

Doke, C M; Malcolm D M; Sikakana, J M; Vilakazi, B W *English – Zulu, Zulu – English Dictionary* Wits University Press, Johannesburg

Nyembezi, C L S *Zulu Proverbs* (A very useful book on Zulu proverbs together with their meaning and usage) Wits University Press, Johannesburg

Elliot, A *Sons of Zulu* (Beautifully illustrated survey of Zulu life and customs) Collins, London

Goslin, B du P *Conversational Zulu for Beginners* Shuter & Shooter, Pietermaritzburg

Goslin, B du P *An Interactive Computerized Language Course in Zulu* Cum Laude Educational Software, Pretoria

Krige, E J *Social System of the Zulus* Shuter & Shooter, Pietermaritzburg

Ritter, E A *Shaka Zulu* Allen Lane/Penguin Books, London

GLOSSARY

–akha *build*
–akhawundi (i(li)-, ama-)
  account
–ala *refuse*
–alukazi (is-, iz-) *old women*
amamenazi *manners*
amehlo *eyes*
–amukela *accept*
–amukeleka *be acceptable*
–amukeli (um-, ab-) *receptionist*
–amukelwa *be accepted*
–andla (is-, iz-) *hand*
–anele *be enough*
–anelisiwe *be satisfied*
–anti (u-, o) *auntie*
–anyanisi (u-, o-) *onion*
–aphula *break*
–Apreli (u-) *April*
–ayina *iron*
–ayiskhrimu (u-, o-) *ice cream*
–azi *know*
–azisa *introduce*

–baba *be dry*
  iwayini emhlophe ebabayo
  dry white wine
–baba (u-, o-) *father, sir*
–bala (um-, imi-) *colour*
–baleka *run away*
–bamba *hold*
–bambekile *be busy*
–banda *be cold*
–bane (isi-, izi-) *light*
–banga (i(li)-, ama-) *school
  standard*
–bani? (u-, o-) *who?*
bese *and then*
–bhala *write*
–bhala (i(li)-, ama-) *wheelbarrow*
–bhalisa *register, make a
  reservation*
–bhanana (u-, o-) *banana*
–bhange (i(li)-, ama-) *bank
  (commercial)*

–bhanselo (um-) *small something (= tip)*
–bhantshi (i(li)-, ama-) *jacket*
–bhasi (i(li)-, ama-) *bus*
–bhasikidi (i(li)-, ama-) *basket*
–Bhayibheli (i(li)-, ama-) *Bible*
–bhayisikili (i(li)-, ama-) *bicycle*
–bhayisikobho (i(li)-, ama-) *cinema*
–bhede (um-, imi) *bed*
–bhedlela (isi-, izi-) *hospital*
–bhejane (u-, o-) *Black rhinoceros*
–bheka *look after*
–bhema *smoke*
  Akubhenywa lapha *No smoking (allowed) here*
–bhishi (i(li)-, ama-) *beach*
–bhiya (u-, o-) *beer*
–bhodlela (i(li)-, ama-) *bottle*
–bhontshisi (u-, o-) *bean*
–bhotela (i(li)-, ama-) *butter*
–bhubesi (i(li)-, ama-) *lion*
–bhuka *book (accommodation)*
–bhuku (i(li)-, ama-) *book*
–bhukuda *swim*
–bhulakufesi (i(li)-ama-) *breakfast*
–bhulukwe (i(li)-, ama-) *trousers*
–Bhunu (i(li)-, ama-) *Afrikaner*
–Bhunu (isi) *Afrikaans*
–bhuti (u-, o-) *brother*
–bi (adj) *bad*
–bi (izi-) *dirt*
–bika *report (verb)*
–bila *boil*
–bili (adj) *two*

–bisi (u(lu)-) *milk*
–biza *call*
–boleka *borrow, lend*
–bomvu *brown, red*
–bona *see*
  sawubona/sakubona/sanibona/
  sanibonani *(form of greeting)*
  sobonana futhi *we'll see each other again*
–bonga *give thanks, say thank you*
–bongo (isi-, izi-) *surname*
–buhlungu *be painful, be sore*
–bukela *watch*
–bukeza *revise*
–bukhali *be sharp*
–buko (izi-) *spectacles*
–bulala *kill*
–busisa *bless*
–buya *return*
–buyisela *return to*
–buza *ask*
–buzo (um-, imi-) *question*

–cathula toddle *learn to walk*
–cathulo (isi-, izi-) *shoe*
–cela *request*
  Ngicela kini? *How are things at your home?*
–cha *no*
–cinene *be congested (chest)*
–cingo (u(lu)-) *telephone*

–daba (in-, izin-) *affair, news*
  Akunandaba *It doesn't matter*
–dade (u-, o-) *sister*
–dadewethu (u-, o-) *my sister*
–dala (ubu-) *age*
–damu (i(li)- ama-) *dam*
–dawo (in-, izin-) *place*

–dazini (i(li)-, ama-) *dozen*
–de (adj) *long, far*
–debe (u(lu)-, izin-) *lip*
–dethi (i(li)-, ama-) *date*
–diliva *deliver*
–dilowa (i(li)-, ama-) *drawer*
–dinga *need*
–dinwa *be (physically) tired*
–diphozithi (i(li)-, ama-) *deposit*
–Disemba (u-) *December*
–diza (in-, izin-) *aeroplane*
–dla (uku-) *food*
–dlala *play*
   dlala ibhola *play football*
–dlali (um-, aba-) *player*
–dlamini (in-, izin-) *lunch*
–dlebe (in-, izin-) *ear*
–dlela (in-, izin-) *road, way*
   Ngisendleleni *I am on my
   way*
–dlovu (in-, izin-) *elephant*
–dlu (in-, izin-) *house*
–doda (in-, ama-) *man, guy*
–dodana (in-, izin-) *son*
–dokotela (u-, o-) *doctor*
–dokotela wamazinyo *dentist*
–dolobha (i(li)-, ama-) *town*
–dololwane (in-, izin-) *elbow*
–donsa umoya *inhale*
–duba umsebenzi *strike*

–eba *steal*
–eBhayi *Port Elizabeth*
–edlula *pass by*
–edlulisela *hand over to, put
   through to*
   Ngizokwedlulisela
   kumabhalane wakhe *I'll put
   you through to his secretary*

–eduka *stray*
eDukathole *Germiston*
eduze *near*
eGoli *Johannesburg*
–ehlukene *differ from one
   another*
–ehlukile *be different*
–ehluleka *fail, to be unable to*
   Ngehluleka uku... *I am
   unable to ...'*
eJalimani/eGermany *Germany*
–ejwayele *be accustomed to*
eKapa *Cape Province*
ekugcineni *at the end*
ekuseni *in the morning*
eLandani *London*
emahlukandlela *at the cross
   roads*
eMelika *America*
eMgungundlovu/eMalitzboko
   Pietermaritzburg
eMnambithi *Ladysmith (a
   town in KwaZulu-Natal)*
emuva *behind*
emva kwa- *after*
eNatali *Natal*
eNgilandi *England*
entambama *in the afternoon*
–enyuka *ascend*
–enza *do*
–enzansi *at the bottom*
–enzeka *happen*
–ephukile *be broken*
–ephulela *give a discount*
–ephulelo (is-) *discount*
ePitoli *Pretoria*
–eqa *cross a street*
eqinisweni *in fact*

–esaba   *be afraid of*

esitobhini   *at the halt / stop street*

–esula   *wipe off*

–esuthi   *be satisfied with food*
Ngesuthi esentwala   *I'm full (lit. I'm full with food like a body louse)   I've had more than enough to eat*

eThekwini   *Durban*

–ethemba   *trust, hope, believe*

–ethula   *introduce to*

eZulwini   *in heaven*

faka   *put in*
Faka enshuwalensini   *insure*

–falakahlana (im-)   *small change*

–fana (um-, aba-)   *boy*

–fanele   *be fitting, must*
Ngifanele ...   *I must / I ought*

–fasitele (i(li)-, ama-)   *window, windscreen*

–fastela (i(li)-, ama-)   *window, windscreen*

–fazi (um-, aba-)   *women*

–Februwari (u-)   *February*

–fektri (i(li)-, ama-)   *factory*

–fika   *come, arrive*

–filimu (i(li)-, ama-)   *film, movie*

–fisa   *desire, wish*

–fisela   *wish for*
Ngikufisela okuhle kodwa   *I wish (for) you only the best*

–fiva (im-)   *fever*

–fluwenza (im-)   *influenza*

–fomu (i(li)-, ama-)   *form*

–fonela   phone (for) *someone*

–fowabo (um-, aba-)   *his brother*

–fowethu (um-, aba-)   *my brother*

–friji (i(li)-, ama-)   *fridge*

–fuba (isi-, izi-)   *chest*

–fudu (u(lu)-, izim-)   *tortoise*

–fudumele   *be wam*

–fula (um-, imi-)   *river*

–Fulentshi (i(li)-, ama-)   *Frenchman*

–Fulentshi (isi-)   *French language*

–funa   *want*

–funda   *read, learn*

–fundisa   *teach*

–fundisi (um-, aba-)   *minister of religion*

–futhi   *again, once more*

–gadi (in-, izin-)   *garden*

–galaji (i(li)-, ama-)   *garage*

–galofu (i(li)-)   *golf*

–gama (i(li)-, ama-)   *name*

–gane (in-, izin-)   *infant, child*

–garanti (i(li)-, ama-)   *guarantee*

–gazi (i(li)-)   *blood*

–gcina   *come to an end*
Sagcinana isikhathi eside   *We haven't seen each other for a long time*

–gcina   *preserve*

–gcinwa   *be kept*

–gcwalisa   *make full, fill up, fill in, complete a form*

–gcwele   *be full*

–gebengu (izi-, izi-)   *thug, robber, thief*

–geza   *wash*

–gide (in-, izin-)   *padlock*

–gilazi (in-, izin-)   *glass*

–gogo (u-, o-) *grandmother*
–gqekezi (um-, aba-) *burglar*
–gqekezwa *be burgled*
–gula *be ill*
–gulube (in-, izin-) *pig*
–gwaqo (um-, imi-) *road*
–gwayi (u-) *tobacco*
–gxoxo (in-, izin-) *dialogue*

–habhula (i(li)-, ama-) *apple*
–hafu (u-) *half*
Halala! *Congratulations!*
–halalisela *congratulate someone*
–hamba *leave, walk, go*
–hamba (uku-) *to travel, travelling*
hawu *interjection of surprise*
–hembe (i(li)-, ama-) *shirt*
–hhash(i(li)-, ama-) *horse*
hhayi/hhayibo!/hhayikbona! *(interjection of dissent)*
–Hholandi (um-, aba-) *Dutchman*
–hhotela (i(li)-, ama-) *hotel*
–hhovisi (i(li)-, ama-) *office*
–hitha (i(li)-, ama-) *heater*
–hla (um-, imi-) *day*
–hlabamkhosi (izi-, izi-) *burglar alarm*
–hlabelela *sing*
–hlakaniphile *be intelligent*
–hlala *sit, stay*
–hlalisana *share (accommodation), accommodate*
–hlalo (isi-, izi-) *chair*
–hlangana *meet*
–hlangano (um-, imi-) *meeting*
–hlangene na- *include*

–hlanhla (in-, izin-) *good fortune*
–hlanu (adj) *five*
–hlanzi (in- izin-) *fish*
Likhipha inhlanzi emanzini *The sun takes the fish out of the water, i.e. it is very hot*
–hlaza (u-) *vegetables*
–hle (adj) *good, pretty, beautiful*
–hlezi *be sitting*
–hlobo (isi- izi-) *blood relation*
–hlobo (um-, imi-) *kind, nationality*
–hlola *inspect, examine, check*
–hlonipha *respect*
–hlupheka *suffer*
–hola *earn (money)*
–holide (i(li)-, ama-) *holiday*
–hulumeni (u- o-) *government*

i-cooldrinki *cool drink*
i-ID namba *identity number*
impilonde *a long life*
impilontle *a good life*
Impilontle nempilonde *May you have a long and prosperous life!*
Inhloboni? *what kind?*
inkundla yezindiza *airport*
isigxobo seposi *at the post box*
isikhashana *a little while*
isikhwama semali *purse*
isithupha *six*
izolo *yesterday*

–ja (in-, izin-) *dogs*
–jabula *be happy*
–jahe *be in a hurry*
–jaladi (i(li)-, ama-) *yard*
–Jalimane (i(li)-, ama-) *German*

–Jalimane (isi-) *German language*
–jamu (u-) *jam*
–jikela *turn to*
–jinjabhiya (i-) *ginger beer*
–jova *give an injection*
–jovo (um-, imi-) *injection*
–Julayi (u-) *July*
–Juni (u-) *June*

kabi *badly,*
  kabi kakhulu *very bad*
kabili *twice*
kahle *well*
kakhulu *very much*
–kala *weigh*
–kamelo (i(li)-, ama-) *room*
  ikamelo lokudlela *dining room*
kamnandi *nicely, sweetly*
kancane *a little*
kangaka *so much*
KaNgwane *former Swazi Homeland*
kanjalo *in that manner, thus*
kanjani *how?, in what manner?*
–kantolo (in-, izi-) *court*
kanye *together with, once*
–kati (i(li)-, ama-) *cat*
–kebhe (isi-, izi-) *ship*
–khala *cry, complain*
  Kukhala ibhungane *A beetle is buzzing there, i.e. there is nobody there*
–khaliphile *be sharp*
–khanda (i(li)-, ama-) *head*
  Ngiphethwe yikhanda *I've got a headache*

–khanya *shine*
–khasimende (i(li)-, ama-) *customer*
–khathazekile *be worried*
–khathele *be tired*
–khathi (isi-, izi-) *time*
–khawunda (i(li)-, ama-) *counter*
–khaya (i(li)-, ama-) *home*
  ekhaya *at home*
–khefi (i(li)-, ama-) *cafe*
–khehla (i(li)-, ama-) *old man*
–khekhe (i(li)-, ama-) *cake*
–kheli (i(li)-, ama-) *address*
–khemisi (i(li)-, ama-) *chemist*
–kherothi (i(li)-, ama-) *carrot*
–kheshe (u-) *cash*
–khetha *choose*
–khethini (i(li)-, ama-) *curtain*
–khilogramu (i(li)-, ama-) *kilogram*
–khilomitha (i(li)- ama-) *kilometre*
–khipha *take out*
  khipha umoya *exhale*
–khishi (i(li)-, ama-) *kitchen*
–Khisimuzi (u-) *Christmas*
–khiya *lock*
–khiye (u-, o-) *key*
–khiye (isi-, izi-) *key*
–khiyiwe *be locked*
–khofi (i(li)-) *coffee*
–khohlwa *forget*
–khokha *pay*
–kholifulawa (u-, o-) *cauliflower*
–khombisa *show*
khona *there, here, be present, exist*
  Ngikhona *I'm fine*

kukhona ... *there is / are ...*
–khona (i(li)-, ama-) *corner (of street)*
–khonsathi (i(li)-, ama-) *concert*
–khonto (um-, imi-) *spear*
–khonzela *convey someone's greetings*
–khosi (inkosi, amakhosi) *king, chief, paramount chief*
Inkosi yenkantolo *Magistrate*
–khozi (u(lu)-, izin-) *eagle*
–khuhlane (um-, imi-) *common cold*
–khukhamba (i(li)-, ama-) *cucumber*
–khuluma *speak*
–khumbi (i(li)-, ama-) *combi (car)*
–khumbi (um-, imi-) *boat*
–khumbula *remember*
–khumula *undress, take off*
–khuthele *be diligent*
–khwama (isi-, izi-) *small bag*
–khwehlela *cough*
–kilasi (i(li)-, ama-) *class*
–kinga (in-, izin-) *problem*
–klomelo (um-, imi-) *prize*
kodwa *but*
kokubili *both*
–kolo (isi-, izi-) *school*
–komishi (in-, izin-) *cup*
–komo (in-, izin-) *beast, cattle*
–kosazana (in-, ama-) *miss*
–Koshi (isi-, izi-) *Scotsman*
–kosi (in-, ama-) *chief*
–kosikazi (in-, ama-) *wife, madam*

kubiza malini? *what is the price?*
kude *far*
kulungile *it is OK*
kuphela *only*
kusasa *tomorrow*
kusihlwa *at dusk*
kuthangi *day before yesterday*
kuyabiza *it is expensive*
–kwatapheya (u-, o-) *avocado pear*
KwaZulu *Zululand*

–lahlekile *be lost*
–laka (u-) *temper, vicious*
–lala *go to sleep*
–lalela *listen to*
–lambile *be hungry*
–landa *fetch*
–landelayo *follow after*
–langa (i(li)-, ama-) *sun*
–lantshi (i(li)-, ama-) *lunch*
lapha *here*
lapho *there*
–layela *show the way*
–layisense (i(li)-, ama-) lokushayela *driving licence*
–lenze (um-, imi-) *leg*
–letha *bring*
–letisi (u-, o-) *lettuce*
–limele *be injured*
–limi (u(lu)-, izi-) *language*
–linda *wait*
–lingana *fit*
–lisho (i(li)-, ama-) *rickshaw*
–listi (i(li)-, ama-) *list*
ilisti yewayini *wine list*
–lobela *write for (someone)*
–lokwe (i(li)-, ama-) *dress, lady's gown*

luhlaza *under-cooked, green, blue*
–lula *be light, easy*
–lunga *be correct*
–lunga (i(li)-, ama-) *member*
–lungelo (i(li)-, ama-) *right, privilege*
–lungile *be fine / OK*
  Kulungile *It's OK*
–lungisa *put right, make tidy, correct*
–lungu (um-, abe-) *white person*
lutho *nothing*
–lwandle (u-, izi-) *sea*
–lwane (isi-, izi-) *animals*

–ma *stand*
  yima lapha! *stand here!*
–ma (u-, o-) *madam*
–mabhalane (u-, o-) *clerk*
–mabonwakude (u-, o-) *TV, television*
–makhaniki (u-, o-) *mechanic*
–makhaza *be cold*
–makhelwane (u-, o-) *neighbour*
–makhonya (u-, o-) *boss*
–mali (i-) *money*
  malini? *how much money?*
  Kubiza malini? *How much does it cost?*
–malume (u-, o-) *uncle*
–mamukeli (u-, o-) *receptionist*
–mango (u-, o-) *mango*
manje *now*
–manzi *be wet*
–Mashi (u-) *March*
masinya *soon*
–masipala (u-, o-) *municipality*
–masitadi (u-) *mustard*

–mayela (i(li), ama-) *mile*
–mbala muni) *what colour?*
  Mehlomadala! *What a pleasure!, Good gracious!*
–meli (um-, aba-) *lawyer*
–memo (isi-, izi-) *invitation*
–meneja (i(li)-, ama-) *manager*
–meniyu (i(li)-, ama-) *menu*
–mese (um-, imi-) *knife*
–Meyi (u-) *May*
–mfowethu (um-, aba-) *my brother*
–mhlophe *white*
–mhloshana *off-white*
mina *I* (emphasised)
–mnandi *tasty, nice*
–mnyama *black*
–moto (i-, izi-) *car*
–moya (u-) *wind, air*
–mpofu *poor*
–mungumungwane (isi-) *measles*
–mayalezo (umu-, imi-) *message*

–namba (i-, izi-) *number*
namhlanje *today*
nami *I also*
nangu (Cl 1) *here she is*
nanka (Cl 5) *here it is, here they are*
nanku (Cl 3) *here it is*
nansi (Cl 9) *here it is*
nanti (Cl 5) *here it is*
nantu (Cl 11) *here it is*
nasi (Cl 7) *here it is*
–ncane (adj) *small, few*
–nceda *help*
–ncintiswano (um-, imi-) *competition*

–ncwadi (in-, izin-) *book, letter*
–Ndebele (i(li)-, ama-) *Ndebele speaking person*
–Ndebele (isi-) *Ndebele language*
–ndla (ama-) *power, strength*
–nesi (u-, o-) *nurse*
–nga (ama-) *lie (noun)*
 -qamba amanga *tell lies*
 ngabe *maybe*
–ngaka *as big as this*
 ngakanani? *How big, how many?*
–ngaki? *how many?*
 ngakwesobunxele *left-hand side*
 ngakwesokudla *right-hand side*
 ngale *on that side*
 Ngala komgwaqo *On the other side of the street*
 ngale kwa- *across*
 ngamancozuncozu *(pay) in instalments*
–ngane (um-, aba-) *friend*
 ngani? *with what?*
–ngcolile *be dirty*
–ngcono *better*
–ngcwabo (um-, imi-) *funeral*
–ngena *enter*
 ngenhlanhla *fortunately*
 ngeshwa *unfortunately*
 ngeSonto *(on) Sunday*
–Ngisi (i(li)-, ama-) *Englishman*
–Ngisi (isi-) *English language*
–Ngisi (um-, aba-) *Englishman*
 ngoba *because*
 ngokushesha *quickly*

ngoLwesibili *(on) Tuesday*
ngoLwesihlanu *(on) Friday*
ngoLwesine *(on) Thursday*
ngoLwesithathu *(on) Wednesday*
ngoMgqibelo *(on) Saturday*
ngoSombuluko *(on) Monday*
ngovivi *early dawn*
–ngozi (in-, izin-) *danger*
–ngqongqoza *knock*
–ngwe (i-, izi-) *leopard*
–nhloboni? *what kind*
–nina (u-, o-) *their mother*
 nini? *when?*
–njalo *so, like that*
–njani? *how?*
 Kunjani? *How is it?*
–nje *like this*
 njegani? *as what?*
–njiniyela (u-, o-) *engineer*
–nkosikazi (u-, o-) *madam, mrs*
–Nkulunkulu (u-) *God*
–nkwa (isi-, izi-) *bread*
 nokho *nevertheless*
 noma *or*
–nombolo (i-, izi-) *number*
 Inombolo yocingo lwakho *Your telephone number*
–nsundu *brown*
–ntanakho (um-, aba-) *your child*
–ntanami (um-, aba-) *my child*
–ntongomane (i(li)-, ama-) *peanut*
-ntombazane (i-, ama-) *girl*
–ntombazane (in-, ama-) *girl*
–ntu (ubu-) *human nature*
–ntu (um-, aba-) *person*

–ntwana (um-, aba-) *child*
–ntwana (um-, aba-) *child*
–numzane (um-, aba-) *respected man, sir*
–nwele (u(lu)-, izin-) *hair*
nxephe! *pardon! sorry!*
–nyaka (u-) *year*
–nyaka (um-, imi-) *year*
–nyama (in-) *meat*
–nyanga (in-, izin-) *month, moon*
–nyango (um-, imi-) *door*
–nyathi (in-, izin-) *buffalo*
–nye *one*
–nyeni (um-, aba-) *husband*
–nyoni (in-, izin-) *bird*
–nzi (ama-) *water*
–nzima *difficult, heavy*

–oda *order*
–oda (i(li)-, ama-) *order (noun)*
–Oktoba (u-) *October*
okuhle kodwa *only the best*
okuphuzwayo *something to drink*
okwamanje *presently*
–omile *be thirsty*
onke (Cl 6) *all*
–owaseposini *post office official*
–owoyela (u-/i-) *oil*

–pahla (im-, izim-) *goods*
–paka *park (verb)*
–pasipoti (i(li)-, ama-) *passport*
–patho (im-) *treatment*
–Pedi (i(li)-, ama-) *Pedi-speaking person*
–Pedi (isi-) *Pedi (Northern Sothi) language*
–pelepele (u-) *pepper*

–pensele (i(li)-, ama-) *pencil*
–pentshisi (i(li)-, ama-) *peach*
–pesheli (isi-, izi-) *special*
–phakamisa *recommend, propose, suggest, raise*
phakathi kwa- *inside / between*
–phakela *dish out for*
–phakethe (i(li)-, ama-) *packet*
phambi kwa- *before*
phambili *in front*
–phambuka *leave the main road*
phandle *outside*
phansi *beneath, down*
phansi kwa- *under, below*
–phaseji (i(li)-, ama-) *passage*
–phasela (i(li)-, ama-) *parcel*
–phasile *passed*
–phathela *bring for*
–phathi (um-, aba-) *manager, person in charge*
–phayinaphu (u-, o-) *pineapple*
–phazamisa *bother*
–pheka *cook*
–phelele *be complete*
–phelile *be finished*
–phendula *answer*
–phepha (i(li)-, ama-) *paper*
–phephandaba (i(li)-, ama-) *newspaper*
phesheya *overseas*
–phethe *hold / have on you*
–phethwe *suffer from*
–phetroli (u-) *petrol*
phezu kwa- *on top of*
–phi?/kuphi? *where?*
–phikisa *deny*
–phila *live*

Ngiyaphila *I'm fine*
Ngisaphila *I'm still OK*
–philisi (i(li), ama-) *pill*
–phimbo (um-, imi-) *throat*
–phinda *do again, repeat*
–phinifo (i(li)-, ama-) *pinafore*
–phiwa *be given*
–pho (isi-, izi-) *gift*
–phola *get well*
–pholisa *cure*
–phopho (u-, o-) *paw-paw*
–phosiso (isi-, izi-) *mistake*
–phoyisa (i(li)-, ama-)
 policeman
–phuma *come from, come out*
–phumula *rest*
–phuthini (u-, o-) *pudding,*
 sweets
–phuthuma *hurry, be urgent*
 yindaba ephuthumayo
 urgent matter
–phuza *drink (verb)*
–phuzo (isi-, izi-) *drink*
–polisiteshi (i(li)-, ama-) *police*
 station
–popola *examine with*
 stethoscope
–posa *post*
–posi (i(li)-, ama-) *mail, post*
–posihhovisi (i(li)-, ama-) *post*
 office
–posikhadi (i(li)-, ama-) *post*
 card
–pulamu (i(li)-, ama-) *plum*
–pulazi (i(li)-, ama-) *farm*
–puleti (i(li)-, ama-) *dish*
–punu (isi- izi-) *spoon*

–qala *begin*

–qala *begin, start*
–qanda (i(li)-, ama-) *egg*
–qaphela *be careful*
–qasha *hire*
–qeda *complete, finish*
–qgoke *wear*
–qhubeka *carry on, continue*
–qinile *be hard, be tough*
–qinisile *be correct, be true, be*
 certain
–qiniso (i(li)-, ama-) *truth*
–qonda *understand*
 Qonda ngqo! *Go straight*
 ahead!
–qotho *be honest*

–randi (i(li)-, ama-) *Rand*
 (money)
–rediyo (i(li)-, ama-) *radio*
–rejista *register*
–restouranti (i(li)-, ama-)
 restaurant
–risidi (i(li)- ama-) *receipt*
–robhoti (i(li)-, ama-) *traffic*
 light

–sa (umu-) *kindness*
–sakazana (u-, o-) *(sugar)*
 pocket
–sakazo (um-, imi-) *radio*
–sala *stay, remain*
–saladi (i(li)-, ama-) *salad*
–sango (i(li)-, ama-) *gate*
–sangu (in-, izin-) *dagga,*
 marijuana
–sawoti (u-) *salt*
–sayina *sign (signature)*
–sayini (i(li)- ama-) *signature*
-sayitsheni (u-, o-) *sergeant*
–sayizi (u-, o-) *size*

Sayizi bani? *What size?*
–sebenza *work*
–sebenzi (isi-, izi-) *worker*
–sebenzi (um-, imi-) *work (noun)*
–sebenzisa *use*
–sendiwishi (i(li)-, ama-) *sandwich*
–sha (adj) *new, young*
–shadile *be married*
–shado (um-, imi-) *wedding*
–shalofu (i(li)-, ama-) *shelf*
–shanela *sweep*
–shantshi (i(li)-, ama-) *charge office*
–shaya *hit*
 Shaya itelegilamu *Send a telegram*
 Shaya isiZulu *Speak Zulu*
–shayela *drive (a car)*
–shayela imoto *drive a car*
–shayisa *knock off work*
–sheke (i(li)-, ama-) *cheque*
–shesha *hurry*
–shini (um-, imi-) *machine*
–shintshi (u-) *change (money)*
–shisa *be hot*
 Kushisa kakhulu *It's very hot*
–shiya *leave behind*
–shizi (u-) *cheese*
–sho *mean*
–sho (isi-, izi-) *saying*
–sho (umu-, imi-) *sentence*
–shona *die*
–shukela (u-) *sugar*
–shumi (i(li)-, ama-) *ten*
–shuwarensi (in-) *insurance*

–sika *cut*
–siko (i(li)-, ama-) *custom*
–siko (i(li)-, ama-) *tradition*
–sindisi (uM-) *Redeemer*
–sinki (u(lu)-, izin-) *wash-basin*
–sisi (u-, o-) *sister*
–sistela (i(li)- ama-) *nursing sister*
–siza *help*
 Ngingakusiza ngani? *With what can I help you?*
–sizo (u(lu)-) *help, assistance*
–sizwa (in-, izin-) *young man*
–so (ubu-) *face*
–soda (u-) *soda water*
–somabhizinizi (u-, o-) *businessman*
–sondo (i(li)-, ama-) *wheels*
–Sonto (i(li)-, ama-) *Sunday, church*
–su (isi-, izi-) *stomach*
–suka *go off, depart from*
–suku (u(lu)-, izin-) *day*
–suku (ubu-) *night*
 ebusuku *at night, in the late evening*
–sukuma *stand up*
–sula *wipe off*
–supamakethe (i(li)-, ama-) *supermarket*
–suthi *be satisfied with food*
–Suthu (Southern) *Sotho language*
–Suthu (um-, abe-) *Sotho person*
–Suthu (um-, abe-) *Sotho-speaking person*
–Swati (isi-) *Swazi language*
–Swati/-Swazi (i(li)-, ama-)

Swazi-speaking person
–swidi (i(li)-, ama-) *sweets*

–taba (in-, izin-) *mountain*
–tafula (i(li)-, ama-) *table*
–tamatisi (u-, o-) *tomato*
–tambo (in-, izin-) *(telephone) line, rope*
–tanki (i(li), ama-) *tank*
–tebhisi (isi-, izi-) *step*
–telegilamu (i(li)-, ama-) *telegram*
–tembu (isi-, izi-) *post office stamp*
–tengo (in-, izin-) *price*
–teshi (isi-, izi-) *station*
–thakathi (um-, aba-) *witch doctor*
–thakazelo (isi-, izi-) *praise name*
–thanda *like*
–thandaza *pray*
–thandekayo *be likeable, dearest*
–thatha *take*
–thandu (adj) *three*
–thekisi (i(li)-, ama-) *taxi*
–thela *pour, put in (liquids)*
–thelo (isi-, izi-) *fruit*
–themperetsha (i-) *temperature*
–thenga *buy*
–thengisa *sell*
–thengisi *salesman*
–thengiswa *sold*
–thi *say*
–thi (umu-, imi-) *medicine*
–thikithi (i(li)-, ama-) *ticket*
thina *we* (emphatic)
–thini (i(li)-, ama-) *tin*

–thisha (u-, o-) *teacher*
–thokozile *be happy*
–thola *get, find*
–thonsela (ama-) *tonsillitis*
–thosi (u-, o-) *toast*
–thosiwe *be toasted*
–thoyilethe (i(li)-, ama-) *toilet*
–thuba (i(li)-, ama-) *opportunity*
–thula *be silent, quiet*
–thumela *send to*
–thuthuthu (isi-, izi-) *motorbike*
–timela (isi-, izi-) *train*
–tiye (i(li)-) *tea*
–to (in-, izin-) *thing*
–tobhi (isi-, izi-) *halt, stop street*
–tofu (isi-, izi-) *stove*
–tolo (isi-, izi-) *store*
–tombi (in-, izin-) *girl*
–tsha (isi-, izi-) *dish*
–tshela *tell*
–tshipisi (ama-) *chips*
–tshudeni (isi-, izi-) *student*
–tshwala (u(bu)-) *traditional beer*
–Tsonga (isi-) *Tsonga language*
–Tsonga (um-, ama-) *Tsonga-speaking person*
–Tswana (isi-) *Tswana language*
–Tswana (um-, abe-) *Tswana-speaking person*

ukuqala *first*
ukuthi *(so) that*
uma *if, when*
umfotho wegazi *blood pressure*
umshini wokuwasha (ozenzelayo) *(automatic) washing machine*

unani? *what is the matter with you?*
Unwele olude! *May you live long!, Cheers!*
usuku lokuzalwa *birthday*

–vakashela *visit*
–vala *close, switch off (e.g. radio)*
–valelisa *say good-bye to*
–valiwe *be closed*
–vela *come from*
–Venda (isi-) *Venda language*
–Venda (um-, ama-) *Venda-speaking person*
–veni (i(li)-, ama-) *light delivery van*
–viki (i(li)-, ama-) *week*
–vilapha *be lazy*
–vota *vote*
–vu (i(li)-) *leave (noun)*
–vuka *wake up*
–valiwe *be closed*
–vuliwe *be open*
–vuma *agree*
–vunyelwa *permitted, allowed*
  Ukubhema akuvunyelwa *Smoking not allowed*
–vuthiwe *be ripe, be done (of food)*
  -vuthwe kakhudlwana *be medium done*
  -vuthwe kancane *be under-cooked, under-done*
  -vuthwe kakhulu *be well-cooked, well-done*
–vuza *leak*

wamalini? *(change) for how much (money)?*

–washi (i(li)-, ama-) *watch*
–wayini (i-) *wine*
wena *you* (emphatic)
–weta (u-, o-) *waiter*
–wina *win*
–wiski (u-) *whisky*
–wola *gather (dirt)*
–wolintshi (i(li)-, ama-) *orange*
Woza! *Come!*
Wozani! *Come (ye)!*

–Xhosa (i(li)-, ama-) *Xhosa-speaking person*
–Xhosa (isi-) *the Xhosa language*
–xolela *pardon, forgive someone*
–xolisa *ask for pardon*
–xolo (u(lu)-) *pardon (me), excuse (me), sorry*
–xosha *dismiss*

–ya *go*
yebo *yes*
yilokho kuphela *it is only that*
yimalini? *what is the price?*
yini ndaba? *why?*
yonke (Cl 9) *all*
yunivesithi (i(li)-, ama-) *university*

–za *come*
  Yiza lapha! *Come here!*
–zali (um-, aba-) *parent*
–zalo (in-) *interest (money)*
–zalwa *be born*
–zama *try*
–zambane (i(li)-, ama-) *potato*
–zi (umu-, imi-) *homestead, village, family*

–zinyo (i(li)-, ama-) *tooth*
–zu (i(li)-) *zoo*
–zulu (i(li)-) *weather, heaven*
–Zulu (isi-) *Zulu language*
–Zulu (um-, ama-) *Zulu-
speaking person*
–zuzwana (um-, ama-) *minute,
short while*

–zwa *hear, understand, feel*
Angizizwa kahle *I don't feel
well*
–zwe (isi-, izi-) *nation*
–zwelana na- *sympathise with*